The Divide Within

Intersections of Realities, Facts, Theories, and Practices

A Volume in
Social Science Education Consortium Book Series

Series Editors:
Gregory L. Samuels and Amy Samuels,
University of Montevallo

Social Science Education Consortium Book Series
Gregory L. Samuels and Amy Samuels, Series Editors

The Divide Within: Intersections of Realities,
Facts, Theories, and Practices (2021),
edited by Tina L. Heafner, Laura K. Handler, and Tracy C. Rock

Democracy at a Crossroads: Reconceptualizing Socio-Political Issues
in Schools and Society (2019),
edited by Gregory Samuels and Amy Samuels

The Divide Within

Intersections of Realities, Facts, Theories, and Practices

Edited by

**Tina L. Heafner, Laura K. Handler,
and Tracy C. Rock**
University of North Carolina at Charlotte

Information Age Publishing, Inc.
Charlotte, North Carolina • www.infoagepub.com

Library of Congress Cataloging-in-Publication Data

CIP data for this book can be found on the Library of Congress website:
http://www.loc.gov/index.html

Paperback: 978-1-64802-300-2
Hardcover: 978-1-64802-301-9
E-Book: 978-1-64802-302-6

Printed in the United States of America.

CONTENTS

INTRODUCTION

Tina L. Heafner, Laura K. Handler, and Tracy C. Rock
University of North Carolina at Charlotte

> Nothing is more wonderful than being free, but nothing is harder
> to learn how to use than freedom.
>
> —Alexis de Tocqueville

> I think the country has to find out what it means by freedom.
> Freedom is a very dangerous thing. Anything else is disastrous.
> But freedom is dangerous. You've got to be taught that your life is
> in your hands.
>
> —— James Baldwin

Globalization, modernization, and technologization have brought rapid
social and economic change while also increasing diversity of democratic
societies. Plurality of democracy, once viewed as a progressive ideology,
has been met in more recent years by the movement of identity politics to
the margins of society. Although social movements demanding recognition on the part of groups that were once invisible to mainstream society
have brought attention to systemic inequities, prejudice, and discriminatory policies, other groups feeling a loss of status and a sense of displacement have pushed back with counterclaims and protests. These conflicting
narratives have fractured society and segmented the populace along narrowly defined identities creating a new era of democracy and isolationism.

The Divide Within: Intersections of Realities, Facts, Theories, and Practices
pp. vii–xiii
Copyright © 2021 by Information Age Publishing

Today in the United States and elsewhere we see the troubling effects of increasingly polarized political discourse: amplified gridlock within government, the politicization and fragmentation of economic and social life, and the suppression of the spread of information and mutual learning across ideological lines. The sociopolitical climate in America is characterized by skepticism, hostility, distrust, claims of fake news, and unwavering opposition. Cavernous divisions among Americans are revealed in rhetoric surrounding controversial issues such as inequality, gun control, and immigration. Moreover, divisions about such issues have become increasingly aligned with partisan identities in recent years and exacerbated by social media isolationist practices. The *divide within* our nation has shifted the narrative of democracy from promoting the common good to protecting the interests of like-minded factions and the preservation of power and privilege.

Most recently, COVID-19 forced us to chart new paths of physical distancing and delivering remote education while simultaneously revealing the cavernous socioeconomic and racial divisions in American society. Pandemics not only affect individuals; they change the world. Disease outbreaks have shaped politics, crushed revolutions, and entrenched racial and economic discrimination. Pandemics have altered societies, affecting personal relationships, the work of artists and intellectuals, and the man-made and natural environments. Stretching across centuries and continents, social, political, and economic structures, population settlement patterns, and the use of natural and human resources have also allowed diseases to flourish. Pandemics are not random events that afflict societies capriciously and without warning; on the contrary, every society produces its own vulnerabilities. To study them is to understand a society's structure, its standard of living, its political and economic priorities, its inequities and pretense. While COVID-19 reveals the tenacity, perseverance, selflessness, and kindness of people, it also serves as a mirror to all things that society has not come to terms with. It has made transparent the digital access divide in America, elevated racial tensions, revealed socioeconomic and racial inequalities, and exacerbated political divisions.

Helping people contextualize the significance of the outbreak of COVID-19 is both critical and timely as communities face unprecedented disruptions with far reaching effects. We are in the midst of an economic recession due to the pandemic-related shutdown. Situating government responses to COVID-19 in historic, geographic, global and economic perspectives will deepen students' understanding of their lived experiences and enhance their civic reasoning skills. But it is also necessary for us to examine more deeply structural inequalities pandemics reveal about society. Although the effects of COVID-19 have been felt by all, struggles and hardships continue to be disproportionately experienced among racial groups.

This current pandemic hits as our country also reaches an unprecedented level of demographic diversity. In 2013, the nation hit a tipping point, where for the first time in history most of the infants born were members of minoritized groups. In 2014 the number of White students fell below 50%, marking this year as the first majority-minority enrollment in U.S. public schools (Hussar & Bailey, 2014). By 2043, the nation is projected to become majority-minority (Krogstad & Fry, 2014). The demographic landscape continues to shift as the racial and ethnic composition is fueled by metropolitan urbanization. More students are living in poverty and in segregated neighborhoods, particularly the country's rapidly growing Latinx school-aged population. For the first time in at least 50 years, a majority of public school students across the country are considered low wealth (Mordechay & Orfield, 2017).

These contexts magnify tensions and challenge the essence of our democracy. The brutal deaths of George Floyd and Breonna Taylor once again laid bare the racist and inequitable treatment of Black people in America. Ensuing protests around the world have sparked a critical reexamination of history and the reverberating, perpetuating effects of systemic racism throughout structures of society. Seemingly overnight, Confederate statues topple in argument of historical atrocities that should not be memorialized, and Juneteeth rises in prominence in recognition of historical events that deserve national celebration of independence and freedom. Despite COVID-19, civic activism persists through mask-wearing protests, arts-inspired murals, and nonstop technology-driven media, hashtags, and webinars.

As social scientists committed to critical inquiry as well as human rights and democratic governance, we must challenge and push against societal structures and curriculum as a wary defense of the status quo. All of this is possible, but none of it is automatic. If we want democracy, we have to demand it, and we have to be able to educate children who will make and remake it. Democracy requires continuous effort to thrive, and a constant willingness to broaden and deepen the application of its principles. The future of democracy depends on our ability to show that it is more than a set of bare-minimum defenses against the worst abuses of authoritarian leaders and divisions within democracies that fracture the structures intended to preserve the promise of liberty. Democracy offers a guarantee of the freedom to choose and live out one's own destiny; it is the promise of unalienable rights for all.

*   *   *

When the voices of democracy are silenced, freedom becomes a hollow concept. No man or woman should be sentenced to the shadows of silence.

—— Al Neuharth

*   *   *

In recent decades, researchers focused attention on studying the social, geographic, political, and technological polarization in the United States. Trends manifest in myriad ways, both in politics and in everyday life, and expose the divergence between urban and rural communities, the opportunities afforded the wealthy and the impoverished, the lived experiences of various racial groups, and countless other divides among us. These inquiries also suggest that causes and effects of identity politics and polarization are too complicated to be construed as simple dichotomies and too complex to be studied within the confines of a single discipline. The exploration of such divides, therefore, requires participation and collaboration from scholars in many different fields, particularly those working in the social sciences.

The Social Science Education Consortium recognizes this integrated nature of the social sciences and the importance of education at this societal impasse. In July 2019, the organization hosted its annual conference in Charlotte, North Carolina, to bring together scholars and educators to grapple with these challenging inquiries and interdisciplinary analyses, both at a broad, national level, and also in a more nuanced, local level. Gathering in the heart of the New South, participants collaboratively engaged in these discussions on a walking tour led by a local historian, while visiting museum exhibits such as "K[no]w Justice, K[no]w Peace", and during a panel presentation of local social scientists. This book seeks to leverage the research capacity of participants and the broader social science community to engage dialogue concerning *the divide within* and the intersections of realities, facts, theories, and practices in social science education.

Chapters in *The Divide Within: Intersections of Realities, Facts, Theories, and Practices* consider the following questions:

- In a polarized political climate characterized by skepticism, hostility, and claims of fake news, what common ground can be found in the social sciences to help bridge the *divide within* our nation and the broader global society?
- Considering the intersections among realities, facts and theories within the social sciences as well as within urban and rural educa-

tion studies, what are solution-based practices toward mending the effects of a fractured and polarized society?

- How do urban and rural districts compare in terms of equity, sustaining educational issues, teaching staff, social mobility, et cetera? What are the implications for education and for our nation?
- In what ways may social science education promote theory and pedagogy to drive unity?

ORGANIZATION OF CHAPTERS

The book begins with a broad scope in which to view various aspects of sociopolitical fractures within our nation. From the first chapter, author Wayne Journell initiates an analysis of the broader structures and characteristics of our society that serve as mechanisms for deepening divides among public thought. Through the disciplinary perspectives of psychology and sociology, he presents the contemporary contexts that allow fake news to thrive and proposes implications for educators in order to minimize threats to our democracy. Maintaining a big-picture lens yet shifting focus to the sector of public education, in Chapter 2 Laura Handler and Tracy Rock examine educational policy and initiatives that contribute to the inequitable and segregative environment of schools, along with the divisive rhetoric that influences perceptions of students. Danny Yonto likewise focuses on policy and socioeconomic disparities, yet his work in Chapter 3 is set in the rural contexts of North Carolina. He offers the World Café as a collaborative tool for proposing integrative solutions to community challenges related to education, public health, housing, and transportation.

Shifting focus to teachers and teaching, researchers Jessica Norwood, Tina Heafner, and Paul Fitchett then follow in Chapter 4 with a quantitative analysis comparing teacher characteristics in rural, suburban, and urban settings. Looking more closely at a national data set, authors suggest ways that cultural and political differences between urban and rural populations affect teaching and learning experiences. Yvonna Hines, Tina Heafner, and Jeanneine Jones continue the focus on teacher characteristics and influences on students in Chapter 5 by examining the discipline practices in a suburban high school. They find that Black students are disproportionately represented in discipline referrals and are overrepresented in in- and out-of-school suspensions, and they pose important implications that the demographic divide between teachers and students carries for ensuring equity in education. To then round out this section, Dean Vesperman and Jill Leet-Otley bring attention to teacher preparation in Chapter 6. Through a mixed-methods study, the authors detail the transformations of two preservice teachers grappling with concepts of Whiteness, racism, and antiracist teaching, contributing to much-needed understanding of educators' racial identity development.

The five subsequent chapters delve into curriculum and raise important considerations for designing learning experiences for students. In Chapter 7, Wade Morris and Chara Bohan illuminate the interplay of textbooks, statues, and politics in shaping conceptions of history. Through a case study of the Confederate icon John B. Gordon in Georgia, the authors utilize data from a content analysis of Southern history books to demonstrate how combined societal structures perpetuate a legacy of White supremacy. Amy Allen takes a close look at one school's service-learning program in the following chapter, cautioning that without critical reflection, students' experiences could have unintended consequences in promoting a White savior mentality. The authors of Chapter 9, Toni Rochester, Tina Heafner, and Kristen Beach, address learning disparities in history by analyzing pedagogical methods of literacy in middle school. They present the benefits of using discipline-specific reading strategies to support students' development of content knowledge as well as reading comprehension. Finally, the following two chapters encourage international perspectives in curricular approaches. In Chapter 10, Amanda Casto and Greg Wiggan examine the practices and policies of multicultural education established in the Republic of Korea to suggest changes in the ways the United States advances equity and inclusion among its demographically diverse students. In Chapter 11, Portia York, also writing with Greg Wiggan, advocates for arts integration, looking to Canada for an example of the policy and curricular reform that promotes creativity and critical thinking for students of all backgrounds.

As a bookend to this volume, we offer a focus on schools. Jim Davis's chapter uses the social science lens of economics to analyze the perilous state of American democracy. In Chapter 12 the author offers a deep dive into what he argues is one of the most pressing injustices facing the United States: the growing economic inequality manifested through gaps in income and wealth. First providing a solid explanation of economic principles and concepts, he then helps the reader understand how this discipline informs policy and inevitably shapes society. Asserting economic inequality as a looming threat to American democracy, Davis urges citizens to weigh several proposed courses of action in order to once again establish a government and society that meets the needs of its members. In the concluding chapter, Bettie Ray Butler provides recommendations for how to enact restorative justice in schools as a means to bridge the divide between data and solutions. The author provides a theoretical framework for an epistemological change in school discipline practices as a response to the disproportionality of discipline referrals for students of color. Chapter 13 emphasizes the importance of leveraging research to correct injustice and implicit bias in schools. Restorative justice according to the author bridges racialized divides within our society.

As editors, we wish to thank all contributors for their deep level of engagement with content for this book. Additionally, we are grateful for the support of the Social Science Education Consortium, particularly its leaders of Charlie White, Executive Director, and Michael Berson, President. Moving forward, we hope this book serves to inform social scientists, educators, and global citizens alike of the deep complexities of our world. Perhaps more importantly, we hope this book initiates critical conversations and steers positive directions toward equitable solutions that unify the people who walk this world together.

REFERENCES

Hussar, W. J., & Bailey, T. M. (2014). *Projections of education statistics to 2022, 41st edition.* National Center for Education Statistics, Institute of Education Sciences. https://nces.ed.gov/pubs2014/2014051.pdf

Krogstad, J. M., & Fry, R. (2014). *Department of education projects public schools will be 'majority-minority' this fall.* Pew Research Center. https://www.pewresearch.org/fact-tank/2014/08/18/u-s-public-schools-expected-to-be-majority-minority-starting-this-fall/

Mordechay, M., & Orfield, G. (2017). Demographic transformation in a policy vacuum: The changing face of U.S. metropolitan society and challenges for public schools. *The Educational Forum*, 81(2), 193–203. https://doi.org/10.1080/00131725.2017.1280758

CHAPTER 1

EXACERBATING EXISTING DIVIDES

Fake News, Desire, and Partisanship

Wayne Journell
University of North Carolina at Greensboro

ABSTRACT

The term "fake news" has become part of the cultural lexicon in recent years, with many arguing that it poses a serious threat to democracy. This chapter complicates that concern a bit by making the argument that fake news is a byproduct of existing political and social divides that is effective only because of aspects of the human condition. The chapter first defines various types of fake news before discussing the psychosocial processes of motivated reasoning and confirmation bias that allow fake news to be believed and shared. The chapter concludes by briefly describing the polarized and partisan environment found in the United States, particularly on social media, that provides a context in which fake news can thrive.

For the past decade, one of the most watched television shows in the United States has been *The Walking Dead*, a science fiction drama about a

The Divide Within: Intersections of Realities, Facts, Theories, and Practices
pp. 1–24
Copyright © 2021 by Information Age Publishing
All rights of reproduction in any form reserved.

zombie apocalypse. A casual observer of the show might identify the zombies as the catalyst for the destruction of humankind; however, a more sophisticated analysis would recognize that the true monsters are the human survivors. Although the zombies continually make the dire situation the survivors find themselves in worse, the true obstacles to survival are aspects of the human condition that were present well before the start of the apocalypse (Keetly, 2014).

A similar premise can be applied to the phenomenon of fake news. Since President Trump first used those words as a way to disparage media outlets that are critical of him, there has been an obsession about "fake news" negatively impacting U.S. democracy. Certainly, the widespread dissemination of false information, made easier than ever before due to social media, has the potential to affect our political system, perhaps best illustrated by Russian attempts to influence the 2016 presidential election. Yet, much like the zombies in *The Walking Dead*, fake news only exacerbates divides and dispositions that already exist, creating a context in which misinformation can both thrive and be civically disruptive.

This reality creates challenges for civic education. Media literacy has long been a staple of quality social studies instruction, and there has been a renewed interest within the field in light of the 2016 election and the increasing influence of social media on Americans' daily lives (e.g., McGrew et al., 2018; National Council for the Social Studies, 2016, 2019). While it is undoubtedly important to help students identify aspects of fraudulent information online, media literacy strategies alone will not combat the influence of fake news. Given that fake news is a symptom of existing political divides and not a cause, instructional efforts seeking to reduce the effects of fake news must take a comprehensive view that focuses on the psychosocial reasons why fake news works (Journell, 2019).

In this chapter, I explore the relationship between fake news and the psychosocial practices of motivated reasoning and confirmation bias, which are fueled by a desire for reality to fit within one's preconceived worldview. I begin by defining various types of fake news, including the version that Trump has popularized in recent years. Then, I explain how the current political and social context in the United States has created an environment that allows fake news to thrive. Although this chapter does not offer specific instructional recommendations, it is my hope that readers can apply aspects of this discussion to their specific classroom context.[1]

DEFINING FAKE NEWS

On the surface, defining fake news seems like it should be easy: information that can be determined to be verifiably false. However, as Garrett (2019) has noted, the lines between fact and fiction are not always clear, particularly when politicians and other pundits regularly use the term fake news to discredit factual information. Understanding this ambiguity is essential to understanding the proliferation and effectiveness of fake news; therefore, in the remainder of this section, I will outline the various definitions of "fake news" in the current U.S. political context.

Actual Fake News

At one end of the spectrum are outlets that purposefully peddle factually incorrect information in the spirit of comedy or satire. Outlets such as *The Onion* or *The Babylon Bee* do not consider themselves news outlets; rather, they use information from actual news outlets as fodder for their content. The "nightly news" segment on *Saturday Night Live* would also fall into this category. Typically, these types of outlets are not of concern when discussing the civic ramifications of fake news since most people recognize them for what they are. However, it is worth noting that not all satire/comedy outlets are transparent about their intentions. Nowhere on *The Onion*'s homepage, for example, does it explicitly note that its content is satirical in nature. Readers must be "in the know," and it is certainly possible that unwitting social media users may incorrectly consume and share *Onion* articles under the premise that they are factual.

Further along the spectrum are outlets that blend factual content with comedy. Television shows like *The Daily Show*, *Last Week Tonight*, *Real Time with Bill Maher*, and any number of late night talk shows fall into this category. These shows often contain excerpts from news sources, sound bites and other primary source clips, and interviews with politicians or pundits. Moreover, many of these shows engage in extensive research to ensure the factual accuracy of the news content they present (Friedman, 2018). As a result, research has shown such outlets to be sources of accurate, albeit biased, information that often offer more substance than traditional nightly news programs (Baym, 2009), to the point that some scholars have argued that they even have pedagogical potential (Garrett & Schmeichel, 2012; Journell, 2017). However, the stars of these shows uniformly deny being journalists (Steinberg, 2018), and many of the punchlines that emanate from facts either stretch the truth or present outright false information. As with the satirical outlets, these comedic news shows are not typically the targets of fake news accusations because most viewers are in on the joke.

The type of actual fake news that represents a true danger to democracy is misinformation being presented as fact without the subtext of satire or comedy. The most infamous example of this type of fake news is the Russian attempt to influence the 2016 presidential election. The over

Figure 1.1.

3,000 Facebook advertisements, 80,000 Facebook posts on Russian-created pages, and 130,000 tweets (U.S. House of Representatives Permanent Select Committee on Intelligence, n.d.) made by Russian operatives during the 2016 election campaign used a variety of techniques, with much of them relying on factually inaccurate information.[2] Figure 1.1 offers an example of one of their more simplistic efforts, a Photoshopped picture of actor/comedian Aziz Ansari encouraging Democratic voters to cast their ballot via a Twitter hashtag on election day (Wagner, 2017).[3]

Of greater concern is fake news that is harder to debunk. Many of the Russian social media efforts contained a mixture of accurate and inaccurate information. Figure 1.2 provides an illustrative example of such a post.

Although the post did not cite any sources for the "69 percent disapproval rate among all veterans" statistic, available data show that veterans disapproved of Clinton and voted for Trump at a rate in the ballpark of what was stated in the post (CNN, 2016; Confessore, 2016). Also, in 2015, Clinton stated on *The Rachel Maddow Show* that delays in treatment times at Veterans Affairs hospitals were not as widespread as commonly thought, which led to calls for her to apologize to veterans by notable Republicans, including John McCain (Richardson, 2015). However, the last sentence of the post calling for the armed forces to be removed from Clinton's control should she win the presidency in accordance with "amendments to the Constitution" is demonstratively false. There are no

Heart of Texas   👍 Like Page
Sponsored · ✎

Hillary Clinton has a 69 percent disapproval rate among all veterans. Indeed,
there are many reasons for it. First of all, Benghazi: four people died on her
watch and she did not send help. Secondly, Hillary refused to apologize to all
veterans, when she has made several remarks about veterans
"embellishing" the situation at the VA. Finally, Hillary is the only one politician
(except Barack Obama) who is despised by the overwhelming majority of
American veterans. If Hillary becomes the President of the US, the American
army should be withdrawn from Hillary's control according to the
amendments to the Constitution.

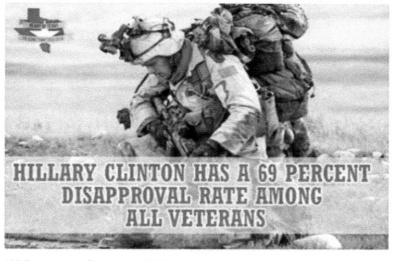

800 Reactions 84 Comments 308 Shares

👍 Like   💬 Comment   ➤ Share

Figure 1.2.

Constitutional amendments that allow for the removal of the president's
role as commander-in-chief of the armed forces while in office.

Of course, the Russians are far from the only source of fake news on the
Internet. It takes minimal technological skill to create memes, posts, or
tweets that have the potential to reach thousands of people, and social
media companies offer few safeguards to prevent the proliferation of false
information online. Figure 3 shows a post created by a random social
media user that went viral in 2018 and was designed to protest the Trump

No this isn't a prison. This is a kids concentration camp in the US.

Figure 1.3.

administration's policy of separating children from their families as they tried to enter the country at the Mexican border. It was spread widely throughout various liberal social media outlets (on one Facebook group, "Millennials for Bernie," it was shared over 9,000 times); however, the photo used in the post was from a 2014 article documenting the conditions of a detention center for unaccompanied minors entering the country illegally during the Obama administration (Kiefer, 2014; Mikkelson, 2018).

The deregulation of social media has also allowed organizations to disseminate false information under the guise of legitimate news. Extremist "news" outlets have thrived on social media. While these outlets occasionally publish factually accurate stories, they also peddle conspiracy theories and other forms of actual fake news to promote their ideological agendas.

A perfect example is *InfoWars*, an outlet run by far-right conspiracy theorist, Alex Jones. Started in 1999, the popularity of *InfoWars* exploded with the rise of social media, leading to a following that numbers in the millions (Southern Poverty Law Center, 2018). Over the years, *InfoWars* has championed a number of seemingly asinine theories that have been shared across social media, including (Hanna, 2017; Madsen, 2016; Quigley, 2017):

- The U.S. government orchestrated the 9/11 attacks, the 2012 Sandy Hook Elementary School shooting, and the 1995 Oklahoma City bombing.
- Former Supreme Court Justice Antonin Scalia was murdered.
- Barack Obama is the global head of Al-Qaeda.
- The U.S. government is using juice boxes and city-controlled water to turn people gay.

It is impossible to quantify the impact *InfoWars* has had on the U.S. political landscape; however, it was influential enough for then-candidate Trump to appear on Jones's radio show in 2015 and praise the host's "amazing" reputation (Bradner, 2015, para. 2). Although *InfoWars* has recently been banned by Facebook, Twitter, Apple, Youtube, and Instagram in their collective crackdown on far-right and anti-Semitic accounts (Lorenz, 2019),[4] the *InfoWars* website and Jones's show are still running strong, and the content they produce can still be used as fodder for user-created fake news.

InfoWars is but one of many pseudo-news organizations that regularly disseminate false, misleading, or heavily biased information on social media. The question becomes, then, why are they believed in lieu of traditional media outlets that have built reputations for delivering accurate information? The answer is that many people seek "news" that affirms what they believe and, conversely, have a predisposition to question or dismiss information that contradicts their worldviews, an aspect of the human condition that Trump has tapped into with his use of the term fake news.

Trump's Version of Fake News

When Trump and his surrogates make claims of fake news, they are conflating accuracy with bias. As Garrett (2019) noted, when a media outlet publishes information that is critical or presents the administration in a negative light, Trump weaponizes the term fake news as a way to dismiss the premise of the story. Whether the story is factually accurate is immaterial; Trump has used the term to discredit stories that can be corroborated by visual or audio evidence (e.g., Blake, 2018; Davis & Rosenberg, 2017; Smith, 2019).

While we can lament the fact that Trump's weaponizing of the term fake news has hastened our descent into a post-truth society (Journell, 2018), there is no question that it has worked as a political tactic. Numerous surveys have shown that Americans' distrust of the mainstream media is at unprecedented levels, particularly among Republicans (e.g., Fischer, 2018; Gallup, 2018; Mitchell & Barthell, 2017), and this rhetoric is amplified on social media (Al-Rawi, 2019). By making the press the enemy, Trump has helped ensure that his political base remains solidified regardless of what facts get reported. If anything, it seems as though fact-based reporting that is critical of Trump only seems to make his supporters more passionate (Peters, 2018).

The civic ramification of this villainification of the mainstream media is that people are more prone to consume and share actual fake news. When basic facts become questioned, it is easy for consumers of media to take the position that what constitutes factual material lies in the eye of the beholder. As a result, they choose to consume what feels "right" without any sense of urgency to ensure whether the media they consume and share is accurate.

In short, Trump's weaponizing of fake news has given license for people to engage in aspects of motivated reasoning and confirmation bias, psychosocial processes to which humans are naturally prone. In the next section, I will discuss these psychosocial processes in greater detail and make the argument that they are the true reasons for the civic crisis we find ourselves in. Trump, social media, and actual fake news have only served to amplify aspects of the human condition in which we all, to varying degrees, find ourselves participating.

MOTIVATED REASONING AND CONFIRMATION BIAS

Imagine if it were being widely shared on social media that actor Tom Hanks, known for iconic roles such as Forest Gump, had been implicated in a child sex ring being operated out of a Washington, DC, pizza restaurant. Most people would likely scoff at the premise of the story and assume it had been conjured up by the editors of *The National Enquirer* so that they would have material to include alongside stories about Elvis Presley sightings and alien abductions.

Yet, when that same story was promulgated about Hillary Clinton and members of her campaign staff during the 2016 election, it went viral among the alt-right recesses of the Internet. People believed the story to the point that the owner of the pizzeria at the center of the fictitious crime received death threats on a regular basis, and a gunman who had been inspired by *InfoWars* videos opened fire in the restaurant in an attempt to "rescue" the nonexistent children being held captive there (Helm, 2017; Ortiz, 2017). Over 3 years after the election, people still believe and circulate the story, now known colloquially as "pizzagate," as evidenced by the attempted arson of the infamous pizzeria in early 2019 (Zadrozny, 2019).

The reason why certain groups of people were quick to believe a seemingly ridiculous story about Hillary Clinton, and why they likely would not have believed a similar story about Tom Hanks, can be explained by two closely related psychosocial concepts: *motivated reasoning* and *confirmation bias*. Both concepts involve individuals' propensity to rationalize new information in ways that reconcile with existing worldviews (Dusso & Kennedy, 2015; Nickerson, 1998; Taber & Lodge, 2016). In short, researchers have found that people actively seek out sources of information that reinforce existing beliefs while avoiding sources that may challenge preconceived worldviews. Motivated reasoning and confirmation bias also make people more likely to uncritically accept false information that fits within their worldview and dismiss factual information that challenges existing understandings (Dusso & Kennedy, 2015). What makes these psychosocial processes particularly insidious and difficult to combat is the fact that most people engage in them unwittingly (Taber & Lodge, 2016).

The idea that Clinton was part of a child sex ring fit within the narrative that Republicans had developed about her and her husband over the previous 25 years. What seems like a preposterous story to most of us makes perfect sense to someone immersed in a culture that has spent the past two decades describing the Clintons as immoral people who have repeatedly broken the law and committed unspeakable acts to create a political dynasty. The individuals who bought into this story did not need to be presented with facts; rather, they were motivated to believe it because it fit within their preconceived notions about who Hillary Clinton was.

Motivated reasoning and confirmation bias are behind much of the fraudulent information that gets shared online. Figure 1.4 offers an illustrative example. The meme is false; Trump never gave that quotation to *People* magazine, nor is there any evidence that he has ever made a similar type of claim (Lacapria, 2017). Yet, that meme was shared widely during the 2016 election and continues to pop up from time to time on various social media outlets. It does not require much Googling to debunk the meme's claim; however, many liberals uncritically share it because it fits within their beliefs about Republicans and the caricature of Trump as a

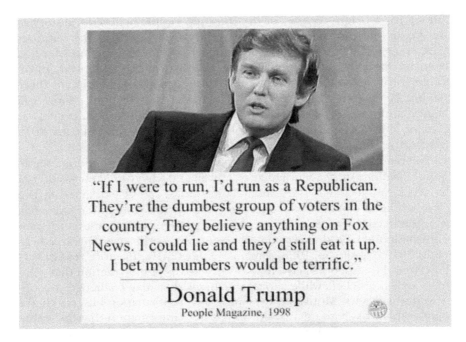

"If I were to run, I'd run as a Republican.
They're the dumbest group of voters in the
country. They believe anything on Fox
News. I could lie and they'd still eat it up.
I bet my numbers would be terrific."

Donald Trump
People Magazine, 1998

Figure 1.4.

conman. Moreover, they *want* the meme to be true because it offers an explanation for what remains, for many liberals, an unconscionable decision by the American electorate (Clinton, 2017; Holloway, 2018).

The seemingly obvious way to combat motivated reasoning and confirmation bias is to provide individuals with accurate information. However, even if we could pierce the ideological echo chambers that often prevent people from accessing factual information, research suggests that it might not make that much of a difference. Another psychosocial concept called the *backfire effect* has been the subject of much debate among psychologists and political scientists (Nyhan & Reifler, 2010; Wood & Porter, 2019). Although experts disagree about the extent to which the backfire effect occurs, there is evidence to suggest that, for some people, encountering factual evidence that challenges preconceived beliefs actually makes those prior views get stronger.

Although anecdotal, I have witnessed a type of backfire effect on social media among friends who have shared a version of the Trump meme shown in Figure 1.4. After posting, someone inevitably tells the original poster that the meme is inaccurate and often includes a link to a fact-checking website as evidence. While some people apologize and take the meme down, in my experience, they are in the minority. Most reply with some variation of the following statement: "Well, even if he didn't say it, you know it's true!" Although they may acknowledge the factual inaccuracy of the meme, they do not dismiss the broader premise, and perhaps most importantly, they do not remove the content, which only perpetuates the false narrative.

Of course, motivated reasoning and confirmation bias do not apply only to inaccurate information. Rather, these processes are perhaps most evident when dealing with factual information. Motivated reasoning and confirmation bias allow people to pick and choose which facts to accept and which facts to ignore. What often gets overlooked in the Russian interference scandal during the 2016 election is that most of the "fake news" that they disseminated was not necessarily fake. Take, for example, Figure 1.5, which is a meme determined to have been planted by Russian operatives.

There is nothing explicitly false in this meme. Although they did not provide a citation, it is not unfathomable that border agents arrested someone who had committed a crime in Honduras. The claim that "rapists, drug dealers, human traffickers, and others" have come across the border is reminiscent of Trump's first official speech as a candidate for president when he claimed that "when Mexico sends its people, they're not sending their best… They're sending people who have lots of problems, and they're bringing those problems with us. They're bringing drugs. They're bringing crime. They're rapists. And some, I assume, are good people" (Schwartz, 2015, para. 3). The issue with both statements is that they are technically not incorrect; there are criminals, including those who commit rape and deal drugs, who illegally enter the United States via the Mexican border.

Where motivated reasoning and confirmation bias come into play, however, is in the assessment of the number and impact of these groups entering the United States. Available data show that both legal and undocumented immigrants are less likely to commit crimes than native-born Americans (Bersani, 2014; Light & Miller, 2018; Nowrasteh, 2018) and that the vast majority of immigrants, both legal and undocumented, contribute positively to American society and the economy (Chen, 2016; Varas, 2018). Yet, the statement on the meme that "the percent of innocent poor families searching for a better life is too small to become an argument for amnesty and Texas warm welcome" is not technically incorrect because, for some people, anything less than a hundred percent poses an unreasonable risk for the security of the United States (Journell, in press). By framing the argument in this way, the meme speaks to those who are already motivated to view immigrants in a negative light, and

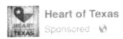

Heart of Texas
Sponsored

👍 Like Page

Border Patrol agents in South Texas arrested an illegal alien from Honduras that had previously been deported and convicted of Rape Second Degree.

Thanks to Obama's and Hillary's policy, illegals come here because they wait for amnesty promised. The wrong course had been chosen by the American government, but all those politicians are too far from the border to see who actually sneaks through it illegally.

Rapists, drug dealers, human traffickers, and others. The percent of innocent poor families searching for a better life is too small to become an argument for amnesty and Texas warm welcome.

3.1K Reactions   89 Comments   1.2K Shares

👍 Like   💬 Comment   ➦ Share

Figure 1.5.

those facts, as incomplete as they may be, serve to confirm individuals' existing biases.

An illustrative example of motivated reasoning and confirmation bias can be found in the response to the video of a confrontation between Trump-supporting students from Covington High School and a tribal elder at a Washington, DC, Indigenous Peoples March in early 2019. An initial video showed the Covington students, who were in town for a March for Life rally and wearing Make America Great Again hats, appearing to mock the tribal elder, Nathan Phillips, in a way that was culturally disrespectful. In particular, one Covington student, Nick Sandmann, was seen smirking just inches from Phillips face.

This initial video went viral, with liberals quick to condemn the Covington students and, by extension, Trump supporters more broadly. In the spirit of full disclosure, I was one of those liberals. I include my own bout with motivated reasoning and confirmation bias to illustrate how easy it is to fall victim to these processes. Even though I pride myself as someone who is inclined to be accuracy motivated (Kahne & Bowyer, 2017; Pennycook & Rand, 2019) and well versed in media literacy strategies, I am also a human with strong beliefs, which means I am not immune to these psychosocial processes. Figure 1.6 shows my Facebook post upon the release of the initial video. I linked to a *HuffPost* article containing the video and explicitly denounced the students, but if I am being honest, my intent was to make a larger point about what I perceived to be racism and bigotry among Trump supporters and the policies of the Trump administration.

My post was initially met with a flurry of comments from likeminded friends who expressed disgust over the students' actions, with one of my friends even going so far as to say that she would "love to punch that kid [Sandmann] in his smug face". Within 24 hours, though, a longer video surfaced, showing that the confrontation was instigated by members of the Black Hebrew Israelites, a far-left group, and that Phillips was the one who approached the Covington students. This second video also went viral, leading many conservatives to condemn liberals like myself for making false accusations of racism.

My own Facebook wall, which I am not displaying here out of respect for my friends' privacy, became a back and forth between those who still believed that the Covington students were bigots and those who believed that they were being victimized simply for wearing pro-Trump apparel. The discourse only intensified when additional videos emerged that showed the Covington students catcalling and cursing at women as they participated in the March for Life Rally. On my wall and across social media, aspects of motivated reasoning, confirmation bias, and the backfire effect were on full display. Despite everyone having seen the same videos, we all came to different conclusions based on our existing beliefs and the strength of our convictions.[5] Writing in the days following the incident, Beauchamp (2019) described these psychosocial processes when he noted that

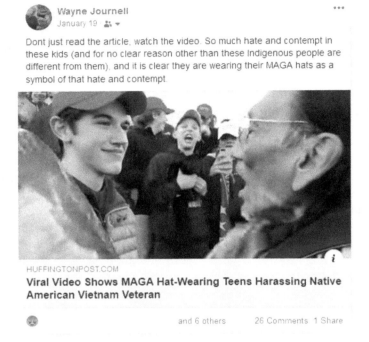

Wayne Journell
January 19

Dont just read the article, watch the video. So much hate and contempt in these kids (and for no clear reason other than these Indigenous people are different from them), and it is clear they are wearing their MAGA hats as a symbol of that hate and contempt.

HUFFINGTONPOST.COM
Viral Video Shows MAGA Hat-Wearing Teens Harassing Native American Vietnam Veteran

and 6 others   26 Comments 1 Share

Figure 1.6.

despite the inherent uncertainty in the footage itself, both sides continue to dig in, accusing the other of willful blindness and bad faith. It's been 4 days since the initial incident.... Still, it's the most divisive and talked-about issue in American public life right now. Why? The answer is that the Covington videos are [a] kind of Rorschach test, showing each side seeing what it wants to in a way that's more revealing about their own worldviews than the actual incident. (paras. 6–7)

The fake news that presents a danger to democracy is reliant on these psychosocial processes. It is human nature that encourages attempts at deception, leads us to believe falsehoods, and makes us jump to conclusions when presented with incomplete information. Of course, humans have always had these attributes, and people have been peddling actual fake news since the beginning of recorded history (Carson, 2018; Manfra, 2019; Woodson et al., 2019). So, why has fake news become such a widespread concern in recent years? The answer is that we are living in a unique period in which extreme partisanship and polarization has coincided with the rise of social media to create a perfect environment for fake news to thrive and cause the most damage.

PARTISANSHIP, POLARIZATION, AND SOCIAL MEDIA

Political polarization is not new to the United States. The nation has always been a collection of diverse beliefs and interests, and since the 1860s, those divisions have largely been regional. The coasts and urban centers tend to be more progressive, and the South, Midwest, and rural areas tend to be more conservative (Journell, 2014; Loewen, 2010). Moreover, these divides extend beyond politics and include social and ideological differences, such as choices of entertainment and the importance of religion (Katz, 2016; Parker et al., 2018). These divides have become so deep that data show that, increasingly, "liberals and conservatives disagree over where they want to live, the kinds of people they want to live around and even whom they would welcome into their families" (Pew Research Center, 2014, para. 4).

In short, the United States remains a deeply polarized nation on many fronts, and politics has increasingly become intertwined in these cultural divides (Abramowitz & Webster, 2016; Pierson & Schlickler, 2020). As a result, the 21st century has seen a sharp rise in *negative partisanship*, which is defined not only by allegiance to one's preferred political party, but also negative perceptions of the opposing party (Abramowitz & McCoy, 2019; Abramowitz & Webster, 2016, 2018). Research shows that sizeable percentages of Democrats and Republicans believe the other is a threat to the nation's well-being (Pew Research Center, 2014) and, as a result, many Americans' connections to their political or ideological identity is stronger than their racial, ethnic, or religious identity (Westwood et al., 2018).

Already isolated from each other geographically and ideologically, liberals and conservatives increasingly self-select into informational echo chambers that align with their worldviews. In theory, the glut of news networks and electronic news outlets available today should make the electorate better informed because people could hear multiple perspectives on a given issue, and social media also has the potential to alleviate ideological divides created by geography. However, most people tend to gravitate to news outlets that affirm existing beliefs and disparage or ignore contrary information, and they surround themselves with others, both in real life and on social media, who share the same political views. As O'Connor and Weatherall (2018) noted, "people like to conform with those around them, and when we are surrounded by peers who hold identical beliefs, the forces of conformity become extremely strong" (pp. 16-17)

The conformity found within these self-selected echo chambers contributes to the rise of fake news by feeding individuals' motivated reasoning and confirmation bias. The extent to which this self-selection of information can skew individuals' perceptions of reality can be found in the comments of Cathy Garnaat, a Republican who attended a constituent town hall with Representative Justin Amash in May 2019. Prior to the town hall, Amash made headlines as the only Congressional Republican to call for the impeachment of President Trump,[6] and at the meeting, Amash defended his position to the surprise of many of his constituents, including Garnaat. When interviewed after the town hall, Garnaat revealed the following:

> I was surprised to hear there was anything negative in the Mueller report at all about President Trump. I hadn't heard that before ... I've mainly listened to conservative news and I hadn't heard anything negative about that report and [that] President Trump has been exonerated. (Caldwell & Moe, 2019, para. 17)

The Mueller report, however, did not exonerate Trump. In fact, the report explicitly stated that "while this report does not conclude the President committed a crime, it also does not exonerate him" (Mueller, 2019, p. 2). This information was not secret; Attorney General William Barr included that quotation in his initial summary of the Mueller report (*The New York Times*, 2019) that was made public, it was widely reported in the mainstream media, and the entire 448-page Mueller report was eventually released to the public. Yet, if one only listened to conservative news outlets or interacted exclusively with conservatives on social media, there was a good chance that the truth would have been omitted or distorted to an extent that the meaning would have been lost. The fact that Trump repeatedly tweeted and stated that the Mueller report provided him with "total exoneration" also likely contributed to this masking of the truth among conservatives (Sarkis, 2019, para. 3).

People, of course, make a choice when they turn on Fox News or MSNBC or download an article from well-known conservative or liberal publications. Social media is more subversive. Certainly, some of the decisions that people make on social media are intentional; for example, when people choose to follow pages like "Millennials for Bernie" or "Veterans for Trump," they likely know what type of content they will be encountering. Social media is unique, though, because it also pushes content on users based on their likes and dislikes as determined by their digital footprints.

We live in an unprecedented era of "big data," and as the Internet continues to consume more aspects of everyday life, more of our thoughts, desires, and fears are captured in the process of electronic surveillance that has come to define life in the 21st century (Garrett, 2016). All social media sites, for example, base their advertisements and other sponsored content on algorithms that track users' online habits. A technical understanding of how algorithms work is beyond the scope of this chapter, but in short, if social media platforms notice that someone clicks on a lot of articles or posts about, say, food recipes, then they should expect to see advertisements about cooking equipment and sponsored pages touting Crockpot recipes regularly showing up in their Facebook and Twitter feeds.[7]

Political propaganda and fake news work the same way. Based on one's click history, a profile is developed, and people can use that information to maximize exposure and impact of a political advertisement, meme, or post. For example, conservative politicians and political action groups are more likely to target someone who regularly visits hunting websites and likes the page of the television show *Last Man Standing* than they are someone who visits environmental conservation websites and likes the page of the television show *Modern Family*.

In other words, fake news is not designed to sway people's opinions; rather, its intent is to intensify existing views. By releasing propaganda and advertisements into echo chambers, the peddlers of fake news and biased information ensure that their products will be liked and shared by the greatest number of people. Take, for example, the meme shown in Figure 1.5. The meme was included in a Russian-sponsored Facebook group that catered to conservatives; as a result, it was viewed over 3,000 times and shared over 1,000 times. Given this strategic placement of fake news on social media platforms, it is not surprising that research has found that fake news is spread faster online than information from legitimate news sources (Lazer et al., 2018; Silverman, 2016). Therefore, while it is up for debate exactly how much influence fake news has on shaping beliefs and affecting political outcomes (Allcott & Gentzkow, 2017), there is no question that the peddlers of fake news have been effective in getting their message in front of people who are more likely to share it and keep it alive on social media.

The idea, then, that fake news just floats around the Internet waiting to be consumed by ignorant individuals is a simplistic and misleading narrative. The dissemination of fake news is purposeful and often implemented with a great deal of precision. As a result, teaching about fake news creates new challenges for educators in that traditional media literacy approaches are not sufficient (Journell, 2019; Mason et al., 2018).

CONCLUSION

A recent survey found that Americans believe fake news is more detrimental to the nation than systemic issues such as racism and sexism, as well as the specific issues of violent crime, climate change, illegal immigration, and terrorism (Mitchell et al., 2019). Given the publicity around fake news over the past 4 years, those results are not surprising, but I would argue that they are shortsighted. The proliferation of fake news online, on television, and out of the mouths of politicians is, without question, a serious societal problem. However, I contend that it is not *the* problem; rather, fake news is a symptom of much larger divides present in U.S. society that are amplified in a largely unregulated social media landscape.

Understanding that distinction is important for educators. If fake news is perceived as the problem, then it is tempting to address it through traditional media literacy approaches. Certainly, research has shown that students are not adept at evaluating the legitimacy of information they encounter online (McGrew et al., 2018) and often rely on inaccurate and heavily biased information in class discussions (Segall et al., 2019). Therefore, I am not suggesting that teachers abandon basic media literacy principles; on the contrary, research has shown that the more media literacy education one receives, the more likely they are to develop dispositions that make them think analytically about media (Kahne & Bowyer, 2017), which is essential to combating the effects of fake news (Pennycook & Rand, 2019). However, in this era of deepfakes and memes generated from the dark recesses of the Internet, many of the traditional media literacy methods have become antiquated.

Addressing fake news in the classroom requires that teachers not only focus on the quality of information being shared, but also the motivation for sharing it. By unpacking the existing societal divides that create a favorable environment for fake news, teachers can provide students with a context for understanding why fake news works and how we all, to varying degrees, are complicit in its effectiveness. Such instruction is challenging because it forces students to grapple with complex ideas, such as worldviews and desires, that cannot be reduced to a simple checklist. However, until we, as a society, can develop a common understanding of the wider problem, fake news will only continue to exacerbate these divides and negatively influence our democratic institutions.

NOTES

1. Although specific instructional strategies are beyond the scope of this chapter, readers interested in practical ideas for the classroom can consult Breakstone et al. (2018); Hauver (2019); Hodgin and Kahne (2019); Journell and Clark (2019); and Manfra and Holmes (2018).

2. To see the full listing of all of the Russian advertisements released by Congress following their investigation into Russian influence in the 2016 election, visit https://intelligence.house.gov/social-media-content/social-media-advertisements.htm

3.   Although it is unclear how many users, if any, were tricked into submitting their votes online based on these types of posts, Twitter has recently taken steps to help ensure that misleading tweets related to voting are quickly removed from the platform (Lomas, 2019).

4.   Despite being blocked, savvy users can still find ways to promote *InfoWars* content on these platforms, and it becomes a continual game of cat and mouse to take them down.

5.   It is worth noting that in early 2020 CNN reached an out-of-court settlement with Sandmann, who had sued CNN and other media organizations for how they depicted him following the first video (Darcy, 2020).

6.   Soon after calling for Trump's impeachment, Amash unaffiliated himself with the Republican Party and became an independent.

7.   Those interested in a better technical understanding of how algorithms work can refer to Cohen (2019).

REFERENCES

Abramowitz, A. I., & McCoy, J. (2019). United States: Racial resentment, negative partisanship, and polarization in Trump's America. *The ANNALS of the American Academy of Political and Social Science, 681*, 137–156.

Abramowitz, A. I., & Webster, S. (2016). The rise of negative partisanship and the nationalization of U.S. elections in the 21st century. *Electoral Studies, 41*, 12–22.

Abramowitz, A. I., & Webster, S. (2018). Negative partisanship: Why Americans dislike parties but behave like rabid partisans. *Political Psychology, 39*, 119–135.

Allcott, H., & Gentzkow, M. (2017). Social media and fake news in the 2016 election. *Journal of Economic Perspectives, 31*, 211–236.

Al-Rawi, A. (2019). Gatekeeping fake news discourses on mainstream media versus social media. *Social Science Computer Review, 37*, 687–704.

Baym, G. (2010). *From Cronkite to Colbert: The evolution of broadcast news.* Paradigm.

Beauchamp, Z. (2019, January 23). The real politics behind the Covington Catholic controversy, explained. *Vox.* https://www.vox.com/policy-and-politics/2019/1/23/18192831/covington-catholic-maga-hat-native-american-nathan-phillips

Bersani, B. E. (2014). An examination of first and second generation immigrant offending trajectories. *Justice Quarterly, 31*, 315–343.

Blake, A. (2018, July 13). Trump denies he said something he said on a tape everyone has heard. *The Washington Post.* https://www.washingtonpost.com/news/the-fix/wp/2018/07/13/trump-denies-he-said-something-that-he-said-on-a-tape-that-everyone-has-heard/?noredirect=on&utm_term=.01818ae7946d

Bradner, E. (2015, December 2). Trump praises 9/11 truther's 'amazing' reputation. *CNN.* https://www.cnn.com/2015/12/02/politics/donald-trump-praises-9-11-truther-alex-jones/index.html

Breakstone, J., McGrew, S., Smith, M., Ortega, T., & Wineburg, S. (2018). Why we need a new approach to teaching digital literacy. *Phi Delta Kappan, 99*(6), 27–32.

Caldwell, L. A., & Moe, A. (2019, May 28). Republican Justin Amash stands by position to start impeachment proceedings despite criticism. *NBC News.* https://www.nbcnews.com/news/us-news/republican-justin-amash-stands-position-start-impeachment-proceedings-despite-criticism-n1011176

Carson, J. (2018, November 28). Fake news: What exactly is it—And how can you spot it? *The Telegraph.* www.telegraph.co.uk/technology/0/fake-news-exactly-has-really-had-influence

Chen, M. (2016, March 14). Undocumented immigrants contribute over $11 billion to our economy each year. *The Nation.* https://www.thenation.com/article/undocumented-immigrants-contribute-over-11-billion-to-our-economy-each-year/

Clinton, H. R. (2017). *What happened.* Simon & Schuster.

CNN. (2016, November 23). Exit polls, 2016. https://www.cnn.com/election/2016/results/exit-polls

Cohen, J. N. (2018). Exploring echo-systems: How algorithms shape immersive media environments. *Journal of Media Literacy Education, 10*(2), 139–151.

Confessore, N. (2016, November 2). Veterans, feeling abandoned, stand by Donald Trump. *The New York Times.* https://www.nytimes.com/2016/11/03/us/politics/donald-trump-veterans.html

Darcy, O. (2020, January 7). CNN settles lawsuit with Nick Sandmann stemming from viral video controversy. *CNN.* https://www.cnn.com/2020/01/07/media/cnn-settles-lawsuit-viral-video/index.html

Davis, J. H., & Rosenberg, M. (2017, January 21). With false claims, Trump attacks media on turnout and intelligence rift. *The New York Times.* https://www.nytimes.com/2017/01/21/us/politics/trump-white-house-briefing-inauguration-crowd-size.html

Dusso, A., & Kennedy, S. S. (2015). Does ignorance matter? The relative importance of civic knowledge and the human tendency to engage in motivated reasoning. *Journal of Public and Nonprofit Affairs, 1,* 59–72.

Fischer, S. (2018, June 27). 92% of Republicans think media intentionally reports fake news. *Axios.* https://www.axios.com/trump-effect-92-percent-republicans-media-fake-news-9c1bbf70-0054-41dd-b506-0869bb10f08c.html

Friedman, S. (2018, October 22). Why John Oliver takes breaks from 'Last Week Tonight' may be related to all the research involved. *Bustle.* https://www.bustle.com/p/why-john-oliver-takes-breaks-from-last-week-tonight-may-be-related-to-all-the-research-involved-12635285

Gallup. (2018). *Indicators of news media trust.* Gallup and Knight Foundation.

Garrett, H. J. (2016). Big data, surveillance, and the unprecedented conditions of citizenship. In W. Journell (Ed.), *Teaching social studies in an era of divisiveness: The challenges of discussing social issues in a non-partisan way* (pp. 127–142). Rowman & Littlefield.

Garrett, H. J. (2019). Why does fake news work? On the psychosocial dynamics of learning, belief, and citizenship. In W. Journell (Ed.), *Unpacking fake news: An educator's guide to navigating the media with students* (pp. 15–29). College Press.

Garrett, H. J., & Schmeichel, M. (2012). Using "The Daily Show" to promote media literacy. *Social Education, 76,* 211–215.

Hanna, J. (2017, January 27). What is Infowars? *CNN.* https://www.cnn.com/2017/01/27/politics/infowars-explainer/index.html

Hauver, J. (2019). Two truths and fake news: Lessons for young learners. In W. Journell (Ed.), *Unpacking fake news: An educator's guide to navigating the media with students* (pp. 126–137). Teachers College Press.

Helm, B. (2017). Pizzagate nearly destroyed my restaurant. Then my customers helped me fight back. *Inc.* https://www.inc.com/magazine/201707/burt-helm/how-i-did-it-james-alefantis-comet-ping-pong.html

Hodgin, E., & Kahne, J. (2019). Judging credibility in un-credible times: Three educational approaches for the digital age. In W. Journell (Ed.), *Unpacking fake news: An educator's guide to navigating the media with students* (pp. 92–108). Teachers College Press.

Holloway, C. (2018, September 30). The great revolt: Understanding real Trump voters. *Public Discourse.* https://www.thepublicdiscourse.com/2018/09/43720/

Journell, W. (2014). Teaching politics in the U.S. history classroom. *The History Teacher, 48,* 55–69.

Journell, W. (2017). *Teaching politics in secondary education: Engaging with contentious issues.* State University of New York Press.

Journell, W. (2018). Civic education in a post-truth society: Combating "fake news" and "alternative facts". In J. Clabaugh & T. Lintner (Eds.), *No reluctant citizens: Teaching civics in K–12 classrooms* (pp. 113–129). Information Age.

Journell, W. (Ed.). (2019). *Unpacking fake news: An educator's guide to navigating the media with students.* Teachers College Press.

Journell, W. (in press). The subjectivity of openness: Framing social issues in K–12 education. In T. Hawley & P. Chandler (Eds.), *Handbook on teaching social issues* (2nd ed.). Information Age.

Journell, W., & Clark, C. H. (2019). Political memes and the limits of media literacy. In W. Journell (Ed.), *Unpacking fake news: An educator's guide to navigating the media with students* (pp. 109–125). Teachers College Press.

Kahne, J., & Bowyer, B. (2017). Educating for democracy in a partisan age: Confronting the challenges of motivated reasoning and misinformation. *American Educational Research Journal, 54,* 3–34.

Katz, J. (2016, December 27). 'Duck Dynasty' vs 'Modern Family': 50 maps of the U.S. cultural divide. *The New York Times.* https://www.nytimes.com/interactive/2016/12/26/upshot/duck-dynasty-vs-modern-family-television-maps.html

Keetley, D. (Ed.). (2014). *"We're all infected": Essays on AMC's The Walking Dead and the fate of the human.* McFarland & Company.

Kiefer, M. (2014, June 18). First peek: Immigrant children flood detention center. *The Arizona Republic.* https://www.azcentral.com/story/news/politics/immigration/2014/06/18/arizona-immigrant-children-holding-area-tour/10780449/

Lacapria, K. (2017, November 30). Did Donald Trump say Republicans are the "dumbest group of voters"? *Snopes.* http://www.snopes.com/fact-check/1998-trump-people-quote/

Lazer, D. M. J., Baum, M. A., Benkler, Y., Berinsky, A. J., Greenhill, K. M., Menczer, F., Metzger, M. J., Nyhan, B., Pennycook, G., Rothschild, D., Schudson, M., Sloman, S. A., Sunstein, C. R., Thorson, E. A., Watts, D. J., & Zittrain, J. L. (2018). The science of fake news. *Science, 35,* 1094–1096.

Light, M. T., & Miller, T. (2018). Does undocumented immigration increase violent crime? *Criminology, 56,* 370–401.

Loewen, J. W. (2010). *Teaching what really happened: How to avoid the tyranny of textbooks and get students excited about doing history.* Teachers College Press.

Lomas, N. (2019, April 24). Twitter to offer report option for misleading election tweets. *TechCrunch.* https://techcrunch.com/2019/04/24/twitter-to-offer-report-option-for-misleading-election-tweets/

Lorenz, T. (2019, May 2). Instagram and Facebook ban far-right extremists. *The Atlantic.* https://www.theatlantic.com/technology/archive/2019/05/instagram-and-facebook-ban-far-right-extremists/588607/

Madsen, W. (2016, February 25). Why Scalia's death suggests cover-up. *InfoWars.* http://www.infowars.com/why-scalias-death-suggests-cover-up/

Manfra, M. M. (2019). What's new about fake news? Integrating digital history for media literacy. *Social Education, 83,* 113–117.

Manfra, M. M., & Holmes, C. (2018). Media literacy and fake news in the social studies. *Social Education, 82,* 91–95.

Mason, L. E., Krutka, D. G., & Stoddard, J. (2018). Media literacy, democracy, and the challenge of fake news. *Journal of Media Literacy Education, 10*(2), 1–10.

McGrew, S., Breakstone, J., Ortega, T., Smith, M., & Wineburg, S. (2018). Can students evaluate online sources? Learning from assessments of civic online reasoning. *Theory & Research in Social Education, 46,* 165–193.

Mikkelson, D. (2018, May 27). Is this a photograph of a children's concentration camp in the U.S.? *Snopes.* https://www.snopes.com/fact-check/childrens-concentration-camp/

Mitchell, A., & Barthell, M. (2017, May 10). Americans' attitudes about the news media deeply divided along partisan lines. *Pew Research Center.* https://www.journalism.org/2017/05/10/americans-attitudes-about-the-news-media-deeply-divided-along-partisan-lines/

Mitchell, A., Gottfried, J., Fedeli, S., Stocking, G., & Walker, M. (2019, June 5). Many Americans say made-up news is a critical problem that needs to be fixed. *Pew Research Center.* https://www.journalism.org/2019/06/05/many-americans-say-made-up-news-is-a-critical-problem-that-needs-to-be-fixed/

Mueller, R. S. (2019). *Report on the investigation into Russian interference in the 2016 Presidential Election, Volume II of II.* U.S. Department of Justice.

National Council for the Social Studies. (2016). Media literacy. *Social Education, 80,* 183-185.

National Council for the Social Studies. (2019). Youth, social media, and digital civic engagement. *Social Education, 83,* 164–166.

Nickerson, R. S. (1998). Confirmation bias: A ubiquitous phenomenon in many guises. *Review of General Psychology, 2,* 175–220.

Nowrasteh, A. (2018, February 26). Criminal immigrants in Texas: Illegal immigrant conviction and arrest rates for homicide, sexual assault, larceny, and other crimes. *Cato Institute.* https://www.cato.org/publications/immigration-research-policy-brief/criminal-immigrants-texas-illegal-immigrant

Nyhan, B., & Reifler, J. (2010). When corrections fail: The persistence of political misperceptions. *Political Behavior, 32,* 303–330.

O'Connor, C., & Weatherall, J. O. (2018). *The misinformation age: How false beliefs spread.* Yale University Press.

Ortiz, E. (2017, June 22). 'Pizzagate' gunman Edgar Maddison Welch sentenced to four years in prison. *NBC News.* https://www.nbcnews.com/news/us-news/pizzagate-gunman-edgar-maddison-welch-sentenced-four-years-prison-n775621

Parker, K., Horowitz, J. M., Brown, A., Fry, R., Cohn, D., & Igielnik, R. (2018, May 22). What unites and divides urban, suburban, and rural communities. *Pew Research Center.* https://www.pewsocialtrends.org/2018/05/22/what-unites-and-divides-urban-suburban-and-rural-communities/

Pennycook, G., & Rand, D. G. (2019). Lazy, not biased: Susceptibility to partisan fake news is better explained by lack of reasoning than motivated reasoning. *Cognition, 188,* 39–50.

Peters, J. W. (2018, June 23). As critics assail Trump, his supporters dig in deeper. *The New York Times.* https://www.nytimes.com/2018/06/23/us/politics/republican-voters-trump.html

Pew Research Center. (2014, June 12). Political polarization in the American public. http://www.people-press.org/2014/06/12/political-polarization-in-the-american-public/

Pierson, P., & Schickler, E. (2020). Madison's constitution under stress: A developmental analysis of political polarization. *Annual Review of Political Science.* Advance online publication. https://doi.org/10.1146/annurev-polisci-050718-033629

Quigley, A. (2017, June 16). Who is Alex Jones? His top five conspiracy theories ahead of NBC's Megyn Kelly interview. *Newsweek.* www.newsweek.com/who-alex-jones-his-top-five-conspiracy-theories-aheads-nbc-megyn-kelly-626633

Richardson, B. (2015, November 10). McCain: Hillary remarks about VA 'shameful.' *The Hill.* https://thehill.com/policy/defense/259750-mccain-hillary-remarks-about-va-shameful

Sarkis, S. (2019, March 24). Trump puts exoneration in all caps—Almost as if he were exonerated. *Forbes.* https://www.forbes.com/sites/stephaniesarkis/2019/03/24/trump-puts-exoneration-in-caps-almost-as-if-he-were-exonerated/#4a9b6ba42e01

Schwartz, I. (2015, June 16). Trump: Mexico not sending us their best; criminals, drug dealers and rapists are crossing border. *RealClearPolitics.* https://www.realclearpolitics.com/video/2015/06/16/trump_mexico_not_sending_us_their_best_criminals_drug_dealers_and_rapists_are_crossing_border.html

Segall, A., Crocco, M. S., Halvorsen, A-L, & Jacobsen, R. (2019). Teaching in the twilight zone of misinformation, disinformation, alternative facts, and fake news. In W. Journell (Ed.), *Unpacking fake news: An educator's guide to navigating the media with students* (pp. 74–91). Teachers College Press.

Silverman, C. (2016, November 16). This analysis shows how viral fake election news stories outperformed real news on Facebook. *Buzzfeed.* https://www

.buzzfeednews.com/article/craigsilverman/viral-fake-election-news-outperformed-real-news-on-facebook

Smith, A. (2019, June 2). Trump denies he called Meghan Markle 'nasty' despite audio of remark. *NBC News.* https://www.nbcnews.com/politics/donald-trump/trump-denies-he-called-meghan-markle-nasty-despite-audio-remark-n1012881

Southern Poverty Law Center. (2018). Alex Jones. http://www.splcenter.org/fighting-hate/extremist-files/individual/alex-jones

Steinberg, B. (2018, February 16). And now this: John Oliver just might be a journalist. *Variety.* https://variety.com/2018/tv/news/john-oliver-journalist-hbo-last-week-tonight-1202702144/

Taber, C. S., & Lodge, M. (2016). The illusion of choice in democratic politics: The unconscious impact of motivated political reasoning. *Advances in Political Psychology, 37*, 61–85.

The New York Times. (2019, March 24). Read Attorney General William Barr's summary of the Mueller report. https://www.nytimes.com/interactive/2019/03/24/us/politics/barr-letter-mueller-report.html

Varas, J. (2018, March 7). Restricting legal immigration to America won't help our economy. *The Hill.* http://thehill.com/opinion/immigration/377216-restricting-legal-immigration-to-america-wont-help-our-economy

Wagner, K. (2017, October 31). These are some of the tweets and Facebook ads Russia used to try and influence the 2016 Presidential Election. *Vox.* https://www.vox.com/2017/10/31/16587174/fake-ads-news-propaganda-congress-facebook-twitter-google-tech-hearing

Westwood, S. J., Iyengar, S., Walgrave, S., Leonisio, R., Miller, L., & Strijbis, O. (2018). The tie that divides: Cross-national evidence of the primacy of partyism. *European Journal of Political Research, 57*, 333–354.

Wood, T., & Porter, E. (2019). The elusive backfire effect: Mass attitudes' steadfast factual adherence. *Political Behavior, 41*, 135–163.

Woodson, A. N., King, L. J., & Kim, E. (2019). Real recognize real: Thoughts on race, fake news, and naming our truths. In W. Journell (Ed.), *Unpacking fake news: An educator's guide to navigating the media with students* (pp. 30–41). Teachers College Press.

U. S. House of Representatives Permanent Select Committee on Intelligence. (n.d.). Exposing Russia's effort to sow discord online: The internet research agency and advertisements. https://intelligence.house.gov/social-media-content/

Zadrozny, B. (2019, February 1). Fire at 'pizzagate' shop reignites conspiracy theorists who find a home on Facebook. *NBC News.* https://www.nbcnews.com/tech/social-media/fire-pizzagate-shop-reignites-conspiracy-theorists-who-find-home-facebook-n965956

CHAPTER 2

THE NC ACCESS PROGRAM

Remediating or Deepening Divisions in Public Education?

Laura K. Handler and Tracy C. Rock
University of North Carolina Charlotte

ABSTRACT

The splintering of democratic aims in our nation even persists through our current system of public education, as the continued expansion of charter schools presents new challenges of divisions across funding, enrollment, and high-quality educational opportunity. In the context of a state whose charter school enrollments demonstrate trends of increasing segregation and inequity, the North Carolina Advancing Charter Collaboration and Excellence for Student Success (NC ACCESS) program was established to improve academic opportunities for "educationally disadvantaged" students. Through the analysis presented in this chapter, we critically examine the stated intentions, submitted applications, and initial participation of charter schools in this 5-year program. In doing so, we problematize its purpose, question its potential outcomes, and caution its unintended consequences, particularly in the broader focus of remediating existing current educational inequities.

The Divide Within: Intersections of Realities, Facts, Theories, and Practices
pp. 39–58
Copyright © 2021 by Information Age Publishing

INTRODUCTION

As asserted by the theme of this book, *the divide within*, the polarization of groups within the United States spans across political ideologies, geography, religion, citizenship, and race. The splintering of democratic aims even persists through the nation's system of public education, as the continued expansion of charter schools presents new challenges of divisions across funding, enrollment, and high-quality educational opportunity. While originally intended to support innovation of public education, the political polarization now associated with charter schools in particular, leads to problematic paths of collaboration and communication toward this collective aim. Furthermore, evidence of the growing divisions among populations attending public charters and traditional public schools (TPSs) is shown in numerous reports of segregation exacerbated by school choice (Ayscue et al., 2018; Hawn Nelson, 2017; Lareau & Goyette, 2014; Rotberg & Glazer, 2018).

In North Carolina, the first charter schools opened their doors in 1997, yet a 100-school cap limited enrollment and growth for over 2 decades. In conjunction with Race to the Top initiatives, however, the state legislature lifted the cap in 2011, and the charter school sector has since rapidly expanded to include 184 schools and more than 109,000 students (just over 7% of public school attendees) during the 2018–2019 school year. With relatively minimal regulation in this expansion, enrollment trends show charters in North Carolina serving disproportionately higher numbers of affluent White students than TPSs (Ladd et al., 2015; Malkus, 2016). In the Charlotte region, the second largest metropolitan area in the state, over a third of charters are segregated by race, nearly half are racially isolated (60% or more, double the district percentage) White, and under a quarter are hypersegregated (over 80%) Black (Hawn Nelson, 2017). According to the North Carolina Department of Public Instruction's Charter School Annual Report of 2016, 12% of Hispanics were knowledgeable about charters, and, similarly in a qualitative report, Latinx parents commonly responded to inquiries about charters with, "What charters?" (Handler, 2018, p. 114).

Recognizing the need to address this racial and economic segregation, the state recently applied for and was awarded $26.6 million in federal funding to support charters to serve more "educationally disadvantaged"[1] students. The North Carolina Advancing Charter Collaboration and Excellence for Student Success (NC ACCESS) program designates "educationally disadvantaged" (EDS) to include students who are economically disadvantaged (ED), homeless or unaccompanied youth, English learners (EL), and students with disabilities (SWD; North Carolina State Board of Education, n.d.). Other goals of the program are to develop a cohort of school leaders knowledgeable of best practices in serving educationally disadvantaged students, and to increase collaboration between public charter and TPSs. Given the current context of charter schools in the state—not representative of state populations, highly segregated by race and income, and more in competition than collaboration with TPSs—we sought to critically examine how the NC ACCESS program might remediate these divisions. Analyzing applications of the nine charter schools awarded funding, we questioned how their proposed plans might address the barriers currently restricting certain populations from attending charters, and simultaneously attempt to meet the needs of such diverse "educationally disadvantaged" students.

To begin the chapter, we briefly review the political, demographic, and academic contexts of public schools—both traditional and charters—in the national setting of the United States and then more narrowly in the state setting of North Carolina. From this situated framework we lead into a description of the NC ACCESS program, including its objectives and planned procedures to support the state's charter schools' recruitment and service of "educationally disadvantaged" students. After detailing the methods of our research, we present the three major themes of our analysis. We conclude the chapter with a discussion of the implications of our findings, returning again to the broad contexts of the deep divisions within the American public school sectors, and pose recommendations for continued work that explicitly prioritizes equity and integration in the educational experiences of our nation's youth.

LITERATURE REVIEW

Charter Schools in the United States

With Kentucky most recently approving legislation in 2017, now 44 states and the District of Columbia have enacted charter school laws (Education Commission of the United States, 2019). Nationally, there are more than 7,000 charter schools enrolling over three million students across K–12 levels (David & Hesla, 2018). While these numbers still only constitute roughly 7% of the overall student population (National Center for Education Statistics, 2019), in some school districts (i.e., Orleans Parish, District of Columbia) and states (Arizona, California) that percentage is much higher. Since 2015, charter school enrollment has surpassed that of magnet schools (National Center for Education Statistics, 2015), a specialized form of public schools which were introduced in the 1970s as a voluntary form of desegregation.

The rise of charter schools reflects a trend in national educational policies designed to employ school choice as a reform strategy to address perceived failings of the public school system and improve academic achievement. While numerous researchers have attempted to measure and compare charter schools and TPSs, evidence is largely inconclusive, noting great variance in policies, schools, and programs across the nation due to differences in the state charter school laws governing them (i.e., Center for Research on Education Outcomes, 2013; Jabbar et al., 2017). The authors of several studies also emphasize significant differences among the populations attending charters and TPSs, calling attention to the link between academic achievement and student demographics, most notably class and race (Ladd et al., 2015; Malkus, 2016). Rather than oversimplify analyses with broad generalizations about the performance and characteristics of charters and TPSs, there is an increasing need for a more nuanced understanding of schools at the state and local levels, where these particulars and contexts can be more thoroughly examined and explained.

Charter Schools in North Carolina

As presented in the introduction, the establishment and growth of charter schools in North Carolina is unique to the political, social, and economic contexts of the state. Following the lifting of the 100-school cap in 2011, North Carolina Senate Bill 8 was passed in 2013, containing several provisions that eased a rapid advancement of charter schools (Mickelson et al., 2018). Though the 2018 Charter Schools Annual Report notes an increase in racial diversity among charter school population, it acknowledges continued growth needed to eliminate differences from traditional public schools. Stating "there is no mechanism by which schools can guarantee racial and ethnic balance" (p. 10), no consequence is in place for charters that do not "reasonably reflect" the general population, as the state's charter law, G.S. 115C-218.45(e), mandates. Four of the state's 187 charter schools have voluntarily applied and received approval for use of a weighted lottery to attain a more diverse student body.

Additionally, the annual report notes North Carolina charter schools have a higher percentage of schools receiving a school performance grade of A than TPSs, and they also have a higher percentage of schools receiving a school performance grade of F than TPSs. These performance ratings reflect the racial and economic isolation present in the North Carolina charter sector. Between 1997 and 2017, 60 charter schools closed, some prior to opening their doors, with a majority due to financial reasons. Fiscal challenges, however, are often related to low enrollment numbers, particularly after receiving poor performance ratings (Doss Helms, 2018). The first charter to be closed for poor academic performance was in 2012, with only three additional charter nonrenewals or revocations since then (Center for Community Self-Help et al., 2014). Three of these four had populations predominantly comprised of students of color and students of poverty. Most recently, the state general assembly approved House Bill 514, which allows the municipalities surrounding Charlotte—with Whiter, wealthier populations—to establish their own charter schools. Critics fear this law will draw students away from the larger urban school district and contribute to further resegregation of public schools (Osborne, 2019).

Overview of the NC ACCESS Program

In 2018, the North Carolina Department of Public Instruction was one of eight states awarded a Charter School Program grant from the U.S. Department of Education for approximately $26,600,000 to implement the NC ACCESS Program. Through the grant, the program's objectives were outlined as the following:

- Objective 1: Increase the number of educationally disadvantaged students attending high-quality charter schools and expand the number of high-quality charter schools available to educationally disadvantaged students;
- Objective 2: Develop a cadre of 100 charter school leaders who can develop and demonstrate best practices in serving educationally disadvantaged students; and
- Objective 3: Broadly disseminate best practices in serving educationally disadvantaged students and foster collaboration in the charter school community and between charter schools and traditional public schools.

These objectives would be met through a subgrant program that would provide funding to support the startup and expansion of high-quality charter schools wishing to serve educationally disadvantaged students; a year-long fellowship program with professional development and support for participants; and the development of a community of 100 charter school leaders that will demonstrate and share best practices in serving educationally disadvantaged students (NC State Board of Education, n.d.).

Core Elements of the NC ACCESS Subgrant Program

For each of the 5 years of the federal Charter School Program award, the NC ACCESS Program plans to award subgrants to North Carolina charter schools that propose comprehensive plans to increase the number of educationally disadvantaged students attending high-quality charter schools. The NC ACCESS Program defined educationally disadvantaged students as students who are economically disadvantaged, homeless or unaccompanied youth, English learners, and students with disabilities (NC State Board of Education, n.d.). It is important to point out that educationally disadvantaged students as defined by these grants expands the focus beyond the broad conception of serving economically disadvantaged students to call additional specific attention to the needs of homeless, unaccompanied youth, English learners, as well as students with disabilities. There are 4 types of subgrants identified through the NC ACCESS program: (a) planning and implementation; (b) implementation only; (c) expansion; and (d) replication. Table 2.1 presents the basic criteria for eligibility and priority consideration of each type of subgrant.

Review Process of NC ACCESS Applications

In the spring of 2019, each first year subgrant application was reviewed by a team of NC ACCESS Program team members and external evaluators using the scoring rubric and a recommendation was made to the Charter School Advisory Board (CSAB). Recommendations for approval or denial were based on the completed application which included school information, signed assurances, enrollment projections, application narrative, budget, budget narrative, logic model, and appendices. There was a total of 100 possible points on the scoring rubric (see Appendix A) with at least 80 points required to meet the standard for approval. The application narrative, constituting 60 points, was assessed by reviewers focusing on the following elements: (a) aggressive recruitment plan of educationally disadvantaged students, including a weighted lottery; (b) SMART goals and statement on how they will eliminate barriers; (c) education, discipline and school climate plan tailored to educationally disadvantaged students; (d) implementation of a parent/community advisory council; (e) budget and budget narrative for the duration of the grant; (f) marketing and recruitment plan; (g) plan to provide transportation; (h) comprehensive plan to provide free and reduced lunch; (i) school closure plan. The State Board of Education and the Charter School Advisory Board approved all eligibility criteria and determined the final approval of all subgrant awards. The Charter School Advisory Board made a recommendation for the approval of subgrants to the State Board of Education on June 6, 2019.

**Table 2.1.   Types of Subgrants
With Eligibility Criteria for NC ACCESS Program**

Type	Total # to be Awarded	Description
Planning and implementation	12 across 5 years	• Available to approved schools in their planning year • Must have a comprehensive plan for recruiting and serving a high education population • Schools operated by a charter management organization or education management organization will be required to submit performance data for other schools operated by the organization
Implementation only	10 across 5 years	• Available to schools in years 1-3 • Must have a comprehensive plan for recruiting and serving a high education population • If school-level data is available it should be provided from the initial years of operation. • Must have achieved at least "B" school performance grade (SPG) and met or exceeded growth for at least 2 of the last 3 years
Expansion	18 across 5 years	• Available to high-quality charter schools operating for at least 3 years to expand enrollment/grade levels or replicate • Must have achieved at least "B" SPG and met or exceeded growth for at least 2 of the last 3 years; or a school with "C" SPG for 3 years must have met or exceeded growth for all three years prior to application • Must support a significant increase in the EDS • Priority consideration given for the following: o serving greater than 40% ED; EL o graduation rate greater than the state average; o Title I status; o ED, EL, and SWD proficiency rates greater than the state average; and o "A" or "A+NG" SPG and met or exceeded growth for 3 consecutive years
Replication	10 across 5 years	

METHODS

For this analysis we collected several publicly-available documents to critically examine the divisions within and among public charter schools in North Carolina, and the proposed methods of the NC ACCESS program to address them. First, we accessed North Carolina's application to the federal grant Expanding Opportunity Through Quality Charter Schools Program, which was used to establish the NC ACCESS initiative. This document expressed the state's purpose and intention in creating the program and helped to stage subsequent document analyses. The Office of Charter Schools, under the State Board of Education, offers all documents, presentations, and minutes of their meetings, from which we obtained additional details of the NC ACCESS program as well as individual applications, reviewers' comments, and the recommendations made to the State of approval/rejection of funding. Finally, we used demographic information about charter schools of NC available through state reports, School Report Cards, National Center for Education Statistics, and websites of individual schools themselves to serve as contextual information about the populations enrolled, school locations, and student achievement.

As written, recorded material, the Charter School Program applications in particular proved to be an advantageous source of insight for us into the NC ACCESS program and how applying charter schools interpreted its purposes and requirements to serve "educationally disadvantaged" students. These materials were valuable not just for the information they directly contained, but the clues they indirectly conveyed (Mogalakwe, 2006). Yin (2014) reminds researchers that documents were written for a specific purpose other than the analysis being done; thus, we aimed to "listen" to implicit messages (p. 74) in the grant writers' understandings, perceptions, and approaches to serving "educationally disadvantaged" students.

Independently, we each began reviewing the applications for a first level of holistic coding (Dey, 1993; Saldaña, 2016) to generate initial themes or issues present in the data. This preparatory approach set us up for a second, more detailed, cycle of analysis of the applications. After discussing our exploratory descriptors, we created a table to focus our analysis on the applications' strategies to reduce barriers to enrollment and participation in charter schools based on criteria listed in the application narrative. We added a second column for researcher notes to fuel the critical analysis of the application. Here we recorded questions, noted reviewers' comments and limitations, and any other ideas generated in this second iteration of review. From these notes we created the focused codes (Charmaz, 2014; Saldaña, 2016) used in the development of Table 2.2, which aided the interpretation of the data (Miles & Huberman, 1994). Together we compared our analyses and discussed inconsistencies or alternative interpretations of the data to finalize the table. Our discussions of Table 2.2 led us to conduct an additional round of pattern coding (Miles et al., 2014; Saldaña, 2016) of all data. We grouped categories into larger themes and verified these emerging themes represented consistent patterns in the data; these themes are elaborated upon in the following section.

FINDINGS

Approach to Break Down Barriers

The stated purpose of the NC ACCESS program and these charter school subgrant applications was to plan for strategies to increase the number of educationally disadvantaged students being served by charter schools in the state, and ultimately to create leadership and collaboration in disseminating best practices in educating them. While the NC ACCESS program specifies educationally disadvantaged students to include students who are economically disadvantaged, homeless or unaccompanied youth, English learners, and students with disabilities, a persistent theme across the data was the very general reference to "educationally disadvantaged" students used throughout program goals and likewise applied by charter school applications. In very few instances are these distinct populations of students distinguishably addressed in the applications. Consequently, the contexts of their educational needs and services are often overgeneralized and lumped together, raising questions of the knowledge, experience, and capacities of schools to effectively meet this goal of the program.

Most frequently, "educationally disadvantaged" appears to be used interchangeably with reference to economically disadvantaged students. In the Endeavor Academy application, a reviewer questions, "Is the assumption that English language learner students are also economically disadvantaged?" (p. 214). Two applications, operated by the same charter management organization, explicitly state, "In analyzing the data, economically disadvantaged student populations served as a proxy for educationally disadvantaged students." Projected enrollments, a requirement of the subgrant application, are rarely broken down by specific education populations, lessening the credibility of strategies mentioned to target certain groups of people. For example, not one application identifies homeless students or considered the support needed through McKinney-Vento provisions. Similarly, few schools cite the professional development and supports needed for exceptional children populations, let alone begin to address the diversity within this subgroup of students. External reviewers comment explicitly on this need to address specific populations in two of the applications.

While some schools' proposed strategies may directly connect to the proxied economically disadvantaged population the school is targeting, they are frequently accompanied by deficit language. An external reviewer calls attention to this in one application: "The strategies identified in Question 6 are not academically focused, they start with a deficit model by emphasizing the no suspension policy as if that is the primary strategy that will be the main driver of the school's success" (p. 100). In another application, both of the school's mentioned support strategies—training through Ruby Payne's "Understanding Poverty" program and the hiring of a mental health professional "who will provide direct support and advise [sic] the administration and staff on strategies for engaging with students who may exhibit negative behaviors as a result of trauma or a mental crisis or illness"—largely focus on the assumed detriment students from working-class or impoverished families will bring to the school and ignore the educational benefits of creating an economically diverse learning environment. Furthermore, the lumping of so many different groups of students together as "educationally disadvantaged" dangerously promotes an "othering" of individuals who are not of the normed White, middle-class, dominant lifestyle.

In contrast, two applications are more specific and intentional in identifying the student population they intended to attract and serve. Noting both a significant rise in Hispanic residents as well as a majority population of lower socioeconomic households, the Somerset School is recruiting low-income Hispanic and African American families. Their curricular decisions—from a dual-language immersion program to Dream Builders professional development for staff to looping students with the same teacher—reference the academic and affective benefits of and for their specific population. Reviewers do, however, caution the school's seemingly numerous ambitions—also emphasizing the sciences, art, and technology in adopting a STREAM focus—and a lack of detail surrounding some of the programmatic elements, particularly of the dual-language program. One other school, Blue Ridge Charter, is very much targeting English language learner populations "of modest economic backgrounds" in their metropolitan area, and strives to build upon the strengths and assets of the community. Their stated strategies—having a dean of culture, employing a positive behavioral interventions and supports model, and using the Triple P Program (Positive Parenting Program)—also appear to assume an assets approach to education specific to their targeted populations. These inconsistencies across the applications cultivate a lack of confidence in our minds that many of these funded projects have an approach that will address the needs of educationally disadvantaged students or that is innovative of what currently exists with the TPSs.

Capacity to Break Down Barriers

In order to receive funding, the subgrant narrative requires applicants to describe the strategies they would use to break down known barriers for educationally disadvantaged students to enroll and attend their charter school. These barriers range from access to information about the school to enrollment procedures to transportation and successful participation and supports. Examining these proposed plans across schools' applications in Table 2.2, we identified a theme of capacity of these schools to adequately address these barriers, even with the proposed funding.

In several instances, reviewers note a lack of specificity in the applicant's plans, and comment that additional details were needed—these are coded "Incomplete" in the table. Frequently this occurs with explanations of the implementation of the school's weighted lottery, which is a requirement for participation in the program. Key information is missing, such as what percentage of seats would be set aside for educationally disadvantaged students. Though all NC charter schools were originally designed to use a weighted lottery, this mandate was waived, and as previously mentioned, only four of the state's 184 charter schools in 2018–2019 applied to institute one. Participants of this grant seem to be in need of more guidance of this necessary process. Reviewers also question the lack of important details in several applicants' transportation plans, including the missing line item in the budget for the proposed purchase of the school bus, or whether busing services would be extended beyond the applicant's proposed five mile bus zone radius of the school.

Another area of frequent limitations in applications are in plans to provide sufficient academic and emotional support for educationally disadvantaged students. While some schools describe significant supports such as a year-round academic calendar, additional tutoring opportunities, and mental health therapists, others are lacking details on plans for school culture and discipline, or specifics of how "buzzwords" (Reviewer, The Somerset School, p. 100) of concepts such as culturally responsive pedagogy and inclusive learning environments would be implemented, particularly in connection to professional development plans. Although the NC ACCESS program aims to promote charter schools' expertise in serving educationally disadvantaged students, several applications reference getting support from local educational agencies in this section of the application narrative. Furthermore, the named strategies—such as a Communities in Schools Success Coach—are not innovative in comparison to what TPSs offer. A reviewer of Tarheel State Charter notes, "Curriculum is not much more innovative than instructional materials used by LEAs" (p. 128). With seven out of nine schools awarded the NC ACCESS grant being in the first 3 years of existence, these noted limitations again raise questions of their capacity to successfully mitigate these barriers.

In other instances, schools' proposed plans prove potentially problematic beyond the first years of implementation, as numbers of educationally disadvantaged students increase. Coded "Limited" in Table 2.2, these

Table 2.2. Coding Matrix of Subgrant Application Narratives' Addressing of Known Barriers to Charter School Participation

Barrier	TPS	Blue Ridge Charter	Children First Charter	Common Ground Charter	Endeavor Academy	Global Citizens Academy	Growing Minds Academy	Polk Academy	The Somerset School	Tarheel State Charter
Transportation	Yes	Incomplete	Yes	Incomplete	Yes	Limited	Limited	Limited	Yes	Incomplete
Location of school in close proximity to students' homes	Yes	Yes	Yes	Incomplete	Yes	Yes	Yes	Yes	Yes	Yes
Free/reduced lunch	Yes	Limited	Limited	Limited	Yes	Limited	Limited	Limited	Yes	Limited
Simple and accessible enrollment processes	N/A	Incomplete	Yes	Incomplete	Yes	Limited	Limited	Limited	Yes	Incomplete
Access to information and application process	N/A	Yes	Incomplete	Yes	Yes	Incomplete	Yes	Yes	Yes	Incomplete
School schedule that aligns with parent work schedules	Yes	Yes	Yes	Yes	Yes	Yes	Yes	Yes	Yes	Yes
Access to before- and after-school programming	Yes	Yes	Yes	Yes	Yes	Yes	Incomplete	Incomplete	Yes	Yes
Sufficient academic and emotional support for EDS	Yes	Yes	Yes	Incomplete	Incomplete	Yes	Incomplete	Incomplete	Incomplete	Incomplete

plans would need to be revisited, as often they require alternatives and significant changes to the initially proposed plan in order to accommodate higher numbers. For example, to address the transportation barrier, The Global Citizens Academy plans on recruiting educationally disadvantaged students within walking distance of the school, then conduct "a comprehensive transportation needs assessment" in the 2022–2023 school year. Two other schools' applications similarly lack adequate plans for alleviating this significant barrier to charter school attendance in future years, as reviewers question if the proposed vehicles have the capacity to support proposed numbers of educationally disadvantaged students. Only three schools have viable strategies for providing free or reduced lunch for students, as often the proposed strategies are questioned by reviewers of being scalable to the projected population needs. These supports are mandated by law for TPSs to provide and create a significant barrier for educationally disadvantaged students to attend charter schools. Therefore, we found that many of the successful NC ACCESS subgrant applications were incomplete or limited in their ability to demonstrate that barriers would be eliminated over time to sustain their ability to serve the educationally disadvantaged student population they intend to recruit.

Desire to Break Down Barriers

Zooming out from subgrant application narratives, we analyzed the overall outcomes of the first year of the NC ACCESS program to determine if the grant was successful in their intent to increase and expand the educational opportunities for educationally disadvantaged students. The program was designed to leverage existing interest in charter school development by stimulating the startup and expansion of additional high-quality charter school options that have a *desire* to increase the educational opportunities for educationally disadvantaged students. We questioned if the grant could be an effective mechanism to motivate charter schools to seek opportunities to significantly increase the educationally disadvantaged populations in NC charter schools.

Table 2.3 displays the projected schedule of subgrant awards for years one through five of the NC ACCESS federal grant. The highlighted columns display the data from the first year of grant implementation. In alignment with the projections, the NC ACCESS program met the intended schedule for the granting of Planning and Implementation subgrants and exceeded the number of Implementation Only grants by awarding four rather than the projected two. In the Expansion and Replication subgrant types, the program did not meet Year One projections.

**Table 2.3.   Projected Schedule of Subgrant Awards
With Submitted and Actual Awards Granted in Year 1**

Subgrant Type	Projected Year 1	Submitted Year 1	Awarded Year 1	(P) Year 2	(P) Year 3	(P) Year 4	(P) Year 5	Projected Total	Maximum Award Amount
Planning and implementation	3	5	3	3	3	3	0	12	$400,000
Implementation only	2	5	4	2	2	2	2	10	$250,000
Expansion	3	2	2	4	4	4	4	18	$600,000
Replication	2	0	0	2	2	2	2	10	$600,000

Note: Each grant award funded for maximum amount allowed in Year 1.

There were only two Expansion grants submitted and approved, which fell short of the projected three awards. There were no Replication subgrants submitted in Year One with the projections set to approve two.

The strong showing in the Planning and Implementation and Implementation Only types of grant submissions could suggest a successful overall outcome of Year One. It is likely that the actual number of awards might vary from the projections with the need for flexibility to allow for the strongest grant submissions to be awarded on a year-to-year basis. However, when analyzing this data it is important to acknowledge the shortfall in grant submissions and awards in the categories of Expansion and Replication. While the Expansion type subgrants came close to meeting the projections and are represented in the Year One grant cycle, the Replication type subgrants were absent from the pool of submissions. This raises the question of why there were no Replication subgrants submitted. There could be a variety of reasons that influenced existing charter schools' decision to not apply in Year One that we are unable to determine. However, there are two interpretations of this data that are worth exploring as the objectives of the grant are more fully understood within the context of market theory of school choice.

First, as presented earlier, there are clear eligibility requirements for existing charter schools that must be met for grant approval. To be eligible for a Replication or Expansion type subgrant, the high-quality charter school must have been operating for at least three years with at least a "B" School Performance Grade and met or exceeded growth for at least two of the last 3 years. Fewer than one third of the 184 current charter schools in operation met this additional criteria. The subgrants also provided priority status for high-quality charter schools that: (a) serve greater than 40%

educationally disadvantaged; (b) have a graduation rate greater than the state average; (c) have Title I status; and (d) have educationally disadvantaged, English learners, and students with disabilities proficiency rates greater than the state average. Did this priority consideration marginalize many high-performing charter schools from applying for the grant? When analyzing the applications it was noted that none of the submitted and accepted applications qualified for priority status based on the set criteria; however, when determining whether to submit a grant the awareness that the charter school may not be competitive without priority status may have discouraged some from participating in Year One. Are these eligibility and priority consideration requirements what kept charter schools from applying? Will there be more eligible/potential applicants in later years of the grant?

Alternatively, the low to nonexistent applicant pool for Expansion and Replication subgrants may reflect an actual lack of desire to significantly increase the educationally disadvantaged populations in many of the high-quality NC charter schools. Of the eligible schools, only two submitted Replication grants and zero submitted Expansion grants. The success of the grant program was based on its ability to leverage interest and tap the desire of startup and expansion sites to serve educationally disadvantaged populations, yet this Year One data does not suggest that there is such a strong desire among existing NC charter schools to pursue this effort. This trend is consistent to the charter school sector's previous response to the state's offering of waivers to allow for the use of weighted lotteries to increase the number of educationally disadvantaged students—only four charter schools applied. The NC ACCESS Year One data in 2019 does not demonstrate that the funding incentive encouraged broader appeal among the high-quality charter schools to implement a weighted lottery in order to guarantee more racial and ethnic access and balance within these school sites.

DISCUSSION

The purpose of this study was to critically examine one state's initiative to remediate current divisions among the populations of students attending its high-quality charter schools. More specifically, in the context of a highly segregative and disproportionately representative charter school sector, the NC ACCESS program sought to improve the access to and experience of "educationally disadvantaged" students in charter schools by incentivizing support for charter schools to address known barriers and challenges. As detailed in the previous section, we find numerous limitations in the subgrant applications of these charter schools, and we problematize the approach, capacity, and desire of this program and participating charter schools to truly dismantle the barriers involved in such divisions.

Returning to the big picture impact of this program, it is important to situate its goals within the larger context that 70% of NC charter schools are either hypersegregated White (enrolling more than 80% White students) or hypersegregated Black (enrolling more than 80% Black students) (Hawn Nelson, 2017). Even if the NC ACCESS grant were to meet the expected goal of funding a total of 18 Expansion subgrants and 10 Replication subgrants in the 5-year period, this would only work to ameliorate divisions in student populations in 28 out of the 184 (15%) operating charter schools in the state. Furthermore, over the duration of the grant, two of these participating charter schools' populations are not even projected to meet the demographic percentages of their local education agencies. Neither the opportunity to utilize weighted lotteries nor the monetary incentive offered through NC ACCESS appears to have the potential to bring significant movement or change to the reality of these divisions. It seems the real problem lies in there is no consequence for charters that do not "reasonably reflect" the general population, as the state's charter law, G.S. 115C-218.45(e), mandates, and the free market principles of school choice have no systematic mechanisms in place to demand actions for the greater good of our educational system.

Therefore, our findings urge us to question the alignment of the stated purpose of the NC ACCESS program to the problem it seeks to address. With an objective to "increase the number of educationally disadvantaged students attending high-quality charter schools", rather than to create an integrated sector of schools, we argue this program has missed the opportunity to address systemic inequities or to position the benefits of diversity in education. Our analysis calls attention to the "othering" and deficit language found in the program approach, the shortcomings of strategies to alleviate barriers, and the minimal charter school response to the opportunity, all of which point more toward perpetuating divisions rather than alleviating them. We anticipate any gains in numbers of "educationally disadvantaged" students in charter schools to validate the continued expansion of the charter system, serving as a bright spot that blinds the inequities inherent in a market-based system (Ayscue et al., 2018; Condliffe et al., 2015; Handler, 2018; Horsford, 2016; Patillo, 2015). Given, among many actions, the state legislature's recent advocacy to extend and expand the two piloted virtual charter schools, despite D ratings for all 3 years of the two schools' existence (Hui, 2019), this premonition does not seem a stretch. We question whether the grant program is an effective use of federal funds to counteract the current trends of segregation within charter schools or simply part of the Trump administration's national agenda to promote school choice (Ayscue et al., 2018).

Such obscured objectives are not new to educational programs and policies, particularly in regard to equity and school choice. Analyzing segregation, race, and charter schools, Brookings Institute researchers Whitehurst and colleagues (2016) previously argued:

> Policymaking is always a balancing act, and requires a careful weighing of different objectives that may not always run easily together. Reducing school segregation and improving the quality of schools serving minority students are both important goals, but they are not necessarily the same. Policy should be based on a clear idea of what goals we are trying to achieve, and on the best evidence for how to reach them. (p. 6)

If the goal of the NC Board of Education is to have an educational system that equitably serves the public good of a multicultural, democratic society, then the associated policy decisions and the utilization of funds must not only prioritize educational achievement outcomes for all our youth but also the integration of its members amidst class, race, ethnicity, language, ability, and citizenship. Research has consistently shown that integrated schools benefit the educational system in a myriad of ways (Johnson & Nazaryan, 2019; Mickelson, 2014; Mickelson & Nkomo, 2012). We must recognize and resist the power of privilege and segregation and work to create a system that prioritizes and incentivizes an integrated approach to educating all of our children.

NOTE

1. Throughout the chapter, the authors problematize the use of this term, "educationally disadvantaged". When used in the context of the State's operationalizing of the term, it does not appear in quotes; however, to draw attention to the authors' questioning of the use of the term, quotation marks are used.

REFERENCES

Ayscue, J., Hawn Nelson, A., Mickelson, R. A., Giersch, J., & Bottia, M. C. (2018). *Charters as a driver of resegregation.* Civil Rights Project/Proyecto Derechos Civiles. https://www.civilrightsproject.ucla.edu/research/k-12-education/integration-and-diversity/charters-as-a-driver-of-resegregation/Charters-as-a-Driver-of-Resegregation-012518.pdf

Center for Community Self-Help, A.J. Fletcher Foundation, & Public Impact. (2014). *North Carolina charter schools: Excellence and equity through collaboration.*

https://publicimpact.com/wp-content/uploads/2014/07/NC_Charter_ Schools_Excellence_and_Equity_through_Collaboration_Full-Report-Public_Impact.pdf

Center for Research on Education Outcomes. (2013). *National charter school study.* Stanford University. http://credo.stanford.edu/documents/ NCSS%202013%20Final%20Draft.pdf

Charmaz, K. (2014). *Constructing grounded theory* (2nd ed.). SAGE.

Condliffe, B. F., Boyd, M. L., & DeLuca, S. (2015). Stuck in school: How social context shapes school choice for inner-city students. *Teachers College Record, 117*(3), 1–36.

David, R., & Hesla, K. (2018). *Estimated charter school enrollment, 2017-2018.* National Alliance for Public Charter Schools. https://www.publiccharters.org/ sites/default/files/documents/2018-03/FINAL%20Estimated%20Public %20Charter%20School%20Enrollment%2C%202017-18.pdf

Dey, I. (1993). (1993). *Qualitative data analysis: A user friendly guide for social science.* Routledge. https://doi.org/10.4324/9780203412497

Education Commission of the United States. (2019). 50-state comparison: Charter school policies. https://www.ecs.org/charter-school-policies/

Handler, L. K. (2018). *School choice and the Latinx community: Increased opportunity/ exclusion in Mecklenburg County* (Publication No. 10836991) [Doctoral dissertation, The University of North Carolina Charlotte]. ProQuest.

Hawn Nelson, A. (2017, January 5). *As charters and choice expand, so does segregation.* University of North Carolina Charlotte Urban Institute. https://ui.uncc.edu/ story/cms-and-charters-school-choice-outcomes-segregation#_edn13

Helms, A. D. (2018, December 19). Amid NC charter school growth, enrollment in Charlotte schools is feast or famine. *The Charlotte Observer.* https:// www.charlotteobserver.com/news/local/education/article222960410.html

Horsford, S. D. (2016). Social justice for the advantaged: Freedom from racial equality post-*Milliken. Teachers College Record, 118*(3), 1–18.

Hui, T. K. (2019, July 29). Governor vetoes bill letting NC virtual charter schools add more students. *The News & Observer.* https://www.newsobserver.com/news/ politics-government/article233258417.html

Jabbar, H., Fong, C. J., Germain, E., Li, D., Sanchez, J. D., Sun, W.-L., & DeVall, M. (2017, April). *The competitive effects of school choice on student outcomes: A systematic review and meta-analysis* [paper presentation]. American Educational Research Association Annual Meeting, San Antonio, TX.

Johnson, R. C., & Nazaryan, A. (2019). *Children of the dream: Why school integration works.* Basic Books & Russell Sage Foundation.

Ladd, H. T., Clotfelter, C. T., & Holbein, J. B. (2015). *The growing segmentation of the charter school sector in North Carolina* (National Bureau of Economic Research Working Paper 21078). National Center for Analysis of Longitudinal Data in Education Research. https://caldercenter.org/sites/default/files/ WP%20133_0.pdf

Lareau, A., & Goyette, K. (2014). *Choosing homes, choosing schools: Residential segregation and the search for a good school.* Russell Sage Foundation.

Malkus, N. (2016b). *Unlike their neighbors: Comparisons of charter and traditional public schools across states.* American Enterprise Institute. http://www.aei.org/spotlight/unlike-their-neighbors-charter-schools/

Mickelson, R. A. (2014). The problem of the color lines in twenty-first-century sociology of education: Researching and theorizing demographic change, segregation, and school outcomes. *Social Currents, 1*(2), 157–165. https://doi.org/10.1177/2329496514524544

Mickelson, R. A., Giersch, J., Hawn Nelson, A., & Bottia, M. C. (2018). Do charter schools undermine efforts to create racially and economically diverse public schools? In I. C. Rotger & J. L. Glazer (Eds.), *Choosing charters: Better schools or more segregation?* (pp. 116–132). Teachers College Press.

Mickelson, R. A., & Nkomo, M. (2012). Integrated schooling, life course outcomes, and social cohesion in multiethnic democratic societies. *Review of Research in Education, 36,* 197–238. https://doi.org/10.3102/0091732X11422667

Miles, M. B., & Huberman, A. M. (1994). *Qualitative data analysis: An expanded sourcebook.* SAGE.

Miles, M. B., Huberman, A. M., & Saldaña, J. (2014). *Qualitative data analysis: A methods sourcebook* (3rd ed.). Sage.

Mogalakwe, M. (2006). The use of documentary research methods in social research. *African Sociology Review, 10*(1), 221–230. http://www.jstor.org/stable/afrisocirevi.10.1.221

National Center for Education Statistics. (2015). Enrollment and percentage distribution of enrollment in public elementary and secondary schools, by race/ethnicity and region: Selected years, fall 1995 through fall 2025. *Digest of Education Statistics.* https://nces.ed.gov/programs/digest/d15/tables/dt15_203.50.asp

National Center for Education Statistics. (2019). Public school charter enrollment. *The condition of education.* https://nces.ed.gov/programs/coe/indicator_cgb.asp

North Carolina State Board of Education. (n.d.). *NC ACCESS Program.* http://www.ncpublicschools.org/charterschools/ncaccess/

Osborne, M. (2019, January 25). *Charter schools in North Carolina: An overview.* North Carolina Center for Public Policy Research. https://nccppr.org/charter-schools-in-north-carolina-an-overview/

Pattillo, M. (2015). Everyday politics of school choice in the black community. *Du Bois Review, 12*(1), 41–71. https://doi.org/10.1017/S1742058X15000016

Rotberg, I. C., & Glazer, J. L. (2018). *Choosing charters: Better schools or more segregation?* Teachers College Press.

Saldaña, J. (2016). *The coding manual for qualitative researchers* (3rd ed.). SAGE.

Whitehurst, G. (2016). *Education choice and competition index 2015: Summary and commentary.* http://www.brookings.edu/~/media/multimedia/interactives/2016/ecci/final/ecci_2015_final.pdf

Whitehurst, G. J., Reeves, R. V., & Rodrigue, E. (2016). *Segregation, race, and charter schools: What do we know?* Center on Children and Families at Brookings. https://www.brookings.edu/wp-content/uploads/2016/10/ccf_20161021segregation_version-10_211.pdf

Yin, R. K. (2014). *Case study research: Design and methods* (4th ed.). SAGE.

Appendix A: Scoring Rubric for NC ACCESS Subgrant Applications

Standards	Elements	Criteria
General	• Application Contact Information, Signed Assurances, and Certification	• Must be complete to meet standard
Technical	• Enrollment projections • Application Narrative • Budget, Budget Narrative, and Logic Model • Competitive Preference Standards • (4 possible standards)	• Up to 10 points • Up to 60 points • Up to 30 points • Up to 3 points per standard
Priority	• Priority Consideration Status • (4 possible standards)	• Used for priority status, if applicable

CHAPTER 3

SOCIOECONOMIC DISPARITIES

A Case Study Addressing
the Urban/Rural Divide Using a World Café

Daniel A. Yonto
Georgia Southern University

ABSTRACT

Socioeconomic disparities have been noted in studies across rural and urban areas of all sizes. These disparities often translate into neighborhoods with contrasting socioeconomic opportunities and weak social mobility. However, what we know is mainly based on limited case studies conducted from specific disciplinary perspectives. To this end, this study adopts an interdisciplinary multidimensional initiative for tackling socioeconomic disparities through integrated solutions in education, public health, housing, and transportation at the community level. The focus of this chapter identifies how a World Café creates opportunities for interactive conversation, reciprocal exchange, and diverse communication. With the use of this tool, a research network identified urgent community needs in one rural community in North Carolina. Despite current research being disciplinary and geographically fragmented, the goal of the World Café seeks to produce actionable research by leveraging disciplinary expertise through strong partnerships.

The Divide Within: Intersections of Realities, Facts, Theories, and Practices
pp. 59–78

INTRODUCTION

The American Dream for many rural communities—the idea that if one works hard enough, a better economic future awaits—is becoming a faint reality. Instead, many rural communities across the U.S. are seeing a reduction in the opportunity for individuals and households to move up the social ladder (Chetty et al., 2014). With most of the social mobility research focusing on urban areas (Parker et al., 2018), there is a lack of consensus on how the 60 million people who live in rural America confront social mobility challenges (Goetz et al., 2018; Krause & Reeves, 2017; McKeag et al., 2018). Even though rural communities account for a fairly small portion of the population in the United States, evidence suggests that certain rural areas operate as "mobility traps," or places where residents are less likely to succeed due to being born to disadvantaged circumstances (Corak, 2017).

With a great deal of variation across the nation in upward mobility (Florida, 2018), rural communities tend to be worse off compared to their urban counterparts on a number of important indicators. For instance, rural communities tend to have lower incomes (Miller et al., 2019), lower levels of educational attainment (Garcia, 2015), and limited access to health insurance and health care providers (Foutz et al., 2017). Additional costs include many rural counties more likely to be persistently poor, with at least a 20% poverty rate continuing for at least 30 years (Pender et al., 2019). Moreover, examining the variation in mortality rates between rural or urban communities uncovers a distinct rural disadvantage (Dobis et al., 2020), with premature death rates consistently higher in rural counties than in urban ones (Case & Deaton, 2015). With few rural communities achieving growth that improve conditions across the socioeconomic spectrum, the need for improving social mobility has become urgent to curtail socioeconomic disparities.

In order to analyze this dynamic and its implications, this chapter's research presents a case study of social mobility in one rural region: Watauga County, North Carolina (NC). The analysis seeks to understand the complexities of social mobility by engaging in an interdisciplinary, multidimensional initiative for tackling socioeconomic disparities through a nuanced understanding of the rural context. To that end, the chapter details how The World Café (TWC) method creates opportunities for interactive conversation, reciprocal exchange, and diverse communication in traditionally overlooked communities. Although the research only touches one rural community in NC, the goal is to work towards a future where every person has an equal opportunity to build a better economic life. With the use of a TWC, social scientists and policymakers have access to a tool that helps to improve our understanding of what differentiates rural areas from their urban counterparts. This research also highlights the need for analytical approaches that look beyond efforts to homogenize rural areas in research designs, focusing instead on how local context and culture produce social phenomena (Lowe, 2012).

The chapter begins by reviewing the literature on social mobility and how a lack of communication across stakeholders creates barriers to develop coordinated programs for tackling socioeconomic disparities. Next, the chapter moves to how rural areas create unique challenges for social mobility solutions, and how a TWC can facilitate multiple stakeholders shaping the development of rural communities. The study area is then outlined to form a comprehensive understanding of social mobility challenges existing in Watauga County. Finally, the chapter ends by dissecting how a TWC bridges the problems faced by local stakeholders when addressing social mobility in rural contexts.

LITERATURE REVIEW

Social Mobility

Recently, nongovernmental organizations across the U.S. have started working together to coordinate efforts in the areas of education, public health, housing, and transportation for disadvantaged communities (Leading on Opportunity, 2017). It has become clear that the societal goals of social equity and equal access to opportunity cannot be achieved by piecemeal, single-sector policies (OECD, 2018). The U.S. Department of Housing and Urban Development addressed this notion in a recent report, highlighting the need for coordinated school, housing, and transportation planning to support students attending low-quality, high-poverty schools (Housing and Urban Development, 2016). There are strong interdependencies between education/learning, health, housing, and transportation-related challenges experienced in disadvantaged communities and the solutions that each of these areas can contribute towards lowering socioeconomic disparities and enhancing community-based opportunities (Nikolaev & Burns, 2014).

Research has shown that socioeconomic disparities are a thorny problem to tackle and that simple, unidimensional, solutions are bound to overlook tipping points in the longitudinal dynamics of communities, mitigating and compounding effects, as well as contextual effects such as historical factors, ethnicity, spatial dependence effects, stereotypes, and value systems (American Psychological Association, 2008). Only recently has the "Culture of Health" paradigm shifted attention to holistic and integrated approaches, which are proving effective in improving the health and well-being of communities, rather than of groups of individuals (National Science Foundation, 2011).

A key issue is the development of human capital in ways that accelerate economic development and reduce inequality in the 21st century. However, there are barriers to how education as a key form of human capital is organized and supported (Adelman & Taylor, 2017). Social disparities affecting pre-K–12 education and learning are reflected in resource allocation to schools, personnel training, and academic supports (Odden et al., 2008). Of particular concern is the impact of social disparity on student reading achievement and implications for high school graduation and readiness to enter the workforce (Meece et al., 2013). Students living in poverty are at increased risk of special education placement (National Research Council, 2002), which has the potential to impact future employment and quality of life. Conditions of the home environment, including environmental hazards, nutrition, and parent education also impact student performance in school (Byun et al., 2012). Compounding this reality, students in disadvantaged areas are more likely to experience negative environmental influences, transportation and digital isolation that hamper academic performance (Murphy, 2013). Interdisciplinary research designed to understand and address social inequities in a local context is critical for developing integrated solutions effective within targeted communities.

From a public health perspective, social disparities are linked to health disparities (Adler et al., 1994), environmental injustices (Brulle & Pellow, 2006), and neighborhood disparities such as food deserts and lack of access to water infrastructure (Frieden, 2010). Recent studies of NC have documented disparities in access to municipal water supply and sanitation infrastructure and have estimated that these disparities increase risks of multiple adverse health outcomes (Carolinas Healthcare System, 2017). At the same time, evidence is mounting that local solutions developed with community engagement can mitigate these pathways (National Academies of Sciences, Engineering, & Medicine, 2017). Again, this requires integrated, community-based, and community-driven solutions.

Additionally, finding decent, secure, and affordable rental housing is increasingly difficult. In recent years wages have stagnated while rents have continued to climb, resulting in sharp increases in the number of rent-burdened households, overcrowded households, and households that lack basic kitchen and bathroom facilities. A 2017 report on rental housing conditions in NC, published by UNC-CH's Center for Urban and Regional Studies, indicates that over half a million of the state's households suffer from one or more of these conditions (Center for Urban and Regional Studies, 2017). From a societal perspective, housing deficits increase public health care costs while lowering productivity and increasing reliance on social support programs (Pollack & Lynch, 2009). From an individual perspective, they undermine the ability of families in the state to lead happy and productive lives (Schaff et al., 2013).

Social mobility and transportation mobility are often seen as correlates so that better integration of new and more traditional mobility systems is a point of priority. While lower-income households may not be able to afford other means of transport than public systems, these services have been found not to be equitably distributed in space or equally accessible by all communities (Agrawal et al., 2011). Additionally, large-scale transit investments in U.S. urban and suburban areas have induced neighborhood changes and have led to gentrification (Nilsson & Delmelle, 2018), and displacement of lower-income households (Bardaka et al., 2018). Cities such as San Francisco and Denver have already implemented coordinated transportation and housing planning to mitigate gentrification pressures (Bardaka & Delgado, 2019).

Rural Social Mobility Challenges

Rural areas, defined as "not urban" according to the U.S. Census, range from small towns sparsely populated to communities of up to 50,000 people outside of urban areas (Fields et al., 2016). With 97% of the land area labeled as rural in the United States, only 20% of the U.S. population resides in these regions (Fields et al., 2016). Although rural populations are diverse, common themes that emerged from the literature included: limited access to services and resources when compared to urban communities, greater distance needed to travel to receive services, geographic isolation from service centers, and limited public transportation (Riebschleger et al., 2015; Rishel et al., 2016). The barriers rural residents experience created by these obstacles result from many community members, unlike their urban counterparts, not being able to take advantage of economic activities, educational opportunities, and diversities of metropolitan areas (Mitchell, 2019).

The U.S. Department of Agriculture's *Rural America at a Glance* highlighted the severity of these trends by correlating rural areas with the lowest levels of educational attainment to higher poverty, child poverty, unemployment, and population loss compared to urban areas (Pender et al., 2019). However, these barriers run deeper than economic indicators (San Antonio, 2016). In a review of the literature, Crockett et al. (2000) illuminated the psychosocial adjustment of rural youth, which they found was often oriented around a central challenge: "the need to reconcile attachments to family and place with a desire for educational and occupational mobility," at a time when rural demographic are rapidly changing

(p. 46). Unfortunately, these types of decisions turn into what Krause and Reeves (2017) identified as "mobility traps," where are residents unlikely to move up the social ladder due to the disadvantaged circumstances into which they were born.

Flora and Arnold (2012) discussed this tension as rural communities trying to preserve its heritage and adapting to outcomes shaped by global forces. The cost, reported by the Robert Wood Johnson Foundation and the University of Wisconsin Population Health Institute, included rural communities with high levels of child poverty and income inequality were often less healthy than those with lower levels of child poverty and income inequality (Housing Assistance Council, 2015). The implication is that rural areas with high levels of poverty and low income impact a family or individual's ability to access quality housing, education, food, and child-care (Lahr et al., 2019a).

Notably, mortality rates from all of the leading causes of death in the United States—heart disease, stroke, cancer, unintentional injury, and chronic lower respiratory disease—are higher in rural than in urban communities (Kozhimannil et al., 2019). With an aging baby boomer population retiring in rural areas (Cromartie, 2018), another major challenge emerged when rural health clinics provided limited access to care coordinators, social workers, and case managers, which could make it difficult for clinics and rural communities to address broader social determinants of health (Lahr et al., 2019b). The problem this created was a lack of coordination and communication that influenced a clinic's ability to successfully connect patients with specialty services and more advanced care.

In a comprehensive review of rural transportation, the Rural Health Research Center from the University of Minnesota stressed that public transportation was a barrier for accessing health care because service was nonexistent or included low-frequency small coverage bus systems (Henning-Smith et al., 2017). While access to transportation impacts the use of healthcare services in both urban and rural settings, the challenge is that individuals who do not have access to reliable transportation tend to delay or forgo necessary appointments and preventative care (Henning-Smith et al., 2017). Thus, residents in rural areas are at higher risks of missing appointments that could lead to healthier lives. Moreover, the demand for more flexible transportation services are required as hospital consolidations moved a wider range of services from local hospitals to specialty centers (Henning-Smith et al., 2017). Coupled with an aging population or retired residents, these concerns make transportation an issue of significant concern for rural health stakeholders nationwide.

The policy implications for these circumstances is that rural communities must find a way to build partnerships that cross traditional organizational and sector boundary lines. However, amid all the resources and services state and local agencies provide rural communities, many well-intended administrators are unaware of the work others are doing in the same community (Marohn, 2020). Rural communities also experienced a separation between agencies and departments that govern education services (Cohen-Vogel et al., 2020). The problem with institutional silos is that separate state and local districts often lead to different policies and approaches toward supporting education instruction, which often cause people to ignore the big picture (McNair, 2004). This disconnect among rural areas suggests that a major barrier to the development of coordinated programs for tackling socioeconomic disparities was the lack of communication across stakeholders. Instead, improved collaboration between agencies is needed to build bridges across silos to improve communication between departments and ensure that they are working efficiently toward the same goals.

WHAT IS A WORLD CAFÉ?

TWC is an increasingly popular step-by-step conversation process that has been used internationally by various stakeholders to engage large groups of people and to foster dialogue on important issues (Storey & Taylor, 2011; Thunberg, 2011). TWC involves concurrent and timed roundtable discussions that focus on a predetermined set of questions (Brown et al., 1997). According to Brown (2001), the café metaphor describes the contextual setting of informal seating at multiple small tables to encourage conversation. The world symbolizes an inclusive format to facilitate the communication of large numbers of people at one time. As shown in Table 3.1, TWC has seven design principles that are meant to be used together in a progressive format (Brown & Isaacs, 2005). TWC hosts are tasked with demonstrating the capacity to procure, weave, and connect ideas emerging from the group's dialogue (Brown, 2001).

Table 3.1. World Café Principles
for Hosting Conversations That Matter

P1	Setting the parameters of meeting and defining the themes or discussion questions
P2	Creating an hospitable space or a welcoming physical setup of the meeting
P3	Exploring questions that matter
P4	Encouraging everyone's contribution
P5	Connecting diverse perspectives through "cross-pollination" of ideas
P6	Listening together for patterns and insights
P7	Sharing, or gathering, collective discoveries

The above stated purpose of TWC as a vehicle for meaning-making positions it as a critical and inductive approach to knowledge creation (Estacio & Karic, 2016). A growing number of community settings, corporate, governmental, health, educational, not-for-profit, and faith environments have reportedly benefited from the transformative capacities of TWC (Lorenzetti et al., 2016). Furthermore, the transformative potential of TWC as a method is evidenced in Brown's (2002) notes on the usefulness of TWC in developing dynamic and action-oriented community networks, and its capacity to foster the cocreation of knowledge and authentic dialogues among people who may not have otherwise met.

Given that a major barrier to social mobility in rural areas extended from the development of coordinated programs, the purpose of this study was to examine and analyze how TWC created an effective vehicle to address difficult and intractable problems through meaningful conversation, thereby influencing social change. To this end, this study engaged in an interdisciplinary multidimensional initiative for tackling socioeconomic disparities in one NC community through integrated solutions in education, public health, housing, and transportation at the community level.

METHODS

Context

This research is part of a larger statewide study of economic mobility across NC. The site of Watauga County, depicted in Figure 3.1, was strategically selected because income inequality has historically been the highest in the state (Berner, 2015). What made Watauga County particularly interesting were the towns of Boone and Blowing Rock, popular vacation and retirement communities, which acted as islands of opportunity surrounded by a sea of lower income neighborhoods (Berner, 2015). According to 2018 U.S. Census estimates, the county has a population of 55,945 residents, with 20% living in poverty. Despite having some of the highest poverty levels in the state, the county also contains Appalachian State University, which has a current enrollment of 19,000 students. The demographics of Watauga County are 94% White, 1.9% Black, and 1.2% Asian. (U.S. Census, 2018).

Another unique aspect of Watauga County was the terrain and scattered population. Situated in the Blue Ridge Mountains, there existed a low density, rural population that has seen an increase in its retirement community (Appalachian District Health Department, 2017). Moreover, the leading causes of death were largely due to chronic diseases such as obesity, smoking, and physical inactivity (Appalachian District Health Department, 2017). Given this evidence, the need for improving social

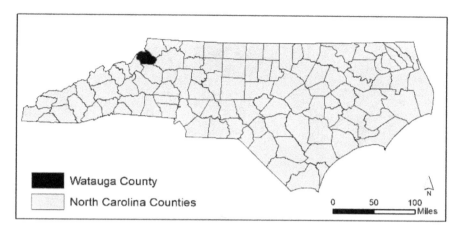

Figure 3.1.   Watauga County, focus area for socioeconomic disparities research.

mobility and curtailing socioeconomic disparities in Watauga become a priority. To develop successful integrated solutions, however, researchers, government officials, nongovernmental entities, and community stakeholders must engage collectively.

Event Promotion

The study employed a snowball sample method to generate a list of practitioner and academics to invite to the forum. The first step consisted of compiling a list of all faculty members at Appalachian State University in the Planning, Geography, Public Administration, Business, Education, and Public Health Departments. Faculty members received a personalized invitation to attend the forum if their research interests broadly touched on the following key words: equity, transportation, community development, community planning, education, public health, community health, affordable housing, or aging. If a faculty member replied, the next step was to ask if they knew an additional nonprofit or local government staff member that would be interested in attending the forum. The process continued in this way until a total of 87 invitations were sent out from April 13–May 23, 2018.

Event Attendees

Thirty-eight community stakeholders attended the forum on June 1, 2018 at Appalachian State University's Plemmons Student Union in

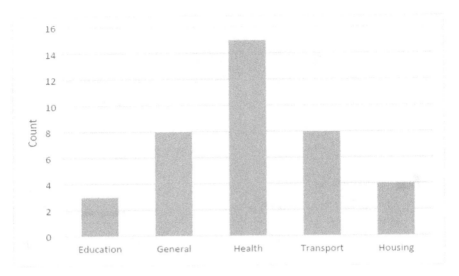

Figure 3.2.   Distribution of attendees by self-reported discipline concentration.

Boone, NC. Out of the 38 community participants, 22 participants were academics and 18 were community practitioners. As shown in Figure 3.2, the majority of attendees concentrated in either public health or transportation. Out of the 18 community practitioners, 4 local government administrators attended, including representatives from the health department, planning department, affordable housing task force member, and the transportation planning director. Nonprofit stakeholders included participants from the Hospitality House, Women's Fund of the Blue Ridge, Western Youth Network, Area Agency on Aging, King Street Church, and the Watauga Compassionate Community Initiative.

Community stakeholders were greeted at the forum by TWC host Dr. Tracy W. Smith. Dr. Smith is a Professor in the Department of Curriculum and Instruction at Appalachian State University and is an expert in conducting TWC workshops across the globe. TWC lasted approximately 3 hours and emphasized the importance of research in finding integrated solutions to social mobility challenges in Watauga County.

Discussion Tables

The room was set up with five themed discussion tables. The thematic approach stimulated discussion around combining different ideas to form integrated solutions, such as: health/transportation, health/education, transportation/housing, transportation/education and education/housing. Given the four components in the study, the following questions were (1) What are the major problems in Watauga County? (2) Who are the necessary players, stakeholders, or interest groups? (3) What if we…?

The first question explored the major research questions in social mobility specific to Western NC. Participants were encouraged to think about the institutional challenges that accompany these problems. The second question aimed at identifying who are the groups of people that should be involved in the discussion on social mobility. As the discussion matured, tables were instructed to ask "who is also missing" from their conversation. Finally, the third question stimulated participant's imagination. For instance, "what if we" had no restriction on resources, what possible solutions could our community come up with.

Data Capture

The ability of TWC as an active engagement tool meant that a large quantity of information was generated as part of the process. The methods used to capture participants' views and insights ensured TWC process was not interrupted were video, tablecloths, and the synthesis wall.

Tablecloth

Participants were encouraged to write or draw their ideas on the butcher paper laid out on the tables to more clearly express their ideas from the questions. In this way, participants pushed past traditional institutional or department silos and engaged with one another to discuss challenges and opportunities of the region's lack of social mobility. The tablecloth option to add to the discussion also acted as a way to record participant responses who did not feel comfortable speaking at the table. Three rounds of table discussion, lasting 20 to 25 minutes each, were held with each table focusing on a different theme. After each round, participants then rotated to the next table, where they were asked another question. The table hosts, volunteers who stayed at each table, shared the responses of the previous group and encouraged participation to add their thoughts to the table.

Synthesis Wall

After the final round table, Dr. Smith brought the group back together to synthesize the conversation and assess how TWC facilitated discussion. Participants were asked to take their ideas from the tablecloths, or ideas that they now had from the round table session, and transfer them onto sticky notes and place them on the synthesis wall, as shown in Figure 3.3,

Figure 3.3.   Sample of sticky notes placed into themes on the synthesis wall.

to sort into themes. The synthesis at this point was done without talking, so participants had to interact with other by reading what they had to say and use sticky notes to post additional comments. Once natural themes emerged from stakeholders' responses, Dr. Smith connected the themes and facilitated group discussion.

FINDINGS

TWC can produce a variety of information from attendees in a variety of ways. These data can be analyzed flexibly, depending on the specific aims of the research question. For the purpose of this chapter, a qualitative thematic analysis (Braun & Clarke, 2008) was used to organize the following data. Before the analysis could start, any video audio gathered from the discussion was transcribed and summarized into a report sent out to all attendees to review. As this chapter focuses on TWC as a method, two themes are only discussed below to provide examples of the types of conversations generated by this tool.

Theme 1: Improving Transportation Services

Transportation access emerged as the forums most important topic. Forum attendees saw an opportunity for the Watauga region to implement a prototype regional ride-sharing system that could assist the aging population reach medical appointments on time, especially time sensitive appointments such as dialysis. Participants at the round tables emphasized that the system could be combined with transit-oriented development policies aimed at integrating new developments in the region into a more effective transit system. As Watauga County lacks transportation infrastructure such as Uber, Lift, or e-bikes, one participant reflected on how their county could "build an integrated multi-modal (e.g., school bus, AppalCart, Bikesharing, ebike) transportation system that can give every community 24 hour access to transportation."

Craig Hughes, Transportation Director of AppalCart, provided context to the group by addressing the agency's role in maximizing mobility in the region. Hughes clarified how the rural transit agency struggled to acquire multiple funding sources for AppalCart to become fare free in 2005. Despite the overwhelming transportation demands, the synthesis allowed Hughes to identify future ridership priorities that focused on aging rural residents and alternative transportation choices to increase regional mobility.

Theme 2: Community Health

As discussions around transportation dominated the forum, TWC provided community stakeholders the opportunity to link different ways to identify how the future of their community could be addressed. With this, a second theme emerged that discussed how community health agencies contributed to the future of Watauga County's success. When addressing problems in public health, one participant asked, "How can we create program to educate citizens about healthcare options in the area and connect them to these services?" This suggestion came after the participant learned of the community's growing aging population. With an increasing elderly community, the group became skeptical that the marketing being done about services in the area could reach people in the rural region. This led one respondent to reply that they would appreciate "more community world cafés as a listening session for action planning for social determinants of health."

Brisa Hernandez, director of community research for Atrium Health, emphasized how social determinants of health related to conditions in which people are born, grow, live, work, and age. According to Hernandez, when a community focuses on the reduction of inequalities, then positive community outcomes tend to follow. What made this interaction interesting was how naturally it flowed from sorting an idea on the synthesis wall to generating conversation within the group.

DISCUSSION

This chapter provides an account of how TWC can be a useful tool that encourages reflection on social mobility in rural communities. The vision of the chapter is to act as a resource for rural communities that hope to identify what factors are at the core of their community's vision of success. Enabling participants to engage in dialogue with individual from practitioner and academic backgrounds illustrates the power of the interdisciplinary work. If these types of meetings were held in a more traditional forum style setting, it is possible that the community stakeholders may not have had the same kind of participation. However, with TWC's focus on synthesizing ideas and building off each other, a diverse set of ideas was able to emerge and cluster into themes for the group to discuss. In this way, TWC acts as a crucial tool for policymakers, community organizers, or academics to address the problem of social mobility.

Participant reflections that emerged from TWC aligned with previous research on social mobility in rural communities that address transportation and health concerns (Henning-Smith et al., 2017). When combined with emerging population trends in rural communities (Lahr et al., 2019b), this evidence confirms that TWC serves as an ideal method to bring different stakeholders together to discuss the priorities of their community. With the help of TWC, different departments across Watauga County connected how health and transportation need improvements to address an aging population. Transportation issues continued to resurface during the discussion to address very specific requests (fix specific streets, provide more bus routes, and extending bus route hours) to the innovative ideas (incorporate faith-based organizations to increase elderly mobility for hospital visits). Ultimately, TWC provided an opportunity for stakeholders to bridge traditional divides and build partnerships that cross traditional organizational and sector boundary lines.

As with any research there are limitations to TWC. First, several respondents pointed out that the concerns of affordable housing and education may not have been adequately addressed in the group discussion. As previously shown in Table 3.1, most attendees were from the transportation or health field. Thus, group discussion may have focused on rural priorities that one could represent only these two concentration's interests. Second, we did not collect pre- or post-survey evaluations from the respondents. Instead, the chapter relied on qualitative data from the actual day of TWC. Despite generating discussion across traditionally separate groups, there was no quantitative data to confirm the chapters' findings. Finally, the chapter's sampling method to generate an attendance list could have been improved by ensuring a more balanced turnout attended TWC.

CONCLUSION

A major barrier to the development of coordinated programs for tackling socioeconomic disparities in rural areas is the multidimensionality of government entities and the lack of communication across departments and stakeholders. To bridge these divides, TWC provided a unique method that brought multiple stakeholders together and focused on integrated solutions to social mobility in a forum on socio-economic disparities in Watauga County, NC. Through back-and-forth discussion, results identified gaps that drive academic research and prioritize future community investments. Additionally, it added a nuanced understanding to what differentiates rural NC areas from other parts of the state by emphasizing the geographic isolation of Watauga County and the lack of transportation opportunities residents in the region faced.

Moreover, TWC created opportunities for interactive conversation, reciprocal exchange, and diverse communication. It departed from the conventional meeting approach, which is typically somber, formal, and unilateral. The paper tablecloths and synthesis wall indicated that the discussion method in this study effectively facilitates experience sharing among the participants. Generating collective insights in multiple ways can enable participants to engage with the topic in the manner in which they feel most comfortable. TWC method recognized differences in people's preferences regarding how they like to express their views and opinions. Participants call for mobile world cafés across the region provides evidence that the effort was worth the time to find ways to increase social mobility in their community.

However, residential segregation, income inequality, local school quality, family structure, and social capital continue to plague upward mobility in the United States. Dissecting these factors, our café created a path towards upward mobility by focusing on building partnerships that cross traditional organizational and sector boundary lines. Looking towards the future, a more inclusive society in the U.S. will require facing a history of income and spatial inequality and moving towards one where all people thrive.

REFERENCES

Adelman, H., & Taylor, L. (2017). *Addressing Barriers to Learning: In the Classroom and Schoolwide*. https://eric.ed.gov/?id=ED586985

Adler, N. E., Boyce, T., Chesney, M. A., Cohen, S., Folkman, S., Kahn, R. L., & Syme, S. L. (1994). Socioeconomic status and health. The challenge of the gradient. *American Psychologist. 49(1)*, 15–24.

Agrawal, A. W., Blumenberg, E., Abel, S., Pierce, G., & Darrah, C. N. (2011). *Getting around when you're just getting by: The travel behavior and transportation expenditures of low-income adults*. Mineta Transportation Institute.

American Psychological Association. (2008). *Report of the Task Force on the Implementation of the Multicultural Guidelines*. http://www.apa.org/pi/

Appalachian District Health Department. (2017). *2017 Community Health Report Alleghany County*. https://www.apphealthcare.com/wpfb-file/alleghany-county-community-health-report-2017-pdf/

Bardaka, E., & Delgado, J. (2019). Comparing the travel behavior of affordable and market-rate housing residents in the transit-rich neighborhoods of Denver, CO. *Travel Behavior and Society, 15*(1), 74–87.

Bardaka, E., Delgado, M. S., & Florax, R. J. G. M. (2018). Causal identification of transit-induced gentrification and spatial spillover effects: The case of the Denver light rail. *Journal of Transport Geography, 71*(1), 15–31.

Berner, M. (2015). *CED winners and losers in the same space: Income inequality in North Carolina*. UNC School of Government. https://ced.sog.unc.edu/ced-winners-and-losers-in-the-same-space-income-inequality-in-north-carolina/

Braun, V., & Clarke, V. (2008). Using thematic analysis in psychology. *Qualitative Research in Psychology, 3*(2), 77–101.

Brown, J. (2001). *The world café: Living knowledge through conversations that matter* (Publication No. 276286326) [Unpublished doctoral dissertation], Fielding Graduate University, ProQuest.

Brown, J. (2002). *The world café: A resource guide for hosting conversations that matter*. Whole Systems Associates. http://www.meadowlark.co/world_cafe_resource_guide.pdf

Brown, J., & Isaacs, D. (2005). *The World Café: Shaping our futures through conversations that matter*. Berrett Koehler.

Brown, J., Isaacs, D., & Margulies, N. (1997). *The World Café: Creating the future, one conversation at a time*. http://www.the worldcafe.com/articles/TWC.pdf

Brown, J., Isaacs, D., & Margulies, N. (1997). *The World Café: Creating the future one conversation at a time*. Whole Systems Associates.

Brulle, R. J., & Pellow, D. N. (2006). Environmental justice: Human health and environmental inequalities. *Annual Review of Public Health, 27*(1), 103–124.

Byun, S. Y., Irvin, M. J., & Meece, J. L. (2012). Predictors of bachelor's degree completion among rural students at four-year institutions. *Review of Higher Education, 35*(3), 463–484.

Carolinas HealthCare System. (2017). *Mapping social determinants of health*. https://unc.maps.arcgis.com/apps/MapJournal/index.html?appid=9cf5798305d74352a9721b9ffab7da87

Case, A., & Deaton, A. (2015). Rising morbidity and mortality in midlife among white non-Hispanic Americans in the 21st century. *Proceedings of the National Academy of Sciences, 112*(49), 15078–15083.

Center for Urban and Regional Studies. (2017). *Innovations in housing: Third interim Moving Forward assessment*. https://curs.unc.edu/files/2017/12/CURS-Interim-MF-Report-2017.pdf

Chetty, R., Hendren, N., Kline, P., & Saez, E. (2014). Where is the land of opportunity? The geography of intergenerational mobility in the United States. *Q.J.E. 129*(4), 1553–1623.

Cohen-Vogel, L., Sadler, J. R., Little, M., & Merril, B. (2020). (Mis)Alignment of instructional policy supports in Pre-K and Kindergarten: Evidence from rural districts in North Carolina. *Early Childhood Research Quarterly*. https://doi.org/ 10.1016/ j.ecresq. 2019.11.001

Corak, M. (2017). *Divided landscapes of economic Opportunity: The Canadian geography of intergenerational income mobility* (Working Papers 2017-043). Human Capital and Economic Opportunity Working Group.

Crockett, L. J., Shanahan, M. J., & Jackson-Newsom, J. (2000). Rural youth: Ecological and life course perspectives. In R. Montemayor, G. R. Adams, & T. P. Gulotta (Eds.), *Adolescent diversity in ethnic, economic, and cultural contexts: Advances in adolescent development* (pp. 43–74). SAGE.

Cromartie, J. (2018). *Rural America at a Glance, 2018*. United States Department of Agriculture   https://www.ers.usda.gov/webdocs/publications/90556/eib-200.pdf?v=5899.2

Dobis, E. A., Stephens, H. M., Skidmore, M., & Goetz, S. J. (2020). Explaining the spatial variation in American life expectancy. *Social Science & Medicine, 246*(1), 1–10.

Estacio, E. V., & Karic, T. (2016) The World Café: An innovative method to facilitate reflections on internationalisation in higher education. *Journal of Further and Higher Education, 40*(6), 731–745.

Fields, A., Holder, K. A., & Burd, C. (2016). *Life off the highway: A snapshot of rural America*. U.S. Census Bureau. https://www.census.gov/ newsroom/ blogs/ random-samplings/2016 /12/ life_off_the_highway.html

Flora, C., & Arnold, N. (2012). *State of the Science report: Community development*. Research & Training Center on Disability in Rural Communities. http:// rtc.ruralinstitute.umt.edu/sos_conference/wp-content/uploads/2012/03/ Flora031312.pdf

Florida, R. (2018). Some rural areas are better for economic mobility. *The Atlantic*. https://www.citylab.com/equity/2018/10/rural-areas-are-better-economic-mobility/571840/

Foutz, J., Artiga, J., & Garfield, R. (2017). *The role of Medicaid in rural America*. Kaiser Family Foundation. https://www.kff.org/medicaid/issue-brief/the-role-of-medicaid-in-rural-america/

Frieden, T. R. (2010). A framework for public health action: The health impact pyramid. *American Journal of Public Health, 100*(1), 590–595.

Garcia, E. (2015). *Inequalities at the starting gate: Cognitive and noncognitive skills gaps between 2010–2011 kindergarten classmates*. Economic Policy Institute. https:// www.epi.org/publication/inequalities-at-the-starting-gate-cognitive-and-noncognitive-gaps-in-the-2010-2011-kindergarten-class/

Goetz, S. J., Partridge, M. D., & Stephens, H. M. (2018). The economic status of rural America in the President Trump era and beyond. *Applied Economic Perspectives and Policy, 40*(1), 97–118.

Henning-Smith, C., Evenson, A., Corbett, A., Kozhimannil, K., & Moscovice, I. (2017). *Rural transportation: Challenges and opportunities* [Policy Brief]. University of Minnesota Rural Health Research Center. http://rhrc.umn.edu/wp-content/files_mf/1518734252UMRHRCTransportationChallenges.pdf

Housing Assistance Council. (2015). *Rural research note: Poverty and substandard housing linked to poor health ratings.* Housing Assistance Council. http://www.ruralhome.org/storage/documents/publications/rrnotes/rrn-county-health-rankings.pdf

Housing and Urban Development. (2016). *Breaking down barriers: Housing, neighborhoods, and schools of opportunity.* Office of Policy Development and Research, U.S. Department of Housing and Urban Development. https://www.huduser.gov/portal/sites/default/files/pdf/insight-4.pdf

Kozhimannil, K. B., Interrante, J. D., Henning-Smith, C., & Admon, L. K. (2019). Rural-urban differences in severe maternal morbidity and mortality in the US, 2007–15. *Health Affairs, 38*(12), 2077–2085.

Krause, E., & Reeves, R. (2017). *Rural dreams: Upward mobility in America's countryside.* Brookings Institute. https://www.brookings.edu/wp-content/uploads/2017/08/es_20170905_ruralmobility.pdf

Lahr, M., Neprash, H., Henning-Smith, C., Tuttle, M. S., & Hernandez, A. (2019a). *Access to specialty care for Medicare beneficiaries in rural communities* [Policy Brief]. University of Minnesota Rural Health Research Center. https://3pea7g1qp8f3t9ooe3z3npx1-wpengine.netdna-ssl.com/wp-content/uploads/2019/12/UMN-Access-to-Specialty-Care_12.4.pdf

Lahr, M., Henning-Smith, C., Hernandez, A., & Neprash, H. (2019b). *Access and capacity to care for Medicare beneficiaries in rural health clinics* [Policy Brief]. University of Minnesota Rural Health Research Center. http://rhrc.umn.edu/wp-content/uploads/2019/12/UMN-access-to-care-RHCS-policy-brief-12.10.19.pdf

Leading on Opportunity. (2017). The Charlotte-Mecklenburg opportunity task force report. https://www.fftc.org/sites/default/files/2018-05/LeadingOnOpportunity_ Report.pdf

Lorenzetti, L. A., Azulai, A., & Walsh, C. A. (2016). Addressing power in conversation. *Journal of Transformative Education, 14*(3), 200–219.

Lowe, P. (2012). The agency of rural research in comparative context. In M. Shucksmith, D. L. Brown, S. Shortall, J. Vergunst, & M. E. Warner (Eds.), *Rural transformations and rural policies in the US and UK* (pp. 18–38). Routledge.

Marohn, C. (2020). *Strong towns: A bottom-up revolution to rebuild American prosperity.* Wiley & Sons.

McKeag, M., Sokis, M. Ramos, l. & Breen, B. (2018). *Social mobility in rural America. Insights from communities whose young people are climbing the income ladder.* National 4-H Council. https://www.bridgespan.org/bridgespan/Images/articles/social-mobility-in-rural-america/social-mobility-in-rural-america.pdf

McNair, R. (2004). *Breaking down the silos: Interprofessional education and interprofessionalism for an effective rural health care workforce.* Paper presented at Alice Springs, NT, Australia.

Meece, J. L., Hutchins, B. C., Byun, S., Farmer, T. W., Irvin, M. J., & Weiss, M. (2013). Preparing for adulthood: A recent examination of the alignment of rural youth's future educational and vocational aspirations. *Journal of Educational and Developmental Psychology*, *3*(2), 175–192.

Miller, P., Votruba-Drzal, E., & Coley, R. L. (2019). Poverty and academic achievement across the urban to rural landscape: Associations with community resources and stressors. *The Russell Sage Foundation Journal of the Social Sciences*, *5*(2), 106–122.

Mitchell, A. S. (2019). Attached, addicted, and adrift: Understanding the rural opioid crisis. *Families in Society: The Journal of Contemporary Social Services*, *100*(1), 80–92.

Murphy, J. (2013). The architecture of school improvement. *Journal of Educational Administration*, *51*(3), 252–263.

National Academies of Sciences, Engineering, and Medicine. (2017). *Communities in action: Pathways to health equity*. National Academies Press.

National Science Foundation. (2011). *Rebuilding the mosaic: Fostering research in social, behavioral, and economic sciences at the National Science Foundation in the next decade*. https://www.nsf.gov/pubs/2011/nsf11086/nsf11086.pdf

National Research Council. (2002). *Minority students in special and gifted education*. The National Academies Press.

Nikolaev, B., & Burns, A. (2014). Intergenerational mobility and subjective well-being-Evidence from the general social survey. *Journal of Behavioral and Experimental Economics*, *53*(2014), 82–96.

Nilsson, I., & Delmelle, E. (2018). Transit investments and neighborhood change: On the likelihood of change. *Journal of Transport Geography*, *66*(C), 167–179.

Odden, A., Goertz, M., Goetz, M., Archibald, S., Gross, B., Weiss, M., & Mangan, M. (2008). The cost of instructional improvement: Resource allocation in schools using comprehensive strategies to change classroom practice. *Journal of Education Finance*, *33*(4), 381–405.

OECD. (2018). *A broken social elevator? How to promote social mobility*. https://www.oecd.org/social/soc/Social-mobility-2018-Overview-MainFindings.pdf

Parker, K., Horowitz, J. M., Brown, A., Fry, R., Cohn, D., & Igielnik, R. (2018). *What unites and divides urban, suburban, and rural communities*. Pew Research Center. https://www.pewsocialtrends.org/2018/05/22/what-unites-and-divides-urban-suburban-and-rural-communities/

Pender, J., Hertz, T., Cromartie, J., & Farrigan, T. (2019). *Rural America at a glance, 2019*. United States Department of Agriculture. https://www.ers.usda.gov/publications/pub-details/?pubid=95340

Pollack, C. E., & Lynch, J. (2009). Health status of people undergoing foreclosure in the Philadelphia region. *American Journal of Public Health*, *99*(10), 1833–1839.

Riebschleger, J., Norris, D., Pierce, B., Pond, D. L., & Cummings, C. (2015). Preparing social work students for rural child welfare practice: Emerging curriculum competencies. *Journal of Social Work Education*, *51*(2), S209–S224.

Rishel, C. W., Hartnett, H. P., & Davis, B. L. (2016). Preparing MSW students to provide integrated behavioral health services in rural communities: The importance of relationships in knowledge-building and practice. *Advances in Social Work*, *17*(2), 151–165.

San Antonio, D. M. (2016). The complex decision-making processes of rural emerging adults: Counseling beyond dualism. *Peabody Journal of Education, 91*(2), 246–269.

Schaff, K., Desautels, A., Flournoy, R., Carson, K., Drenick, T., Fujii, D., Lee, A., Luginbuhl, J., Mena, M., Shrago, A., Siegel, A., Stahl, R., Watkins-Tartt, K., Willow, P., Witt, S., Woloshin, D., & Yamashita, B. (2013). Addressing the social determinants of health through the Alameda County, California, Place Matters Policy Initiative. *Public Health Reports, 128*(6_suppl3), 48–53.

Storey, V., & Taylor, R. (2011). Critical friends and the Carnegie Foundation Project on the education doctorate: A Café conversation at the UCEA. *Journal of Alternative Perspectives in the Social Sciences, 3*(1), 849–879.

Thunberg, O. A. (2011). World cafes and dialog seminars as processes for reflective learning in organizations. *Reflective Practice: International and Multidisciplinary Perspectives, 12*(1), 319–333.

U.S. Census Bureau. (2018). *QuickFacts: Watauga County, North Carolina.* https://www.census.gov/quickfacts/wataugacountynorthcarolina

CHAPTER 4

A QUANTITATIVE COMPARISON OF RURAL AND URBAN SCHOOL AND TEACHER CHARACTERISTICS

Jessica Norwood, Tina L. Heafner, and Paul Fitchett
University of North Carolina at Charlotte

ABSTRACT

Utilizing data from the National Center for Education Statistics National Teacher Principal Survey (NTPS) for the 2015–2016 school year, we explored the following research question: What, if any, differences exist in school and teacher characteristics among urban, rural and suburban locations? Results suggest there are many areas of education in which rural students fall short of urban student access and opportunity. Yet, teachers in rural schools indicate greater satisfaction than their urban teacher counterparts. The difference in teacher satisfaction levels and reporting of school problems between urban and rural schools may be a factor of the "Great Divide." Results from our study suggest teachers may be at the heart of change, with implications for rural and urban schools. Through focusing on the "Great Divide" exhibited through survey responses in this study, we conclude that teachers are not immune to the charged cultural and political differences between urban and rural populations.

The Divide Within: Intersections of Realities, Facts, Theories, and Practices
pp. 79–94
Copyright © 2021 by Information Age Publishing

INTRODUCTION

"The Divide Within" the United States, attributed to shifting demographics in urban and rural communities, is reshaping America both geographically and politically. Urban communities have experienced the greatest ethnic and racial changes with the majority of residences identifying as non-White, whereas rural areas remain majority White (Parker et al., 2018). These demographic differences manifest in distinct political differences. According to researchers at the Pew Research Center (Parker et al., 2018), the political ideological gap among urban and rural voters seems to be widening with changes in party leanings. In fact, these researchers found that over half (54%) of rural voters consider themselves aligned with the Republican Party, while 38% of urban voters identify with the Democratic Party.

These political affiliations also signify cultural aspects of rural and urban communities, with 60% of rural residents and 53% of urban residents reporting that there are major value differences between rural and urban areas (Parker et al., 2018). Researchers also found this reflected in people who happen to live in urban or rural areas but identify with the political majorities of the opposite— 64% of Republicans in urban areas believe most rural people share their values, while 60% of Democrats in rural areas believe they differ from the values of most people around them. Less than half (48%) of Republicans in urban areas believe those living in cities share their values (Parker et al., 2018).

"The Divide Within" the United States may be related to such factors as partisanship, social media-enabled bubbles of opinions and information, and a fractured narrative of democracy among various identity groups, which presents an important consideration for social science scholars. Seemingly, conflicting realities between different factions of America have resulted in the polarization of social and political stances, creating a dichotomy in American politics reluctant to compromise. One of these dichotomies, between rural and urban populations, has roots in historical White flight, modern globalization, and amplified White nationalist rhetoric (Ortiz, 2018). While urban centers feel the economic and social pressures of gentrification, declining infrastructure, and institutional racism (Ingraham, 2018), rural areas also contend with the effects of neoliberal policies and globalization that have stripped economic stability from small towns and seemingly diminished cultural identity among rural residents (Vernon-Feagans & Cox, 2013). As a result, increased income and wealth inequality have shaped the socioeconomic lives of rural and urban residents alike. These market-driven economic policies have created rippling effects of widespread poverty in both types of communities through straining social services and employment opportunities (O'Sullivan, 2019). Additionally, there exists a social and cultural divide between mostly White rural residents and minoritized residents of cities rooted in different philosophical and value beliefs about American society and perceptions of each other. In fact, 70% and 65% of rural and urban residents, respectively, believe that people in other types of communities do not understand the stressors in their own communities (Parker et al., 2018). As social science scholars seek to address the divide between polarized groups in the United States, attention to urban and rural contexts may help develop proactive solutions for unification. Moreover, examining differences in educational experiences based on where a student lives may provide insight into what educative gaps may be contributors to urban-rural divisions.

The purpose of this study is to understand the educational contexts of urban and rural communities by assessing similarities and differences in student educational opportunity. By examining school- and teacher-level variables from a large, nationally representative dataset from the National Center for Education Statistics, we hope to offer insight into the challenges, opportunities, similarities, and differences among schools and teachers in urban and rural areas. Through quantitatively identifying patterns within schools and the teaching workforce in rural and urban communities, we intend to inform understanding of rural and urban educational contexts as a microcosm of greater social trends, and to highlight opportunities for public education to approach mending the "divide within." Guiding this research is the following research question: What, if any, differences exist in school and teacher characteristics among urban and rural locations?

LITERATURE REVIEW

Rural Communities and Education

Approximately 15–20% of Americans live in rural areas as of the 2010 Census (Health Resources & Services, 2018), and the majority of land in the United States is considered rural (Parker et al., 2018). Rural areas are also 79% White (Parker et al., 2018) and tend to be older than average (Vernon-Feagans & Cox, 2013). With economies formerly built around thriving industries, globalization and neoliberalism have contributed to automation and outsourcing that have economically depressed many rural communities, leading to greater poverty and subsequent social issues (O'Sullivan, 2019; Parker et al., 2018; Vernon-Feagans & Cox, 2013). Poverty rates in rural areas range from 13.1% in the Northeast to 20.5% in the South (United States Department of Agriculture, 2018). Compounding economic issues is the relative geographic isolation of rural communities, which dampens the availability of public and social services used in more urbanized communities to mediate the effects of poverty (O'Hare, 2009).

In a globalized world, rural residents often feel left behind and forgotten. Rather than associating economic decline with neoliberalism, however, research suggests rural residents feel a disruption in their communities due to a changing population and greater cultural attention to urban areas (Wuthnow, 2018). Seeing changes in their own communities with the arrival of more immigrants, rural residents may often scapegoat minoritized groups in order to inaccurately explain their economic frustrations (O'Sullivan, 2019). These rationales are then exacerbated by politics and media that amplify White nationalist rhetoric.

Education in rural communities is a reflection of the surrounding community and poverty presents a significant issue for schools and individual students. Rural students who come from economically disadvantaged backgrounds tend to have lower academic achievement, increased behavior problems, and eventual difficulties with adult employment (Burchinal & Willoughby, 2013). Schools also experience economic problems with lower tax base opportunities and potential subsidies diverted from schools to economic investors (Groenke & Nespor, 2010). In addition to funding issues, rural schools also struggle to retain quality teachers and support personnel and to provide professional development opportunities for teachers (Burton et al., 2013). Rural schools are also subject to school reform policies designed for urban schools that do not appropriately consider the context of rural schools, such as personnel and data requirements of federal education policy that are structured around larger schools. For example, policy requirements for paraprofessionals and support staff, such as special education aides and school psychologists, do not often take into account the funding limitations unique to small rural schools (Burton et al., 2013). Finally, cultural aspects of rural communities impact rural education, as students tend to have more insular experiences with greater influence from family members than students form more diverse urban areas (Vernon-Feagans & Cox, 2013). The influence of family is particularly important to consider within social science education.

Urban Communities and Education

Urban communities are home to 80% of Americans, largely due to the concentration of job opportunities and subsequent corporate investment into employee talent (Ingraham, 2018). Of those wanting to vacate urban areas, a lack of financial flexibility keeps residents from leaving (Ingraham, 2018). Urban areas are the most diverse locations in the United

States (Parker et al., 2018), and have significantly more foreign-born immigrants compared to rural areas (19% versus 4%, respectively) (United States Census Bureau, 2016). Also squeezed by neoliberal economic policies that have eroded funding for public services, economic stresses have hurt infrastructure investment and revitalization, affordable housing initiatives, and mental health and drug use services (Ingraham, 2018; O'Sullivan, 2019). Unlike rural poverty, which is often overlooked as a social issue, poverty tends to be associated with urban areas (Vernon-Feagans & Cox, 2013). Indeed, as of 2015, the overall poverty rate for American cities was nearly 20% (Kneebone, 2017). Interestingly, however, metropolitan areas across the United States have lower rates of poverty compared to their nearby rural areas. For example, in the South, the poverty rate for rural areas is 20.5% compared to 14.4% for metropolitan areas (United States Department of Agriculture, 2018). Cities, however, also have higher rates of crime, noise pollution, and traffic problems than rural areas (Parker et al., 2018).

Given lack of attention to public works and cultural beliefs about minoritized students rooted in deficit ideology, urban education has long been the center of "failing schools" rhetoric. Urban schools have issues with teacher stability, dropout rates, funding, resegregation, district leadership, discipline disproportionality, gifted and special education disparities, social capital, and test score gaps (Moore & Lewis, 2012). Targeted by the high-stakes standardized testing era, urban schools have faced threats of school closures and takeovers; been handed "failing" labels despite the alignment of test scores to socioeconomic status; and are often charged with teaching curricula disconnected from their students' lives (Moore & Lewis, 2012). Students in urban areas are also prone to the school-to-prison pipeline, particularly Black male youth, leading to significant lifelong implications (Moore & Lewis, 2012).

The Value of Rural and Urban Education

The earning potential varies depending on where one lives, suggesting a disconnect in educational access and opportunity for students educated in rural America. There is an approximate $10K–$20K higher rate for average salaries for urban residents with a bachelor's degree and graduate degree (Joseph, 2017). Six point five million students, more than 20 of the largest urban school districts combined, are educated in rural schools (Joseph, 2017). Just 29% of 18–24 year-olds in rural areas are enrolled in college, compared to 47% of their urban peers, according to the *New York Times* (Pappano, 2017). When looking at the quality of education, 47.2% of rural school districts do not have any secondary students enrolled in advanced placement (AP), while that is only the case in 2.6% of urban districts (Joseph, 2017). These trends may start early in education, as rural schools have difficulty attracting and retaining teachers (Burton et al., 2013). These schools also often experience "rural brain drain" as their most talented young people move into more career-lucrative cities (Carr & Kefalas, 2009) instead of returning to their home communities after college to teach or otherwise work in the area. This limits rural youth's ability to see themselves reflected in higher-income occupations that may otherwise expose and motivate them toward opportunities beyond their understanding.

Assessing the educational opportunities and experiences between urban and rural schools showcase their similar yet distinctly different contexts that have implications for students' life trajectories. Through quantitatively identifying these trends, researchers may be better informed about potential school processes and reform opportunities as well as the social dynamics underlying the urban-rural divide. Using a large dataset from the National Center for Education Statistics, we explored the following research question: What, if any, differences exist in school and teacher characteristics among urban and rural locations?

METHOD

For this study, we utilized data from the National Center for Education Statistics National Teacher Principal Survey (NTPS) for the 2015–2016 school year. The survey measures several areas of context for elementary and secondary education, including teacher and principal preparation, school characteristics, teacher, and principal labor force demographics, working conditions, and professional development (National Center for Education Statistics, 2019). The data for this work included a subsample of 6,240 teachers and principals and was generalizable to the United States teacher workforce for the survey year (Taie & Goldring, 2018).

Data analysis was performed using SPSS Statistics and included variables at the school and teacher levels. At the school level, variables included: school location (urban, suburban, town, and rural), Census region (Northeast, Midwest, South, West), Title I status, charter school designation, school enrollment range, school program type (regular, special program, special education, career/technical, and alternative), and school support staff members (content area specialists and coaches). At the teacher level, variables included: teacher certification type, teacher preparation experience (courses taken and skill readiness), working conditions (resource availability and job security), perceptions of school problems (student tardiness and absences, teacher absences, parent involvement, student preparation, and poverty), and teacher satisfaction.

The data were first screened for missing data, recoded as necessary, and replicate weights were applied for Chi-square analyses. Both descriptive statistics and Chi-square analyses were used to assess relationships between school- and teacher-level variables across school locations.

RESULTS

Descriptive statistics for the school level variables are reported in Table 4.1. Within the school-level sample (principal respondents), 27.4% of schools were in urban locations, 32.3% in suburban locations, 13.4% in town locations, and 27% in rural locations. Concerning school levels, 69% were elementary schools and 21.9% were secondary schools (9.1% were combined). Additionally, 60.7% of schools were designated as Title I and 7.7% were charter schools. The majority of schools, approximately 65%, had enrollments between 200 and 750 students. Most schools (87.2%) were also identified as regular elementary or secondary schools, while 3.7% were considered special programs (such as a science or math, performing arts, or gifted and talented school), 1.5% were special education programs, 1.6% were career/technical schools, and 6% were alternative schools.

Table 4.1.   Descriptive Statistics for School-Level Variables

Variable		Percentage	n (n = 90437)
School location	Urban	27.4	24,777
	Suburban	32.3	29,109
	Town	13.4	12,158
	Rural	27	24,393
School level	Elementary	69	62,364
	Secondary	21.9	19,839
	Combined	9.1	8,234
School type	Regular	87.2	78,832
	Special program	3.7	3,328
	Special education	1.5	1,391
	Career/technical	1.5	1,468
	Alternative	6	5,417
Title I		60.7	54,906
Charter school		7.7	6,923

Note: n is based on weighted sample.

From the teacher-level sample (teacher respondents), 90.7% held a regular state certification, although 18% had received licensure through an alternative certification program. Approximately 80% of teachers had completed teaching methods courses as part of their teacher education program. Additionally, 70% of teachers surveyed indicated they were committed to remaining in teaching. Regarding working conditions, most teachers (approximately 80%) agreed that they had access to necessary materials, but the majority disagreed that they had job security (56.6%) or influence into content standards they teach (62.3%). Additionally, most teachers considered poverty (60%), student unpreparedness (61%), and parent involvement (54%) moderate to serious issues at their schools. Finally, most teachers (75%) reported being satisfied in their work.

Results from Chi-square analyses suggest several statistically significant differences in school- and teacher-level characteristics among urban, suburban, town, and rural schools. These results are reported in Table 4.2. Within census regions, the majority of schools in the Northeast are suburban (47.9%), the majority of schools in the Midwest are rural (30.9), the majority of schools in the South are rural (37.4%), and the majority of schools in the West are urban (34.5%) (χ^2 (3, 3555622) = 21523.273, $p <$ .001). Additionally, 66.3% of rural schools are designated as Title I, compared to 64.9% of urban schools, 63.3% of town schools, and 51.4% of suburban schools (χ^2 (3, 3,555,622) = 18,263.352, $p <$ .001). Of charter schools, 51.8% of charters are located in urban areas, with 27.5% in suburban, 7.4% in town, and 13.4% in rural schools (χ^2 (3, 3,555,622) = 24,255.876, $p <$ .001).

Considering support staff at the school level, urban schools are more likely to have math specialists (25.7% of urban schools compared to 24% of suburban, 18.9% of town, and 17.6% of rural schools). Similarly, urban schools are also more likely to have science specialists (10.7% of urban schools compared to 8.9% of suburban, 6.7% of town, and 4.7% of rural schools). Urban schools are also most likely to have reading coaches (34.6% of urban schools compared to 29% or suburban, 23.6% of town, and 19.4% of rural schools) (χ^2 (3, 3,555,622) = 19,736.632, $p <$ .001). Within school program types, rural schools are least likely to have schools with special program emphasis (1.2% compared to 8.1% in urban), special education emphasis (0.6% compared to 2.2% in urban), or alternative schools (1.2% compared to 2.1% in urban) (χ^2 (9, 3,555,622) = 83,534.831, $p <$ .001).

At the teacher level, results suggest urban schools were most likely to have alternatively certified teachers (22.3%, compared to 16.6% in suburban schools, 14.7% in town schools, and 15.4% in rural schools) (χ^2 (3, 3,555,622) = 21,690.872, $p <$ .001). Of those who most agreed that resources are available, rural teachers agreed most often (39.8%), fol-

Table 4.2.   Chi-square Results for School-Level Variables

Variable		School Location			Chi Square Tests of Independence
		Urban	*Suburban*	*Rural*	
Census regions	Northeast	25.1	47.9	6.7	$\chi^2 = 21,523.273$
	Midwest	20.7	21.1	30.9	$df = 3, 3,555,622$
	South	26.3	28.7	37.4	$p < .001$
	West	34.5	31.4	13.2	
Title I status		64.9	51.4	66.3	$\chi^2 = 18,263.352$ $df = 3, 3,555,622$ $p < .001$
Distribution of charter school locations		51.8	27.5	13.4	$\chi^2 = 24,255.876$ $df = 3, 3,555,622$ $p < .001$
Support Staff	% of schools with math specialist support staff available	25.7	24.0	17.6	$\chi^2 = 19,736.632$ $df = 3, 3,555,622$ $p < .001$
	% of schools with science specialist support staff available	10.7	8.9	4.7	
	% of schools with reading coach available	34.6	29	19.4	
	% of schools with special program emphasis	8.1	3.0	1.3	

Note: "Town" as school location excluded from table.

lowed by suburban and town (37.2% and 37%, respectively), and urban (33.4%) (χ^2 (9, 3,555,623) = 19178.846, p < .001). Similarly, urban teachers were most likely to strongly disagree that resources were available (7.6%), followed by approximately 5% among the other locations. For all variables related to school problems (student tardiness, student absenteeism, class cutting, teacher absenteeism, drop outs, student apathy, parent involvement, poverty, unprepared students, and student health), urban teachers were most likely to report moderate to serious issues (χ^2 (9, 3,555,620) = 92,809.197, p < .001). Among measures of working conditions, urban teachers were also most likely to report dissatisfaction (χ^2 (9, 3,555,622) = 8,555.489, p < .001). These results are reported in Table 4.3.

Table 4.3.   Chi-Square Results For Teacher-Level Characteristics

Variable		School Location			Chi Square Tests of Independence
		Urban	Suburban	Rural	
Certification	% with traditional	77.7	83.4	84.6	$\chi^2 = 21{,}690.872$
	% with alternative	22.3	16.6	15.4	$df = 3, 3{,}555{,}622$
					$p < .001$
Working conditions	% agree resources available	33.4	37.2	39.8	$\chi^2 = 19{,}178.846$ $df = 9, 3{,}555{,}623$ $p < .001$
	% somewhat to strongly agree satisfied	72.2	75.5	78.2	$\chi^2 = 8{,}555.489$ $df = 9, 3{,}555{,}622$ $p < .001$
School problems (% reporting issue is moderate to serious problem)	Student tardiness	53.7	40.7	43.4	$\chi^2 = 92{,}809.197$ $df = 9, 3{,}555{,}620$ $p < .001$
	Student absenteeism	54.3	14.0	55.3	
	Class cutting	22.7	11.5	16.2	
	Teacher absenteeism	16.7	6.8	10.8	
	Dropping out	12.0	6.8	8.1	
	Student apathy	47.3	39.8	42.0	
	Parental involvement	59.6	47.5	53.7	
	Poverty	68.5	47.9	63.2	
	Unpreparedness	66.4	53.5	61.6	
	Student health issues	30.8	19.5	23.5	

Note: "Town" as school location excluded from table.

The following interpretations of the results of the data presented above are purposefully limited to the differences in rural and urban schools. The justification for this is rooted in showcasing the "divide" between these two groups which is the purpose of this study and the focus of this book. Suburban and town were included in the statistical analysis to account for percentage totals in the Chi-square examination of variables at both teacher and school levels.

INTERPRETATIONS

Rural education researchers espouse concern over the largely absent literature base documenting the experiences of rural students. Preliminary results from this research suggest they are right to do so. There are many areas of education in which rural students fall short of urban student access and opportunity. For example, rural students are less likely to have support personnel, such as content specialists and coaches, to help student achievement. Further, rural students are also less likely to have access to charter schools or special program schools compared to urban schools. With comparable poverty levels to urban schools as indicated by the Title I variable, yet less access to support services, rural schools do seem to be forgotten, as rural residents fear (Wuthnow, 2018).

Interestingly, however, despite similar instances of poverty, higher Title I designation, and less access to support personnel and charter school employment, the data suggest teachers in rural schools are more satisfied than their urban schoolteacher counterparts. Urban teachers share concerns about material resources, school problems, and working conditions at higher percentages than rural teachers. Teacher satisfaction is associated with longer teaching careers (Mullis et al., 2017) and higher student achievement (Caprara et al., 2006), invoking the need to examine the potential roots of these different levels.

First, urban and rural schoolteachers report different satisfaction levels with school material resources. This could be the result of tangible differences in resources available to rural versus urban communities. Rural residents are more likely to own their homes, which would provide a greater tax based for neighborhood schools in rural areas (Ingraham, 2018). These funds may then be used to provide additional resources for teachers in rural areas, explaining the differences in teachers' reports as related to funding. Another explanation may be due to a varying distribution of resources between rural and urban schools. Since school reform has targeted urban schools (Payne, 2008), urban school resources may be distributed to help increase test scores more acutely than rural schools, leaving urban teachers less flexibility and/or access to desired materials and subsequent lower satisfaction levels. This would also be associated with autonomy, which is another indicator of satisfaction (Warner-Griffin et al., 2018). Finally, these differences could simply be the result of school size. Because rural schools typical have fewer students in schools and classrooms, the spread of resources across students is less burdensome for teachers to manage, while urban schools may have more difficulty accessing enough resources for larger student bodies.

The frequency of school problems may also contribute to the differences between rural and urban teacher satisfaction. Urban teachers were more likely to rate school problems as more concerning than rural teachers throughout our results, including issues tardiness, absenteeism, cutting class, dropping out, student apathy, parental involvement, poverty, and unpreparedness. This increase in stress may dampen teacher satisfaction levels. Of interest, however, beyond tangible data to corroborate teacher reports, are the perceptions of teachers themselves.

An additional explanation for the difference in teacher satisfaction levels and reporting of school problems between urban and rural schools may be a factor of the "Great Divide" itself. Literature suggests rural communities experience the aforementioned school problems in similar magnitude and frequency compared to their urban counterparts (Vernon-Feagans & Cox, 2013). However, based on the results of our study, there seem to be differences in teacher *perceptions* of these issues that favor rural student populations over urban students. It is worth noting how this trend aligns with the difference between predominantly White teachers working with predominantly White students in rural areas versus predominantly White teachers working with predominantly minoritized students in urban areas. Given approximately 82% of the public teaching force is White, including 88% of rural teachers and 68% of urban teachers, White teachers necessarily must work with students of color (United States Department of Education, 2016). However, deficit-oriented perceptions of students are noted among White teachers working with diverse students (Moore & Lewis, 2012), and the question of whether urban school problems, when compared to rural school problems, may be inflated due to teacher racial bias could help inform bridging the divide between White teachers and the diverse students they serve. Teachers carry their implicit biases with them into their classrooms (Staats, 2016), and these beliefs and attitudes about students of color may impact their perceptions of schools that tap into broad cultural stereotypes and stigmas about urban education. While we do not aim to diminish the experiences and realities of teachers who reported school problems in the survey, the potential impact of teachers' racialized perceptions of students should not be marginalized in a broader discussion of divisions within American culture.

When examining the "Great Divide" between rural and urban contexts, results from our study suggest teachers may be at the heart of change. Teachers are not immune to the charged cultural and political differences between urban and rural populations, which have implications for rural and urban schools. As White teachers work with White students in rural populations, they may be less likely to help White students come to understand not only their own material and cultural conditions, but those of their urban counterparts as well. White teachers then serve a reproductive role in the maintenance of polarized divisions without critical awareness of these differences themselves (Lewis & Landsman, 2006). Similarly, White teachers may also continue traditional approaches to urban education that reinforce perceptions of urban school failure, weakening education offered to urban students while challenging trust in public education for urban populations. Some urban schools, likely the more diverse schools, are products of a history of de jure segregation (Rothstein, 2017). Implicit biases among teachers may contribute to their approach to education in either setting, potentially characterizing the content and delivery of social studies instruction that could otherwise be used to establish greater cultural, sociological, and civic understanding among all students.

CONCLUSION

When seeking to address gaps between rural and urban contexts, locating educational roots can be informative for action. The results from this study suggest that urban and rural schools contend with similar economic issues associated with education, but in different social contexts that translate to different experiences for teachers. Accounting for socioeconomic barriers, the stark differences in race and ethnicity between rural and urban schools are worth attention.

Moving forward, helping teachers come to understand their own implicit and confirmation biases, as well as the history of rural and urban education, may establish teaching philosophies aimed at resisting divides and instead, developing united interests in the preservation of American democratic society (O'Sullivan, 2019). Fostering embedded antiracist and social science education within teacher education programs may be a starting point for all preservice teachers and enacting meaningful professional development opportunities for in-service teachers, including rural and urban educators, may be beneficial for teacher growth in these areas. At the school level, rural schools, with a salient lack of racial and economic diversity, have difficulties educating students to appreciate the values and skills that make our democracy successful- from including an appreciation of diversity to the ability to listen to others, to the vocabulary to reason and articulate one's own viewpoint and the confidence to voice one's opinion with thoughtful reasoning (Kahne & Bowyer, 2017). Every school district that cannot offer equitable learning opportunities commensurate to wealthier and better organized districts, helps erode the pluralistic value of democracy and the American dream. This implies an immediate need for attention to rural schools' development of racial and cultural awareness among their White student bodies that students may not otherwise receive within their daily lives compared to urban students. Additionally, urban students also deserve opportunities within formal education to develop racial self-efficacy, learn multicultural histories, and experience validation within all avenues of teaching and learning. However, while education scholars have recognized and championed this need through critical race studies, critical Whiteness studies are much newer. In other words, while students of color have been doing work in understanding the racial and class implications of diversity in the United States, White students have been largely absent from such considerations (Rogers & Mosley, 2011). As urban schools focus on developing critical race awareness with students of color, rural schools should also be providing the same type of education to their White students. Better understandings of root causes of political beliefs among Whites surrounding minoritized communities may be a stepping stone toward remedying deep-seated factions between rural and urban populations.

Results of this study suggest that "The Divide Within" the United States as manifest in partisanship, social media-enabled bubbles of opinions and information, and a fractured narrative of democracy among various identity groups may be exacerbated by educational divisions in rural and urban communities. This presents an important consideration for social science scholars. Seemingly conflicting realities between different factions of America have not only resulted in the polarization of social and political stances, but also created educational biases that replicate societal divisions.

As social science scholars contend with educational efforts to bridge the "Great Divide" between political parties, geographic locations, and cultural (mis)understandings, data can be utilized to illustrate these divisions in meaningful ways. Through focusing on the "Great Divide" exhibited through urban and rural teachers' survey responses in this study, we hope to have indicated the need for further social science work in this area. In the future, studies highlighting teacher satisfaction between rural schools that serve White versus predominantly students of color will be helpful for informing the conclusions made here, as well as qualitative studies of teachers that may help identify racial literacies at practice in the classroom.

REFERENCES

Burchinal, M., & Willoughby, M. (2013). Poverty and associated social risks: Toward a cumulative risk framework. In L. Vernon-Feagans & M. Cox (Eds.), *The family life* project: An epidemiological and developmental study of young children living in poor *rural communities* (pp. 53–65). Monographs of the Society for Research in Child Development, *78*(5).

Burton, M., Brown, K., & Johnson, A. (2013). Storylines about rural teachers in the United States: A narrative analysis of the literature. *Journal of Research in Rural Education, 28*(12), 1–18.

Carr, P. J., & Kefalas, M. J. (2009, September 21). *The rural brain drain.* The Chronicle of Higher Education. https://www.chronicle.com/article/The-Rural-Brain-Drain/48425

Caprara, G. V., Barbaranelli, C., Steca, A., & Malone, P. S. (2006). Teachers' self-efficacy beliefs as determinants of job satisfaction and students' academic achievement: A study at the school level. *Journal of School Psychology, 44*(6), 473–490.

Groenke, S. L., & Nespor, J. (2010). "The drama of their daily lives": Racist language and struggles over the local in a rural high school. In K. A. Schafft & A. Youngblood Jackson (Eds.), *Rural education for the twenty-first century* (pp. 18–34). The Pennsylvania State University Press.

Health Resources & Services Administration. (2018, December). *Defining rural population.* https://www.hrsa.gov/rural-health/about-us/definition/index.html

Ingraham, C. (2018, December 18). *Americans say there's not much appeal to big-city living. Why do so many of us live there.* The Washington Post. https://www.washingtonpost.com/business/2018/12/18/americans-say-theres-not-much-ppeal-big-city-living-why-do-so-many-us-live-there/?utm_term=.54faefc0e60f

Joseph, M. (2017, June 1). *Crisis is rural American education.* Huffington Post. https://www.huffpost.com/entry/crisis-in-rural-americaneducation_b_59305c2ce4b09e93d7964875

Kahne, J., & Bowyer, B. (2017). Educating for democracy in a partisan age: Confronting the challenges of motivated reasoning and misinformation. *American Education Research Journal, 54*(1), 3–34.

Knapczyk, D., Chapman, C., Rodes, P., & Chung, H. (2001). Teacher preparation in rural communities through distance education. *Teacher Education and Special Education, 24*(4), 402-407.

Kneebone, E. (2017, February 15). *The changing geography of US poverty.* Brookings. https://www.brookings.edu/testimonies/the-changing-geography-of-us-poverty/

Landsman, J., & Lewis, C. W. (2006). *White teachers/diverse classrooms: A guide to building inclusive schools, promoting high expectations, and eliminating racism.* Stylus.

Moore, J. L. & Lewis, C. (2012). *African American students in urban schools: Critical issues and solutions for achievement.* Peter Lang.

Mullis, I. V. S., Martin, M. O., Foy, P., & Hooper, M. (2017). *PIRLS 2016 International Results in Reading.* Boston College, TIMSS & PIRLS International Study Center. http://timssandpirls.bc.edu/pirls2016/international-results/pirls/school-climate/teacher-satisfaction/

National Center for Education Statistics. (2019). *National Teacher and Principal Survey (NTPS).* https://nces.ed.gov/surveys/ntps/overview.asp

O'Hare, W. P. (2005). *The forgotten fifth: Child poverty in rural America.* Carsey Institute Report No. 10. https://scholars.unh.edu/cgi/viewcontent.cgi?article=1075&context=carsey

O'Sullivan, M. (2019). *The leveling: What's next after globalization.* Hachette Book Group.

Ortiz, P. (2018). *An African American and Latinx history of the United States.* Beacon Press.

Pappano, L. (2017, January 31). *Colleges discover the rural student.* New York Times. https://www.nytimes.com/2017/01/31/education/edlife/colleges-discover-rural-student.html

Parker, K., Horowitz, J. M., Brown, A., Fry, R., Cohn, D., & Igielnik, R. (2018, May 22). *Demographic and economic trends in urban, suburban and rural communities.* Pew Research Center. http://www.pewsocialtrends.org/2018/05/22/demographic-and-economic-trends-in-urban-suburban-and-rural-communities/

Payne, C. M. (2008). *So much reform, so little change: The persistence of failure in urban schools.* Harvard Education Press.

Rogers, R. & Mosley, M. (2011). Racial literacy in a second-grade classroom: Critical race theory, Whiteness studies and literacy research. *Reading Research Quarterly, 41*(4), 462–495.

Rothstein, R. (2017). *The color of law: A forgotten history of how our government segregated America.* Liveright.

Staats, C. (2016). Understanding implicit bias: What educators should know. *American Educator, 39*(4), 29–33.

Taie, S., & Goldring, R. (2018). *Characteristics of public elementary and secondary school teachers in the United States: Results from the 2015–16 National Teacher and Principal Survey First Look.* U.S. Department of Education. https://nces.ed.gov/pubs2017/2017070.pdf

United States Census Bureau. (2016, December 8). *New Census data show differences between urban and rural populations.* https://www.census.gov/newsroom/press-releases/2016/cb16-210.html

United States Department of Agriculture. (2018). *Rural poverty and well-being.* United States Department of Agriculture Economic Research Service.https://www.ers.usda.gov/topics/rural-economy-population/rural-poverty-well-being/

United States Department of Education. (2016). *The state of racial diversity in the educator workforce.* https://www2.ed.gov/rschstat/eval/highered/racial-diversity/state-racial-diversity-workforce.pdf

Vernon-Feagans, L., & Cox, M. (Eds.). (2013). Poverty, rurality, parenting, and risk: An introduction. In *The family life project: An epidemiological and developmental study of young children living in poor rural communities* (pp. 1–23). Monographs of the Society for Research in Child Development, *78*(5).

Warner-Griffin, C., Cunningham, B. C., & Noel, A. (2018). *Public school teacher autonomy, satisfaction, job security, and commitment: 1999–2000 and 2011–12.* National Center for Education Statistics. https://nces.ed.gov/pubs2018/2018103.pdf

Wuthnow, R. (2018). *The left behind: Decline and rage in rural America.* Princeton University Press.

CHAPTER 5

DISCIPLINE DISPARITIES

An Analysis of School Discipline Practices in a North Carolina High School

Yvonna Hines-McCoy, Tina L. Heafner, and Jeanneine Jones
University of North Carolina at Charlotte

ABSTRACT

School discipline research has examined the inequitable discipline experiences of Black students for the past 40 years. Black students, according to research, are disciplined at higher rates (and for less serious infractions) than their White counterparts. As a result, Black students are at greater risk of being referred, suspended, and/or expelled from school (Owen et al., 2014; Skiba & Peterson, 2000). The purpose of this study was to examine the school discipline profile and practices in a suburban, predominantly White, North Carolina high school and to explore whether Black students at this school are disproportionately overrepresented in discipline referrals, referrals leading to in-school suspensions, and/or referrals leading to out-of-school suspensions. Findings from this study suggest that they are and indicate a racial divide in which students are disciplined in high school.

The Divide Within: Intersections of Realities, Facts, Theories, and Practices
pp. 95–110

INTRODUCTION

Most people consider education to be the great equalizer, but in reality, is it truly? How can a system that consistently subjects certain groups of students, mainly students of color, to unjust school experiences be considered the epitome of fairness? The same education system charged with uplifting society has a long history of complicit de jure and de facto segregation as well as oppression and inequality (Rothstein, 2017). The system marginalizes, politicizes, and sanitizes school curriculum and content (Brown & Brown, 2010; King, 2017), often silencing the voices of people of color and ignoring racism. School experiences of Black students are frequently perceived as unfair and disconnected from the racialized realities of their lives (Clay & Rubin, 2019). Rarely are students of color able to grapple with the precarious nature of their citizenship status and civic life. Moreover, discipline practices in schools are more likely to adversely affect Black students as compared to their White peers further replicating inequalities and racialized policing in civil society. In fact, Black schoolchildren are suspended at three to four times the rate of White schoolchildren even though they do not misbehave more than them (Skiba et al., 2014). Black students, as a whole, often receive stiffer punishments than White students even for similar offenses (Michie, 2012).

Research shows that suspensions actually increase negativity within the school climate rather than produce positive behavior(s) (Arcia, 2006). Furthermore, suspensions increase the probability of negative school and life outcomes, such as low levels of academic achievement, unemployment, poverty, delinquency, and incarceration. Considering that Black students are disproportionately at risk of suspension, they are also disproportionately at risk of adverse life experiences.

Research consistently documents that Black students, especially Black males, are disciplined at higher rates (and for less serious infractions) than their White counterparts. Black students, consequently, are at greater risk of being referred, suspended, and/or expelled from school (Owen et al., 2014; Skiba & Peterson, 2000). Thus, the purpose of this study was to examine the school discipline profile and practices in a high school located in the southeastern United States and to explore if Black students, in particular, are overrepresented in school discipline practices, and, if so, to what extent (indices of disproportionality).

LITERATURE REVIEW

Racial disparities in school discipline have generated national dialogue since, at least, the 1970s, when the Children's Defense Fund released a report that revealed disproportionate representation of Black students in exclusionary discipline. The Children's Defense Fund (1975) found that Black schoolchildren, on average, are suspended at twice the rate of any other group. Today, school discipline literature continues to document racial disparities between Black children and White children. Currently, Black students are disciplined at higher rates and for less serious infractions than White students, and, as a result, are disproportionately at risk to be suspended or expelled from school (Owen et al., 2014; Skiba & Peterson, 2000). Black students, although overrepresented in exclusionary discipline, do not engage in more severe behaviors than White students (Skiba & Peterson 1999; Townsend, 2000). Instead, they are unjustly targeted and subjected to harsher consequences (Skiba, 2000).

Skiba et al. (2002) suggest that disproportionality in school discipline, or the *discipline gap*, has emerged as the result of institutional racism and implicit bias. Implicit bias, or the beliefs, attitudes, and stereotypes one has about a specific group, influence practitioners' interpretations of student behaviors (sometimes unknowingly). Teachers, for example, may misperceive nonthreatening behaviors illustrated by Black males as hostile considering stereotypical images of Black males as aggressive and/or violent. Race and class, independently and collectively, influence teachers' perceptions and expectations of students, as well as their discipline decisionmaking (Blanchett, 2006).

We use the acronyms ISS and OSS to represent in-school suspension and out-of-school suspension respectively. This study was guided by the following research question: Are Black students disproportionately represented in school disciplinary actions (ISS and OSS) at X High School? When we refer to exclusionary discipline, a practice of punishment for a discipline referral by a teacher or administrator, this relates to a disciplinary sanction that removes a student from his or her typical educational setting. This methodology that was used to conduct this study mimics, to some extent, the methodology commonly employed by researchers examining racial disparities in school discipline.

METHOD

Secondary analysis, or the analysis of data collected in a previous study, allowed researchers to utilize existing datasets to address new research questions. A secondary analysis of quantitative discipline data, originally collected by an urban, southeastern United States school district's division of accountability and research, was used to answer the research question for this study. The dataset included discipline referrals and sanctions (by race/ethnicity and gender) from August 2017 to December 2017 for all schools in the district, including X High School.

Measuring Disproportionality

Discipline disproportionality occurs when groups of students are present in discipline sanctions, such as discipline referrals, ISS, and/or OSS, at higher or lower percentages/rates than their presence in the student population. Disproportionality is calculated by dividing the percentage of Group X with referrals/ISS/OSS by the percentage of Group X in student enrollment. A disproportionality index (DI) of one indicates no disproportionality whereas an index greater than one signifies overrepresentation in discipline referrals/ISS/OSS and an index less than one shows underrepresentation in discipline referrals/ISS/OSS.

RESULTS

The following findings and interpretations relate to the research question that initially guided this study: Are Black students disproportionately represented in school disciplinary actions at X High School? Implications are included to draw attention to several concerns that emerged from the research findings. Recommendations are included to guide future directions.

Racial Composite of School Demographics

As a measure of disproportionality, percentages of discipline infractions are compared with the population distribution at a given school. The demographic composite of X High School is presented in Table 5.1. There were 1,370 students enrolled in X High School at the time of this study. White students comprised the majority of school enrollment (69.9%), while Black students made up 16.5% of the student population. The remaining 13.6% included students who identified as Hispanic or Other.

Table 5.1.   X High School Student Enrollment by Race/Ethnicity and Gender

Percentage of Total Number of Students	White n (%)	Black n (%)	Hispanic n (%)	All Other n (%)
Male students	481 (35.1%)	127 (9.3%)	46 (3.4%)	44 (3.2%)
Female students	477 (34.8%)	99 (7.2%)	55 (4.0%)	41 (3.0%)
Total number (percentage) of students	958 (69.9%)	226 (16.5%)	101 (7.4%)	85 (6.2%)

Note: Total number of students enrolled in X High School is $N = 1,370$.

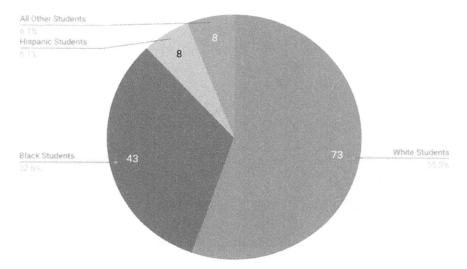

Figure 5.1.   Total number/percentage of referrals by race/ethnicity.

School Discipline Referrals. From August to December 2017, a total of 132 discipline referrals were made at X High School. Figure 5.1 reports the number and percentage of student referrals by race/ethnicity. Of these referrals, 55.3% ($n = 73$) were made for White students with 32.6% ($n = 43$) for Black students. Hispanic and all other students were equal in the number of discipline infractions ($n = 8$, 6.1%).

Black students represent only 16% of the student population at X High School, yet account for roughly 33% of all discipline referrals. The disproportionality index (DI) for Black students was 2.06, a number significantly higher than one. Because their presence in referrals exceeds their presence in the student population, Black students are overrepresented (DI = 2.06) in discipline referrals, and, consequently, at greater risk of being referred than their White counterparts. White students, on the other hand, represent 70% of the student population at X High School, but only 55% of all discipline referrals. The disproportionality index (DI = .79) for White students was lower than one, indicating an underrepresentation in proportion to their representation within the school's student population. As a result, White students are less likely to receive discipline infraction than their Black peers. Similarly, Hispanic students had a disproportionality index lower than one in school referrals (DI = .92); therefore, they too are less likely to be referred. The disproportionality index for all other students was equal to one indicating no disproportionality. To visualize the extent of racial disparities, Figure 5.2 reports the total

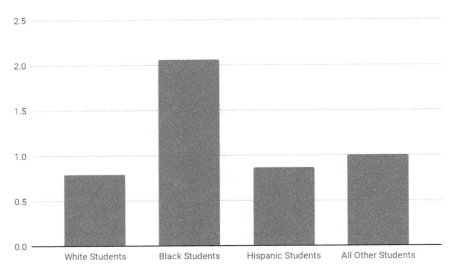

Figure 5.2.   Disproportionality in student referrals by race/ethnicity.

number/percentage of referrals by race/ethnicity (the DI index). Blacks are two times more likely than White, Hispanic, or other students to receive a discipline referral. This finding suggests that race, specifically being Black, is a consideration whether implicit or not, in determining which students are disciplined in X High School.

Race/Ethnicity and Gender in Discipline Referrals. White males at X High School have the most discipline referrals and make up 43% of the total number of infractions. Black males represent a quarter of all referrals and are the second highest group. White females comprise 12% of the referrals, whereas, Black females represent almost 8%. All other males follow with 6% of the overall discipline referrals. The fewest number of infractions are given to Hispanic males and females. Figure 5.3 shows the total number/percentage of referrals by race/ethnicity and gender.

When accounting for race/ethnicity and gender, both Black males and females are disproportionately referred. Black males represent only 9% of the student population, but 25% of all discipline referrals. The disproportionality index for Black males (DI = 2.78) far exceeds all other subgroups of students and is higher than the overall DI for male and female Black students combined (DI = 2.06). Although less disparity exists for Black females, they too are overrepresented in referrals with a disproportionality index of 1.14. White females, despite representing 35% of enrollment, account for only 12% of referrals; they are significantly underrepresented (DI = .34). White males, however, are not. They repre-

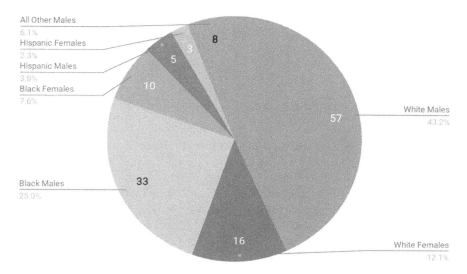

Figure 5.3.   Total number/percentage of referrals by race/ethnicity and gender.

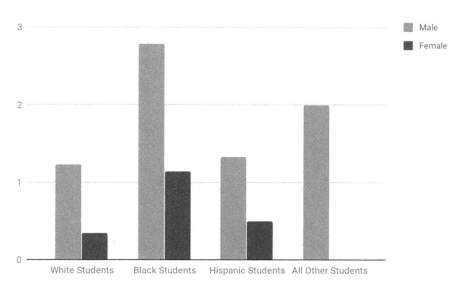

Figure 5.4.   Disproportionality in student referrals by race/ethnicity and gender.

sent 35% of the student population, yet account for 43% of all referrals (DI = 1.23). Figure 5.4 illustrates disproportionality in discipline referrals by race/ethnicity and gender.

Referrals Resulting in In School Suspension (ISS)

Race/Ethnicity and Discipline Referrals Resulting in ISS. From August to December 2017, a total of 67 discipline referrals at X High School resulted in ISS. ISS was the punishment administered for 50.8% of the total number of discipline referrals ($n = 132$). Figure 5.5 reports the number and percentage of student referrals by race/ethnicity that resulted in ISS. Of these ISSs, 56.7% ($n = 38$) were given to White students with 29.9% ($n = 20$) of Black students receiving ISS. White students received ISS for 52% of their discipline referrals; whereas, Black students were given ISS for 46% of their referrals. Approximately 63% of discipline referrals for Hispanic and all other students resulted in ISS for discipline infractions ($n = 5, 4; 7.5\%, 6.0\%$ respectively).

Even though White students account for 57% of referrals that lead to ISS, they make up 70% of student enrollment at X High School. With a

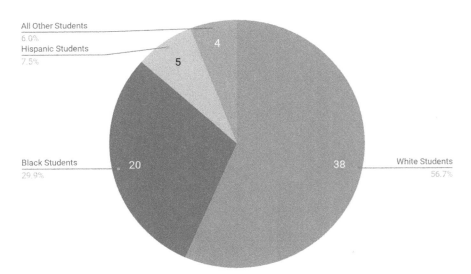

Figure 5.5.   Total number/percentage of student referrals resulting in ISS by race/ethnicity.

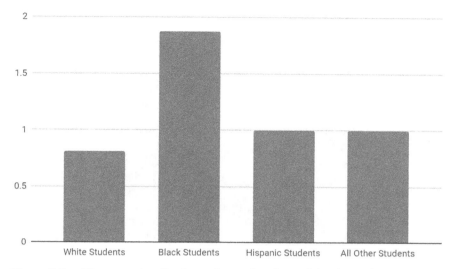

Figure 5.6.   Disproportionality in student referrals resulting in ISS by race/ethnicity.

disproportionality index of .81, White students, unlike their Black counterparts, are less likely to be assigned ISS following a discipline referral. Black students, unsurprisingly, are at greater risk of receiving ISS as punishment for violating rules of conduct (DI = 1.88). Figure 5.6 depicts racial disparities in referrals resulting in ISS by comparing disproportionality indices by race/ethnicity.

Race/Ethnicity and Gender and Discipline Referrals Resulting in ISS. Additional comparisons of discipline practices for X High School were made for the intersectionality of race/ethnicity and gender. Figure 5.7 reports the number and percentage of referrals that resulted in ISS. White (45.6%) and Black (19.1%) males comprised the highest percentages of discipline referrals with ISS followed by Black (11.8%) and White (10.3%) females. Hispanic males and females made up 5.9% and 1.5% of the infractions receiving ISS.

Black males are at greater risk than any other group of students at X High School of receiving ISS following a discipline referral (DI = 2.1). In general, however, males of all races, including White males, are overrepresented in ISS. Black females, on the other hand, with a disproportionality index of 1.71, are the only group of females at X High School that are overrepresented. Figure 5.8 compares disproportionality in referrals resulting in ISS by race/ethnicity and gender.

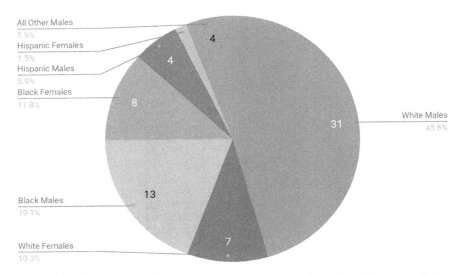

Figure 5.7.   Total number/percentage of referrals resulting in ISS by race/ethnicity and gender.

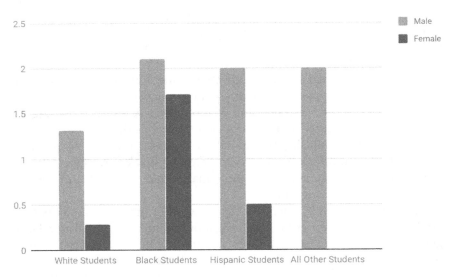

Figure 5.8.   Disproportionality in student referrals resulting in ISS by race/ethnicity and gender.

Referrals Resulting in OSS

Race/Ethnicity and Discipline Referrals Resulting in OSS. From August to December 2017, a total of 40 discipline referrals at X High School resulted in OSS (out-of-school-suspension). OSS was the punishment administered for 30.3% of the total number of discipline referrals (n = 132). Figure 5.9 reports the number and percentage of student referrals by race/ethnicity that resulted in OSS. Of these out-of-school-suspensions, 42.5% (n = 17) were given to White students with 42.5% (n = 19) of Black students receiving OSS. Black students received more OSS than any other student group in X High School. Black students were more likely to receive OSS as a punishment for their discipline referrals as compared White, Hispanic and Other students who received ISS more times than OSS. White students received OSS for 7% of their discipline referrals; whereas, Black students were given ISS for 44% of their referrals. Approximately a quarter to 37% of discipline referrals for Hispanic and all other students resulted in ISS for discipline infractions (n = 1, 3; 2.5%, 7.5% respectively).

Black students make up only 16% of the student population at X High School, but account for almost 50% of discipline referrals resulting in OSS. White students, on the other hand, make up 70% of student enrollment but only 43% of referrals resulting in OSS. Figure 5.10 documents

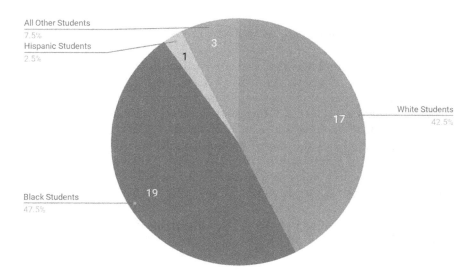

Figure 5.9.   Total number/percentage of referrals resulting in OSS by race/ethnicity.

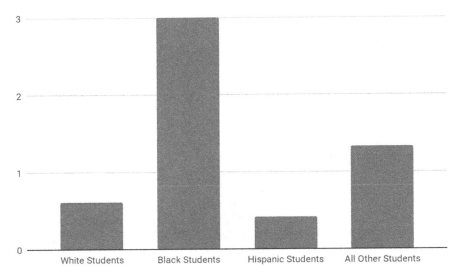

Figure 5.10.   Disproportionality in student referrals resulting in OSS by race/ethnicity.

these punitive discrepancies, as well as the disproportionality index by race/ethnicity.

Race/Ethnicity and Gender and Discipline Referrals Resulting in OSS. Of the forty discipline referrals at X High School resulting in OSS (out-of-school-suspension), most of these were given to male students (87.5%). Figure 5.11 displays the total number/percentage of referrals resulting in OSS by race/ethnicity and gender. Black males received nearly half (42.5%) of the out-of-school-suspensions, with White males representing 37.5% and all other males at 7.5%. Females comprised the remaining OSS discipline referral cases (12.5%) with an equal percentage of Black and White females (5%) receiving out-of-school-suspensions.

Both White and Black females are underrepresented in referrals resulting in OSS. Conversely, all males except Hispanic males, are overrepresented. With a disproportionality index of 4.77, Black males are significantly overrepresented in OSS. The disproportionality index for Black males is more than four times that of White males. Figure 5.12 shows disproportionality (OSS) by race/ethnicity and gender.

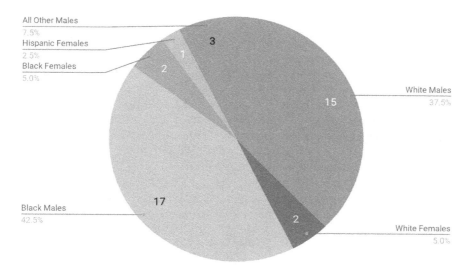

Figure 5.11.   Total number/percentage of student referrals resulting in OSS by race/ethnicity and gender.

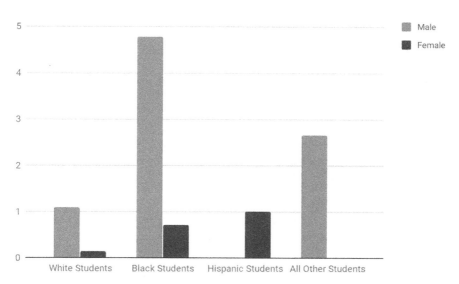

Figure 5.12.   Disproportionality in student referrals resulting in OSS by race/ethnicity and gender.

IMPLICATIONS

Since 1975, the discipline gap, documented initially by the Children's Defense Fund, has garnered significant attention, and, in turn, prompted numerous research studies. The research on school discipline has, for the past 40 years, remained consistent with the Children's Defense Fund's initial findings: Black students, even though they do not engage in more severe behaviors than White students, are disciplined at higher rates, and, as a result, are disproportionately represented in exclusionary discipline (Skiba & Peterson, 1999; Townsend, 2000; Wallace et al., 2008). Findings from this study further supports the research.

This study found that Black students at X High School are overrepresented in all disciplinary actions (referrals, ISS, and OSS), and, consequently, are at greater risk than their White peers of being disciplined for violating rules of conduct. Black males, in particular, are more likely to be disciplined than any other group of students at X High School. Despite representing only 9% of the student population, Black males at X High School account for roughly 25% of all disciplinary referrals and 43% of referrals resulting in an out-of-school suspension. Black males accounted for over 19% of the ISSs and Black females represented the highest number of ISS cases (12%) for all females. The disproportionality index for Black students ranged from two to more than four times that of White students. Of all discipline cases, Black males were more likely to be overrepresented in discipline referrals and more extreme punishments (ISS and OSS).

Findings from this study suggest that teachers' and administrators' disciplinary practices may be implicitly biased against Black students, especially Black males, which, in turn, causes these students to be susceptible to inconsistent and inequitable discipline sanctions. Skiba (2001) argues that this can often be attributed to cultural discontinuity, unfamiliarity, and misunderstandings, as well as the internalization of stereotypes that criminalize Black youth and their behaviors as inappropriate and/or threatening. In light of the discipline gap, which is the product of racial stereotypes and implicit bias, data in this study suggest it may also result in the overuse or misuse of discretionary practices by school officials toward Black students. Complicating matters, administrators at this school utilize discretion when issuing consequences for misbehavior; their actions and subjectivity directly attribute to discipline disparities.

Recommendations

Given the findings and implications from this study, in order to lessen (and ultimately diminish) discipline disparities at this school, it is recommended that culturally responsive classroom management and decision-making are developed and implemented by both teachers and administrators. Culturally responsive classroom managers are aware of their implicit biases and ethnocentric tendencies, as well as knowledgeable about their students' cultural backgrounds and communities (Weinstein et al., 2004). They understand how school (and individual) practices and policies interact to produce inequities, such as racial disparities in school discipline. Culturally responsive classroom managers modify their behaviors to establish cultural synchronization in the classroom, which, research suggests, has the power to close the discipline gap (Monroe, 2006) (assuming disciplinary moments usually occur at the classroom level). Culturally responsive discipline is recommended, too, but because there seems to be a dearth of research on this topic, it is difficult to note what it entails.

CONCLUSION

Research on school discipline disparities continues to emphasize disproportional representation of Black students in disciplinary referrals and suspensions. Findings from this study, although consistent with the literature, furnished implications that deserve deliberate attention from, at minimum, the teachers and administrators at X High School. Black students at X High School, like most Black students throughout the United States, are prone to inequitable discipline sanctions simply because of their race creating a racialized discipline gap. Although beyond the scope of this study, future research should explore teacher, classroom, and/or school characteristics that increase the probability of referrals and suspensions for Black students at X High School. Until then, the teachers and administrators at X High School should administer the suggested recommendations, so that all students, regardless of race, have equitable opportunities for learning.

REFERENCES

Arcia, E. (2006). Achievement and enrollment status of suspended students: Outcomes in a large, multicultural school district. *Education and Urban Society, 38,* 359–369.

Blanchett, W. J. (2006). Disproportionate representation of African American students in special education: Acknowledging the role of White privilege and racism. *Educational Researcher, 35,* 24–28.

Brown, K. D., & Brown, A. L. (2010). Silenced memories: An examination of the sociocultural knowledge on race and racial violence in official school curriculum. *Equity & Excellence in Education, 43*(2), 139–154.

Children's Defense Fund. (1975). *School suspensions: Are they helping children?* Washington Research Project.

Clay, K. L., & Rubin, B. C. (2020) "I look deep into this stuff because it's a part of me": Toward a critically relevant civics education. *Theory & Research in Social Education, 48*(2), 161–181. https://doi.org.10.1080/00933104.2019.1680466

King, L. J. (2017). The status of Black history in U.S. schools and society. *Social Education, 81*(1), 14–18.

Michie, G. (2012). *We don't need another hero: Struggle, hope, and possibility in the age of high-stakes schooling*. Teachers College Press.

Monroe, C. R. (2006). African American boys and the discipline gap: Balancing educator's uneven hand. *Educational Horizons, 84*, 102–111.

Owen, J., Wettach, J., & Hoffman K. (2015). Instead of suspension: Alternative strategies for school discipline. *Duke Center for Child and Family Policy and Duke Law School*. https://www.ednc.org/wp-content/uploads/2015/04/Alternatives_to_Suspension_3_2015.pdf

Rothstein, R. (2017). *The color of law: A forgotten history of how our government segregated America*. Liveright.

Skiba, R. J. (2001). When is disproportionality discrimination? The overrepresentation of Black students in school suspension. In W. Ayers, B. Dohrn, & R. Ayers (Eds.), *Zero tolerance: Resisting the drive for punishment in our schools* (pp. 176–187). New Press.

Skiba, R. J., Arredondo, M. I., & Williams, N. T. (2014). More than a metaphor? The contribution of exclusionary discipline to a school-to-prison pipeline. *Equity & Excellence in Education, 47*, 546–564.

Skiba, R. J., Michael, R. S., Nardo, A. C., & Peterson, R. L. (2002). The color of discipline: Sources of racial and gender disproportionality in school punishment. *Urban Review, 34*, 317–342.

Skiba, R. J., & Peterson, R. L. (1999). The dark side of zero tolerance: Can punishment lead to safe schools? *Phi Delta Kappan, 80*, 372–382.

Skiba, R. J., & Peterson, R. L. (2000). School discipline at a crossroads: From zero tolerance to early response. *Exceptional Children, 66*, 335–347.

Townsend, B. L. (2000). The disproportionate discipline of Black learners: Reducing school suspensions and expulsions. *Exceptional Children, 66*, 381–391.

Wallace, J. M., Jr., Goodkind, S., Wallace, C. M., & Bachman, J.G. (2008). Racial, ethnic, and gender differences in school discipline among U.S. high school students: 1991–2005. *Negro Educational Review, 59*, 47–62.

Weinstein, C., Tomlinson-Clarke, S., & Curran, M. (2004). Toward a conception of culturally responsive classroom management. *Journal of Teacher Education, 55*, 25–38.

CHAPTER 6

PRIMARY CONTRADICTIONS

Qualitative Transformations
of White Social Studies Teacher Identity

Dean P. Vesperman
University of Wisconsin River Falls

Jill Leet-Otley
Luther College

ABSTRACT

Is it possible for preservice social studies teachers to transform their conceptions of race and their identity as White teachers? This mixed-methods study, using critical Whiteness and cultural historical activity theory, focused on two White male preservice social studies teachers and their conceptions of race, racism, and White privilege. We argue that the interaction of the values and beliefs of participants with the values and beliefs of a multicultural education classroom led to the rise of primary contradictions. As the participants grappled with issues of Whiteness, racism, and antiracist teaching, they underwent qualitative transformations, which led to an increased level of racial awareness and cultural competence.

BACKGROUND AND PURPOSE:
THE CONTRADICTIONS OF WHITENESS

Among the greatest challenges facing public education in the United States is the intransigence of systemic racism. The most pressing prob-

The Divide Within: Intersections of Realities, Facts, Theories, and Practices
pp. 111–132

lems, including the achievement gap and the dearth of teachers of color, can be traced to deep-seated racial histories and divisions. One way to begin to dismantle systemic racism is to explicitly teach White preservice teachers (PSTs) the detrimental effects of racism, including how unconscious biases impact students of color.

We recognize there is a significant gap between White preservice teachers' conceptions of themselves and the reality of teaching in increasingly diverse classrooms. As teacher educators in a primarily White institution, it is imperative that we engage our students in careful deliberations around race, racism, and Whiteness to help them move beyond the guilt, shame, and denial that often accompany racial awareness work (Lensmire et al., 2013; Thandeka, 1999). The vast majority of the PSTs at our small, private liberal arts college are White, as are all of the teacher education faculty. It is during the foundation level course on multicultural education that our students receive explicit instruction in how race and culture operate in U.S. schools and society. For some students, this is the first time they are expected to confront racism and their own Whiteness. Others come well-practiced in what Mason (2016) calls *diversity discourse*. They are familiar with terms like White privilege and colorblindness and are eager to engage in social justice discourse, but often lack a deeper understanding of the pernicious nature of White supremacy. Having grown up in Whitestream spaces (Grande, 2004), they often lack the experience and skills to be culturally sustaining educators (Gay, 2010; Ladson-Billings, 1995; Paris, 2012).

Prior course feedback revealed that many students felt significantly impacted by the course, yet we did not know what particular aspects of the course were pushing them to become more culturally and racially conscious. The purpose of this study was to critically examine students' written reflections from the beginning and the end of the course, to help us understand the qualitative transformations of their beliefs. Importantly, the research is a form of praxis (Lather, 1991) as we strive to improve the multicultural education course and our own pedagogy and growth as antiracist teacher educators (Hooks, 1994; Lowenstein, 2009).

THEORETICAL FRAMEWORK

Critical Whiteness Studies

This research is informed by a Critical Whiteness Studies (CWS) framework that recognizes the socially constructed nature of race, the intransigence of Whiteness, and the hegemonic power of White supremacy (Delgado & Stefancic, 1997). As such, we work to deliberately disrupt the racial narratives that have informed many of our students' lives and experiences. This research is also informed by second wave White teacher identity studies (Jupp et al., 2016), which recognizes the complexity of White teacher identity and moves beyond essentialized notions that assume all White PSTs teachers are colorblind and completely resistant to acknowledging their White privilege (Crowley, 2016; Jupp et al., 2016; Lensmire et al., 2013). Instead, we recognize that White preservice teacher identity falls along a continuum of racial consciousness informed by intersecting markers of identity (such as gender and class) and individual sociocultural histories.

Crowley's (2016) explication of *transgressive* and *negotiated White racial knowledge* is particularly germane to our research. Building on Leonardo's (2009) notion of White racial knowledge, Crowley theorized that race-conscious White preservice teachers engaged in transgressive White racial knowledge when they were thinking about race and racism intellectually but began to use negotiated White racial discourse when discussing their actual teaching practice. Negotiated White racial knowledge also surfaced when preservice teachers were confronted with their own complicity in racism.

Cultural-Historical Activity Theory (CHAT)

Our research is also informed by second generation activity theory (Engeström, 1987, 1990). CHAT posits that "collective, artifact-mediated, and object-oriented activity system" is the prime unit of analysis (Engeström, 2001, p. 136), which allows for the critical examination of the subject, culturally mediated artifacts, and the object of the activity (Cole & Engeström, 1993; Engeström, 1987, 1990; Vygotsky, 1978). Therefore, when participants engage in activity there is the possibility of shifts in participants' conceptions: qualitative transformations.

For our research, we focus on two aspects of activity: multivoicedness and contradictions. Every cultural-historical activity is embedded with multiple voices (Engeström, 2001). Thus, as subjects engage in activity they are influenced by their own values, beliefs, and traditions as well as those held by the community (i.e., fellow PSTs, teacher educators, researchers). The interaction of the voice of the subject(s) and the community can lead to qualitative transformations. Next, Engeström (1987, 1990, 2001) argued that qualitative transformations occur as contradictions arise when there is a conflict between the value systems held by the subject(s) and the activity: primary contradictions (Yamagata-Lynch & Haudenschild, 2009). The appearance of primary contradictions leads subjects to try and resolve the contradiction by modifying their existing values, beliefs, norms, and conceptions (Engeström, 1987, 1990; Yamagata-Lynch & Haudenschild, 2009). Thus, primary contradictions cause qualitative transformations.

Multicultural Education Course as Activity

Second generation activity theory allows us to examine the interplay of various factors of our multicultural course as an activity (see Figure 6.1). For the purpose of this chapter, we are focusing on only a few aspects of mediated learning. The object of the activity is for PSTs to critically examine their own identity, culture, and race (Banks, 2009; Crowley, 2016; Delpit, 1995; Ladson-Billings, 2014); to learn more about their intercultural competence (Hammer & Bennett, 2001); to explore their privilege and implicit biases (Banks, 2009; Emdin, 2016; MacIntosh, 2001); and to learn how to construct an equity pedagogy (Banks, 2009; Emdin, 2016; Gay, 2010; Ladson-Billings, 1995).

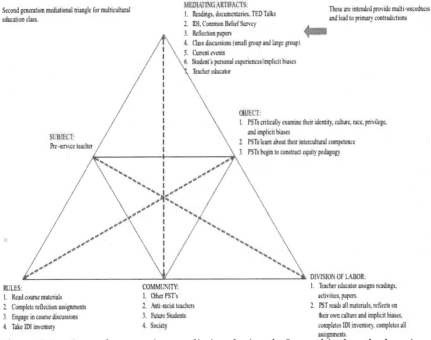

Figure 6.1.   Second generation mediational triangle for multicultural education class

To achieve this object, PSTs use culturally mediated artifacts, such as identity maps and the cultural iceberg model, to explore their identity, culture, and race (Banks, 2009; Delpit, 1995). An essential artifact PSTs are required to complete is the Intercultural Development Inventory (IDI) (Hammer & Bennett, 2001), an assessment of their intercultural competence. In addition, PSTs use readings, current events, TedTalks, documentaries (i.e., *Race: The Power of an Illusion*), and activities (i.e., Implicit Association Test and McIntosh's (2001) *Knapsack of Privilege*, to explore racism, White privilege, and the systemic causes of the opportunity gap (Carter & Welner, 2013; Emdin, 2016; Gay, 2010; McIntosh, 2001).

A key aspect of the course is that the readings and activities reveal multiple points of view, values, beliefs, and traditions related to the community of antiracist teachers. In effect, PSTs are placed into a community of practitioners that includes a community of multicultural citizenship (Banks, 2009; Kymlicka, 1995) and antiracist education (Banks, 2009; Darling-Hammond, 2017; Gay, 2010). These communities guide how PSTs use the aforementioned culturally mediated artifacts.

As PSTs engage with the culturally mediated artifacts and community to achieve the object of activity, they encounter differing perspectives, values, and beliefs about teaching. This leads to the rise of primary contradictions which the subject tries to resolve (Engeström, 1987, 1990). Thus, the intent of the course is to bring about primary contradictions and help subjects resolve the contradictions in such a way that they develop their intercultural competence and deepen their racial knowledge; in other words, that they experience a qualitative transformation towards becoming an antiracist teacher.

RESEARCH METHOD

This case study is part of a larger study on 22 preservice teachers' conceptions of White identity. Participants were enrolled in a multicultural education course in a small liberal arts college in the upper Midwest. This study focused on two White, male, preservice social studies teachers out of the cohort. The first author was the social studies methods instructor at the institution and worked with both participants in following semesters. The second author was the instructor of record for the course and is a certified IDI administrator (Hammer & Bennett, 2001).

This case study used a concurrent mixed methods research design in order to achieve complementarity of the data collected and to provide a more nuanced explanation of this social phenomenon (Greene, 2007; Onwuegbuzie & Johnson, 2006). An enhancement of interpretations of the qualitative findings with quantitative data from the larger study provided a fuller interpretation and understanding of the data collected (Collins et al., 2006; Jang et al., 2008). The qualitative data in this study has supremacy over the quantitative data.

Data Sources

Quantitative data was collected from two sources. The first source of data was from the *Common Beliefs Survey* designed by Teaching Tolerance. The 13-question survey has two sections. The first part required participants to respond to a statement related to race and culture in education on a 5-point Likert scale. The second part required participants to write an explanation of their Likert ranking. The survey was given to 22 participants on the first and last day of the course in order to determine if there had been qualitative shifts in participants' racial awareness and cultural competence by the end of the course. The quantitative data from the larger study was analyzed using a t test to determine if there were significant shifts in participants' responses to the survey.

Additionally, all participants took the IDI during the fifth week of the course (Hammer & Bennett, 2001). The IDI is a 50-item questionnaire developed to assess intercultural competence along a continuum from monocultural (denial, polarization, minimization) to intercultural worldviews (acceptance and adaptation) (see Table 6.1). The assessment is used to determine participants' ability to shift cultural perspective and appropriately adapt their behavior. Part of taking the IDI is participating in a 30 minute debrief session in which a qualified IDI administrator (the second author) discusses the results and the personalized Intercultural Development Plan (IDP) with the participant. The authors decided to use the IDI because it has high cross-cultural validity and reliability (DeJaeghere & Cao, 2009).

Qualitative data was collected from three sources: The *Common Beliefs Survey*, an initial reflection on their own identity, and a final reflection on what they had learned in the course. The authors coded qualitative data separately using grounded theory (Charmaz, 2006; Glaser & Strauss, 1967). This resulted in 20 open codes (Corbin & Strauss, 1990), for example, colorblindness, race visible, focus on teaching, individualism, and education as individual growth. The authors then deliberated over the

Table 6.1.   Intercultural Development Inventory Score Range

Denial	Polarization	Minimization	Acceptance	Adaptation
55–70	70–85	85–115	115–130	130–145

open codes. This deliberation led to the development of three important codes using a constant comparison method (Corbin & Strauss, 1990): pragmatism, Whiteness, and cultural awareness. These codes were then used to conduct multiple rounds of analysis, which revealed two major themes within the qualitative data: pragmatism of teaching and Whiteness.

Participants

Zach

Zach grew up in a diverse city in the Midwest and is the first in his family to attend college. When he was two, his parents divorced. After this divorce, he and his sister lived with their father and faced a period of homelessness until his father purchased a house in a primarily Latinx neighborhood. He attended a Spanish immersion elementary school that was majority Latinx. Zach described being physically and verbally harassed because he was "one of the only Caucasian kids in the school" (Zach, Initial paper). Zach's experience living in a diverse urban environment shaped his thinking in important and unexpected ways. As he describes it:

> Being in this situation I learned and understood what others have gone through and continue to go through based on their race, religion, and political beliefs. From these experiences I no longer judge someone on the skin tone or beliefs, I just accept who they are for the people they are. (Zach, Initial paper)

Zach expresses empathy for people who are mistreated because of their race, religion, or political beliefs rather than resentment for the way he was treated. Although Zach relies on colorblind discourses here, his cultural competence and awareness of how racism impact history were generally more evolved than many of his peers. As the second wave literature on White teacher identity reveals, PSTs who have had significant intercultural experiences, who have had personal experiences with marginalization and discrimination, and/or who come from less privileged backgrounds tend to be more willing to engage in critical conversations around race, racism, and White privilege (Crowley, 2016).

Isaiah

Isaiah grew up in a suburb of a major city in the Midwest and attended a school that was about 80% White. He was raised by a single mother and identifies as middle class. Based on his contributions to class discussions and his writings, we would describe Isaiah as one of the more conservative students in the class. As he describes in his initial "Who am I?" paper:

> I am a proud American whose culture and self-identity reflects the fundamental American principles outlined in our constitution. As a descendant of [a] founding father ... and as the grandson of a WWII paratrooper, I take great personal pride in my nation and its history.... My culture, my identity is utterly American. (Isaiah, Initial paper)

After reading his initial paper, the second author made a concerted effort to get to know Isaiah as she worried that he might be resistant to the topics covered in the course and did not want the course to become disempowering (Ellsworth, 1989). As teacher educators, we must figure out ways to make all our students feel valued and accepted, even as we challenge some of their preconceived beliefs about racism and White supremacy. Although Isaiah was initially quite unaware of White privilege and institutional and systemic racism, he showed significant growth in his cultural competence and White racial knowledge over the course of the semester as evidenced by his final paper and his postsurvey.

FINDINGS

Quantitative Analysis

Quantitative analysis revealed two very important findings for this study. The participants had significant gaps between their perceived orientation and their developmental orientation on their IDIs. This gap influenced how the participants viewed themselves as future educators which allowed us to examine primary contradictions that arose as the participants engaged in particular activities. The other important finding was the shift in participants' responses to questions on the Common Beliefs Survey, which revealed interesting qualitative transformations in their understanding of the pragmatic aspects of teaching.

IDI

The IDI was extremely helpful in thinking about where our students were in terms of their beliefs and readiness to engage in critical discussions about culture and race. The IDI gives two results: A perceived orientation (PO) and a developmental orientation (DO) (see Table 6.1). A PO score that is seven points or higher than the DO score indicates a meaningful difference in a person's perceived versus actual cultural competence (Hammer & Bennett, 2001). Like most people who take the IDI, the two students believed they were farther along in terms of their intercul-

Table 6.2.   Participants' IDI Orientation

Participant	Perceived Orientation	Developmental Orientation	Orientation Gap
Zach	126.837	114.456	12.381
Isaiah	115.471	80.563	34.908

tural development than they actually were. Receiving their individual IDI results had a significant impact on the participants (see Table 6.2).

Zach. Zach's DO score placed him almost out of the minimization perspective and on the cusp of acceptance, while he perceived that he was fully in the acceptance range of cultural competence (Zach, IDI report). Minimization is an orientation that highlights cultural commonalities and minimizes differences as exemplified by the colorblind discourse. Contrastingly, the acceptance orientation recognizes and appreciates cultural differences.

Zach's reflected on his IDI results:

> What I learned about myself from the IDI was that I am on the verge of becoming accepting of others. I hope to achieve this level of acceptance because it'll help improve my communication skills and in today's modern society racism should not be a thing and I do not want to contribute to the already existent racism. (Zach, Final paper)

Zach's response is noteworthy because, unlike many White people who use race evasive discourses (Jupp et al., 2016), he speaks in the first person, "I do not want to contribute to the already existent racism," thus taking ownership of his potential complicity in individual acts of racism. Importantly, his critique does not rise to the level of understanding White complicity in terms of systemic or institutional racism. Nonetheless, it is a pivotal and necessary step in the right direction.

Isaiah. Isaiah's DO score placed him in the middle of the polarization perspective, while his PO score placed him at the beginning of the acceptance perspective. His gap of 34 points is extremely large and speaks to the discrepancy between where Isaiah's intercultural competence is and where he perceives himself to be. The polarization orientation is defined as a judgmental orientation that views cultural differences in terms of "us" and "them" (Isaiah, IDI report).

Unlike Zach, Isaiah displayed some ambivalence about his IDI results as evidenced in his final paper:

> I learned a lot about myself during this course when I took the Intercultural Development Inventory or IDI test. My score was a little surprising to me because of my background and where I grew up. I did not find this test to be an accurate representation of my values because I feel that some of the questions were inherently deceptive in nature.

It appears Isaiah resisted his results on two levels. First, because he grew up outside of a major metropolitan area and attended a high school with some diversity, he believed he would be more interculturally competent than his results suggest. He also struggled to reconcile having a DO in polarization knowing the values that he holds and the person he considers himself to be.

Although the IDI does not make a judgment about where people should be on the continuum, the assumption of the course, and by extension, the education department, is that students will work to move themselves further along the continuum so they can become culturally competent and culturally sustaining teachers (Paris, 2012). In his initial paper Isaiah wrote of having strong core values and beliefs such as "helping others in need ... never hurting anyone unjustly, [and] defending the weak" (Isaiah, Initial paper). His resistance to the results, even after a 30 minute debrief session with a trained IDI administrator, suggests that he is still working through the primary contradictions between his stated values and beliefs and the values and beliefs implicitly and explicitly embedded in the course.

Being confronted with the discrepancy between their perceived intercultural competence and their actual developmental level precipitated significant self-reflection. In Zach's case, he resolved the primary contradiction and appears ready to engage in the work necessary to becoming a more accepting, and thus more culturally competent, teacher. In Isaiah's case, he is still grappling with the primary contradiction between his beliefs and values and the beliefs and values of the multicultural course. Isaiah will require more experiences and activities that challenge his polarized, monocultural worldview.

Pre- and Postsurvey

Statistical analysis of the pre- and postsurveys of all 22 participants revealed shifts in their responses on the Common Beliefs Survey. While there were important shifts in participants' responses to all thirteen questions, two of the thirteen questions revealed significant changes in participants' beliefs (see Table 6.3). Analysis of the two questions with significant shifts focused on how issues of culture and race melded with pedagogical decisions they would have to make as future teachers (see Table 6.4). An

**Table 6.3.   Statistically Significant Shifts
on the Common Beliefs Survey**

	Presurvey		Postsurvey		
	M	SD	M	SD	t Test
Question #3	2.55	1.01	1.55	0.74	3.7468*
Question #12	4.00	0.95	4.64	0.58	2.6664*

Note: *$p < 0.05. N = 22$.

Table 6.4.   Common Beliefs Survey Questions 3 and 12

Question #3	Teachers should adapt their teaching to the distinctive cultures of African American, Latino, Asian and Native American students.
Question #12	With all the pressures to raise student achievement, finding and using examples for the cultural, historic and everyday lived experiences of my students takes away (or could take away) valuable time from teaching and learning what matters most.

analysis of the surveys of the two case study participants mirrored the findings of the larger study.

Qualitative Analysis

Qualitative analysis of the participants' responses on their assigned reflections and written responses on the Common Beliefs Survey revealed several important patterns in the qualitative transformation of the two participants' conceptions of themselves as teachers. These qualitative transformations occurred in two main realms: Whiteness and the pragmatism of teaching.

Whiteness

Second wave teacher identity research has helped the field move beyond seeing White preservice teachers in monolithic terms—as being mostly unaware of and resistant to learning about race, White privilege, and racism (Jupp et al., 2016; Lensmire et al., 2013). At the same time, Mason (2016) cautions that the *diversity discourse* many preservice teachers now subscribe to, often merely reinscribes racism by using code words like "urban" and "poor" to signify racial categories. Furthermore, Crowley (2016) cautions that understanding White privilege is not sufficient; we must work towards greater awareness of White complicity in sustaining the institution of White supremacy that undergirds our education system.

Zach. Zach presents a different trajectory compared to Isaiah in terms of his White racial knowledge and where he started at the beginning of the course (see Figure 6.2). His lived experiences were very much racialized although he professed to seeing things through a colorblind or race-neutral lens. In his initial paper he wrote, "As a result of being one of the only Caucasian kids in the school and class, I was beat and bullied into submission. I was physically and verbally harassed and would often come home with bruises covering my chest." As discussed previously, Zach's experience of being harassed because of his race led him to downplay the significance of race. It is worth noting that he uses the term Caucasian rather than White throughout his initial paper; this can be seen as a way

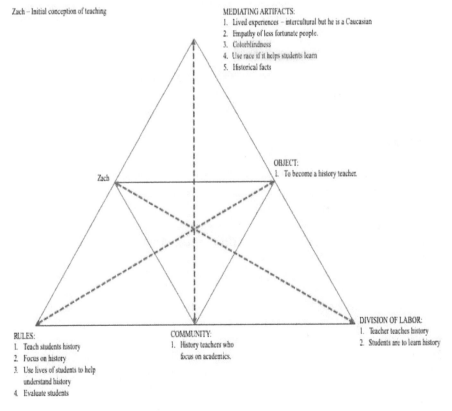

Figure 6.2.   Zach: Initial conception of teaching history.

to obscure his Whiteness because "White" carries a heavier racial burden than the term "Caucasian." In the final paper Zach uses both terms interchangeably, but explicitly refers to himself as a White person. This is a small but significant discursive move towards taking ownership of his Whiteness.

Zach struggled with the concept of colorblindness in a way that is both honest and revealing and is in keeping with his developmental orientation of minimization. In his pre and post survey he agreed with the statement, "I am colorblind when it comes to my teaching," although his written response shifted ever so slightly. On the first survey he wrote, "We are all human." On the second he wrote, "We are all one species," but added, "I see some race because of culture." It appears that he is willing to acknowledge race when thinking about how cultures differ across racial groups. In his final reflection paper, he elaborates,

> A blind spot I have is that I am pretty colorblind. Even though I'm not supposed to believe in colorblindness as a way of acceptance, I do. I believe that being colorblind to race but not culture is important, however, since most experienced educators do not agree with me, I can consider it a fault of my education style.

This is significant because it shows his willingness to modify his teaching to accommodate different cultures, but his lingering resistance to acknowledging the significance of race (see Figure 6.3).

The class took place in fall of 2017 and there was much happening in the news, including police shootings of unarmed black men, the White supremacist march in Charlottesville, and the rise in hate crimes in the United States. We actively incorporated current events into course discussions about racism and equity. In his final paper Zach wrote,

> My thinking about white privilege and racism has changed dramatically over this semester. This is partially due to the class but to a much larger extent, the news and what is happening in the world right now. I realized that racism and white privilege is [sic] more prevalent than ever and is affecting people's rights and lives.

Zach is at once holding on to what seems right about being colorblind—that race should not matter—with his newfound realization that racism and White privilege continue to negatively impact people's rights and lives. Juxtaposing these seemingly disparate beliefs demonstrates just how complicated it is to make sense of Whiteness (Crowley, 2016).

Isaiah. In many ways Isaiah's developing racial awareness followed a familiar trajectory (see Figure 6.4). Prior to the course, he did not think much about racism and White privilege; however, throughout the course,

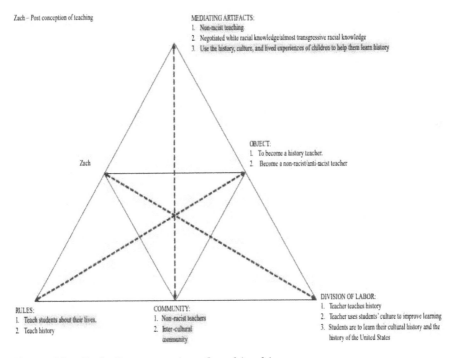

Figure 6.3.   Zach: Postconception of teaching history.

his conceptions shifted. The development of Isaiah's racial consciousness is demonstrated by comparing his responses to the statements that explicitly deal with race on the Common Beliefs Survey. Question #1 states, "I don't think of my students in terms of their race or ethnicity. I am color blind [sic] when it comes to my teaching." On day one of the course Isaiah rated this a 1 (agree strongly) and wrote, "I believe that teachers should focus on teaching their class to the best of their ability and not make any one student or group of students feel left out or unimportant." On the last day of class Isaiah rated this a 4 (disagree) and wrote, "It is important to understand the cultural identity of the students, but not use racial identity as a discriminating factor." He seems to be getting at an important and nuanced point here which is that teachers need to understand the significance of students' cultures (which are often inextricably bound to race), but without engaging in any sort of racial discrimination.

Question #13 of the survey stated, "Talking about race with my colleagues could open up a can of worms; little good is likely to come from it." Although Isaiah rated both of his responses a 3 (neither agree nor dis-

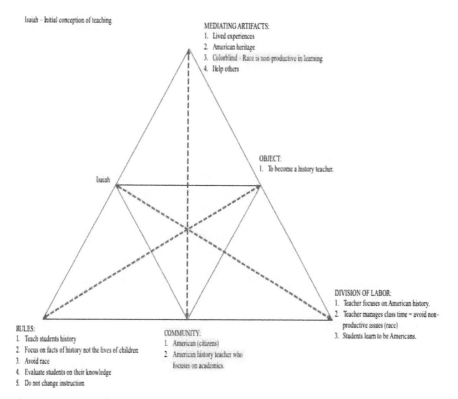

Figure 6.4.   Isaiah: Initial conception of teaching history.

agree), on the presurvey he wrote, "Race is a private issue and while understanding and respecting people of other races is extremely important dwelling on it can be offensive or insensitive." His understanding of race is indicative of a colorblind mentality where race itself is minimized. On the postsurvey, however, he wrote, "Talking about race in a nonabrasive way is critical. But talking about it can be good." Here he shows a willingness to engage with race as long as it is talked about in a "nonabrasive" way. He is no longer colorblind, but he also demonstrates a degree of White fragility (DiAngelo, 2011) that is typical for White preservice teachers.

In his final reflection paper Isaiah documents his learning with the following self-reflection, "My opinions have changed and developed this past semester and now I have a much better idea of the kind of teacher I want to be." He goes on to write:

Of all the lessons learned this semester, White privilege is probably the topic that I had given the least thought to prior to taking this course. As I discussed in my "Who Am I" paper, I don't like to see myself only for the "tip of the iceberg," but if I had to categorize myself I would say I am a middle class White man. (Isaiah, Final paper)

In this passage we can see that Isaiah engages in race visible language although he does so reluctantly. The first step in understanding Whiteness and White privilege is being able to recognize that one has a racial identity. He continues:

White privilege is still an issue in society today even though people do not always realize the inherent uniqueness of opportunity.... Something this course has emphasized is that it is wrong to ignore race and that we as educators need to understand our peers and students and not categorize them based on their skin, culture, or religion. (Isaiah, Final paper)

Although Isaiah names White privilege, he does so in a way that distances him from any kind of ownership. It is an issue that exists "out there" in society somewhere. Likewise, he uses the passive voice to state that *the course* emphasized that it is wrong to ignore race. Importantly, when he says, "We as educators need to understand" and not for example, "I need to understand," he creates a discursive space that alleviates him from some of the burden of Whiteness (see Figure 6.5). Crowley (2016) refers to this type of discourse as negotiated White racial knowledge as opposed to transgressive White racial knowledge. Isaiah is thinking about race in terms of recognizing White privilege and not being colorblind. While these are vital concepts and signal where he is in terms of his White racial knowledge, it is crucial to note that he does not yet think about racism in institutional or systemic terms.

Pragmatism

A key qualitative transformation the two participants revealed was in their conception of teaching. Both participants tended to focus on the pragmatic aspects of teaching: they focused on what they believed would work in the classroom and what would inhibit teaching social studies. Over the course of the semester, their pragmatic conception of teaching changed.

Zach. Initially, Zach focused on the practical aspects of teaching. For him, race was not always something to be considered when teaching. He wrote, "Because I try not to see race but if this were to help them learn I'd agree." Therefore, race was only to be considered if it helped students learn. This was exemplified when he wrote,

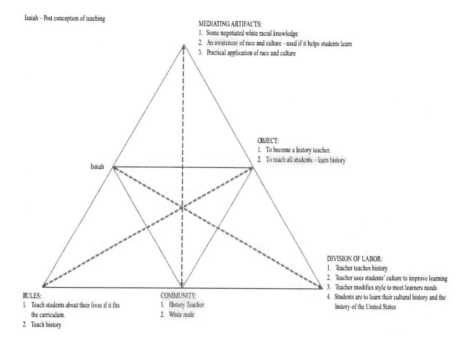

Isaiah – Post conception of teaching

MEDIATING ARTIFACTS:
1. Some negotiated white racial knowledge
2. An awareness of race and culture – used if it helps students learn
3. Practical application of race and culture

OBJECT:
1. To become a history teacher.
2. To reach all students – learn history

Isaiah

DIVISION OF LABOR:
1. Teacher teaches history
2. Teacher uses students' culture to improve learning
3. Teacher modifies style to meet learners needs
4. Students are to learn their cultural history and the history of the United States

RULES:
1. Teach students about their lives if it fits the curriculum.
2. Teach history

COMMUNITY:
1. History Teacher
2. White male

Figure 6.5.   Isaiah: Postconception of teaching history.

> Because they [the cultural, historic and everyday lived experiences of students] are not mutually exclusive. You can use and should use examples from a student's life to help them understand a concept. It'll make it a far quicker and long-lasting knowledge then."

Thus, adapting curriculum should be done only if it pragmatically helps students.

At the end of the course, Zach's conception of teaching had shifted. He noted that teachers should adapt their teaching to the distinctive cultures of their students, but there were limitations to how much. He wrote, "Yes and no [adapting teaching to their students]. Because we need a variety. Yes, we need more of this [discussions of race and culture] in our lessons. However, not completely this." Thus, we should include adaptations for our students of color because that is effective teaching. "Yes, it'll [using examples for the cultural, historic and everyday lived experiences of my students] take more time. However, the quality of education is far more important than the quantity of education." Thus, pragmatic teaching meant including the lives of students into the curriculum. Zach's conception of teaching shifted away from focusing on the individual pragmatic needs of the teacher toward the lived needs of his future students.

Isaiah. Initially, Isaiah rejected adapting the curriculum to his student's identity because it might interfere with the practical aspects of teaching. He wrote, "I believe that education and race are two separate issues. Teaching students should not be focused on anything not related to what is being taught." Thus, issues of race were not to be considered when engaging in the practical aspects of teaching. In fact, it might hamper teaching. He also noted, "I believe that as an educator it is my duty to teach my students to the best of my ability by managing class time and being on track." Thus, students' race and lived experiences should not be considered when teaching because that impedes learning.

At the end of the semester, Isaiah's pragmatic conception of teaching shifted. He argued that issues of race and culture were important to be included in the classroom. For example, in response to a statement about matching teaching styles to learning styles that might differ based on the race and ethnicity of students, Isaiah responded, "Catering the education to the student is vital to student learning." Thus, issues of race and culture should be considered because pragmatically teachers need to teach all of their students. However, there is a caveat: issues of race and culture should only be considered, "Depending on the situation and student make up." Race and culture should be included in the classroom if it fits the practical realities of the curriculum and the student body. Isaiah shifted away from issues of race and ethnicity being a detriment to the social studies classroom toward an acceptance that some of his students might need culturally relevant instruction.

CONCLUSION: IMPLICATIONS

The IDI and the initial reflections revealed that both participants began the activity with a limited conception of themselves as White teachers. They believed it was essential for a teacher to be colorblind. Consequently, Zach and Isaiah argued issues of race should not influence the pedagogical decisions teachers make in the social studies classroom. Teachers should focus on the pragmatic aspects of teaching. Their beliefs conflicted with the beliefs and values embedded in the course, which led to the rise of primary contradictions related to issues of race, privilege, and their own Whiteness. This struggle led both participants to transform their conception of themselves as social studies teachers and their understanding of teaching. They became more aware of their Whiteness and the effect of White privilege on their teaching. However, there were limits to their growing awareness.

To resolve the primary contradiction between Zach's beliefs and those embedded in the activity, he became more aware of his own Whiteness and privilege. However, he still struggled with the complexities of color-blindness. He was reluctant to see race as a source of diversity; instead focusing on the salience of culture. Additionally, Zach intellectually saw the need to be transgressive in describing class practices but did not move beyond negotiated White racial knowledge (Crowley, 2016).

Contrastingly, Isaiah resolved this primary contradiction by moving away from colorblindness and toward a recognition of White privilege. However, he posited White privilege as something that existed outside of his identity. He moved from race evasive discourses toward negotiated White racial knowledge (Crowley, 2016). The participants responded to the primary contradictions by transforming their conception of themselves as White social studies teachers.

Zach and Isaiah both began to recognize that issues of race and culture could not be ignored in the classroom and shifted their conception of teaching social studies. Interestingly, this qualitative transformation occurred along the issue of the pragmatic needs of teaching; however, this transformation was not transgressive. Both participants resolved primary contradictions by moving away from ignoring issues of race and culture in the classroom to being cognizant of the need for them to be pragmatically incorporated into their social studies classroom. The goal of this cognizance was to ensure that all of their students could achieve academically. Significantly, neither participant recognized their essential role in challenging the systemic impacts of racism and White supremacy in their classroom, school, or community. Thus, there were limits to their qualitative transformations of themselves as social studies teachers.

One of the objectives of multicultural courses in teacher education is to disrupt the colorblind discourse many White people have been socialized into believing—that we should not see color (a slippery signifier for race) because race no longer matters. Delpit's (1995) powerful counter narrative, "If one does not see color, then one does not really see children" (p. 177) helps White preservice teachers understand the ongoing salience of race in the lives of students from the global majority. What is often obscured, however, is that race inevitably matters for White people too; that race as a social construct is contingent upon the hierarchy of racism. Too often our students come away from the course with the idea that they should "see race," but they miss, dismiss, or resist the fact that they must also "see racism." That critical lens takes much longer to cultivate. Our multicultural education course is only one semester; we can hardly blame our students if they finish the course without fully developing the knowledge and skills they will need to be culturally sustaining, antiracist educators (Mason, 2016). It behooves us then to continue to challenge racism and White supremacy by deliberately embedding antiracist practices and pedagogies into the remainder of our students' coursework.

Pushing PSTs to think more critically about their own cultural values, norms, and beliefs requires strategic empathy (Matias & Zembylas, 2014) as students grapple with knowledge that disrupts and unsettles some of their preconceived beliefs. At the same time, we must employ a pedagogy of discomfort that enables our students to move outside of their comfort zones without succumbing to guilt, shame, and denial (Matias & Zembylas, 2014). The administration of the IDI and the debrief effectively challenge and support students as they confront the limits of their cultural competence. Both participants entered the activity believing they were more culturally competent; thus, prepared for teaching in diverse classrooms. Working to make sense of this primary contradiction turned out to be a pivotal component of the course. The purpose of critical self-reflection and greater intercultural competence is merely the first step in a larger project to dismantle racism and White supremacy in our classrooms, in our schoolhouses, and in our society writ large.

REFERENCES

Banks, J. (2009). Multicultural education: Dimensions and paradigms. In J. Banks (Ed.), *The Routledge international companion to multicultural education* (pp. 9–32). Routledge.

Carter, P. L., & Welner, K. G. (Eds.). (2013). *Closing the opportunity gap: What America must do to give every child an even chance.* Oxford University Press.

Charmaz, K. (2006). *Constructing grounded theory: A practical guide through qualitative analysis.* Sage.

Cole, M., & Engeström, Y. (1993). A cultural-historical approach to distributed cognition. In G. Salomon (Ed.), *Distributed cognitions: Psychological and educational considerations* (pp. 1–46). Cambridge University Press.

Collins, K. M. T., Onwuegbuzie, A. J., & Sutton, I. L. (2006). A model incorporating the rationale and purpose for conducting mixed-methods research in special education and beyond. *Learning Disabilities: A Contemporary Journal, 4*(1), 67–100.

Corbin, J., & Strauss, A. L. (1990). Grounded theory research: Procedures, canons, and evaluative criteria. *Qualitative Sociology, 13*(1), 3–21.

Crowley, R. M. (2016). Transgressive and negotiated White racial knowledge. *Intercultural Journal of Qualitative Studies in Education, 29*(8), 1016–1029.

Darling-Hammond, L. (2017). Teaching for social justice: Resources, relationships, and anti-racist practice. *Multicultural Perspectives, 19*(3), 133–138.

DeJaeghere, J. G., & Cao, Y. (2009). Developing U.S. teachers' intercultural competence: Does professional development matter? *International Journal of Intercultural Relations, 33*(5), 437–447.

Delgado, R., & Stefancic, J. (Eds.). (1997). *Critical white studies: Looking behind the mirror.* Temple University Press.

Delpit, L. (1995). *Other people's children: Cultural conflict in the classroom.* The New Press.

DiAngelo, R. J. (2011). White fragility. *International Journal of Critical Pedagogy, 3,* 54–70.

Ellsworth, E. (1989). Why doesn't this feel empowering? Working through the repressive myths of critical pedagogy. *Harvard Educational Review, 59*(3), 297–325.

Emdin, C. (2016). *For White folks who teach in the hood ... and the rest of y'all too: Reality pedagogy and urban education.* Beacon Press.

Engeström, Y. (1987). *Learning by expanding: An activity-theoretical approach to developmental research.* Orienta-Konsultit Oy.

Engeström, Y. (1990). *Learning, working and imagining: Twelve studies in activity theory.* Orienta-Konsultit Oy.

Engeström, Y. (2001). Expansive learning at work: Toward an activity theoretical reconceptualization. *Journal of Education and Work, 14*(1), 133–156.

Gay, G. (2010). *Culturally responsive teaching: Theory, research, and practice.* Teachers College Press.

Glaser, B. G., & Strauss, A. L. (1967). *Discovery of grounded theory: Strategies for qualitative research.* Chicago: Aldine.

Grande, S. (2004). *Red pedagogy: Native American social and political thought.* Rowman & Littlefield.

Greene, J. (2007). *Mixed methods in social inquiry.* Jossey-Bass.

Hammer, M. R, & Bennett. M. J. (2001). *The intercultural development inventory manual. Version 2.* Intercultural Communication Institute.

Hooks, B. (1994). *Teaching to transgress: Education as the practice of freedom.* Routledge.

Jang, E. E., McDougall, D. E., Pollon, D., Herbert, M., & Russell, P. (2008). Integrative mixed methods data analytic strategies in research on school success in challenging circumstances. *Journal of Mixed Methods Research, 2*(3), 221–247.

Jupp, J. C., Berry, T. R., & Lensmire, T. J. (2016). Second-wave White teacher identity studies: A review of White teacher identity literatures from 2004 through 2014. *Review of Educational Research, 86,* 1151–1191.

Kymlicka, W. (1995). *Multicultural citizenship.* Oxford Political Theory.

Ladson-Billings, G. (1995). Toward a theory of culturally relevant pedagogy. *American Educational Research Journal, 32*(3), 465–491.

Ladson-Billings, G. (2014). Culturally relevant pedagogy, 2.0: The remix. *Harvard Educational Review, 84*(1), 74–84.

Lather, P. (1991). *Getting smart: Feminist research and pedagogy with/in the postmodern.* Routledge.

Lensmire, T. J., McMannin, S., Tierney, J. D., Lee-Nichols, M. E., Casey, Z. A., Lensmire, A., & Davis, B. M. (2013). McIntosh as synecdoche: How teacher education's focus on white privilege undermines antiracism. *Harvard Educational Review, 83*(3), 410–431.

Leonardo, Z. (2009). *Race, Whiteness, and education.* Routledge.

Lowenstein, K. L. (2009). The work of multicultural teacher education: Reconstructing white teacher candidates as learners. *Review of Educational Research, 79*(1), 163–196.

Mason, A. M. (2016). Taking time, breaking codes: Moments in white teacher candidates' exploration of racism and teacher identity. *International Journal of Qualitative Studies in Education, 29*(8), 1045–1058.

Matias, C. E., & Zembylas, M. (2014). 'When saying you care is not really caring': Emotions of disgust, whiteness ideology, and teacher education. *Critical Studies in Education, 55*(3), 319–337.

McIntosh, P. (2001). Unpacking the invisible knapsack. In M. Andersen & P. Collins (Eds.), *Race, class, and gender* (pp. 95–105). Wadsworth.

Myers, V. (2014, November). *How to overcome our biases? Walk boldly toward them* [Video]. TED Conferences. https://www.ted.com/talks/verna_myers_how_to_overcome_our_biases_walk_boldly_toward_them?

Onwuegbuzie, A. J., & Johnson, R. B. (2006). The validity issue in mixed research. *Research in the Schools, 13*(1), 48–63.

Paris, D. (2012). Culturally sustaining pedagogy: A needed change in stance, terminology, and practice. *Educational Researcher, 41*(3), 93–97.

Thandeka. (1999). *Learning to be white: Money, race, and God in America*. The Continuum International Publishing Group.

Vygotsky, L. S. (1978). *Mind in society: The development of higher psychological processes*. Harvard University Press.

Yamagata-Lynch, L. C., & Haudenschild, M. T. (2009). Using activity systems analysis to identify inner contradictions in teacher professional development. *Teaching and Teacher Education, 25*(3), 507–517.

CHAPTER 7

TEACHING TO A STATUE

John B. Gordon, History Textbooks, and the Creation of a Lost Cause Hero

Wade H. Morris Jr. and Chara Haeussler Bohan
Georgia State University

ABSTRACT

According to a Winthrop University survey conducted in 2018, 80% of White Southerners believed that Confederate statues should remain standing. Our study seeks to understand this continued support for Confederate memorials by examining the interplay between statues and Southern history textbooks published from the 1880s through the 1960s. As a case study, we chose the John B. Gordon equestrian statue located on the Georgia statehouse grounds. We found that local history textbooks evolved over time, reinforcing, and accentuating the imagery on the Gordon statue. For decades, these history textbooks placed more emphasis on Gordon, a relatively obscure Confederate general, than on the wartime experiences of the enslaved. The textbooks also dedicated more words to explaining Gordon's actions at the Battle of Spotsylvania Courthouse—again, a relatively obscure wartime anecdote that was depicted on the statue—than to the Emancipation Proclamation. We believe that this study sheds light on the continued survival of the Lost Cause mythology, the glorification of individual Confederate icons, and the deemphasis on slavery.

The Divide Within: Intersections of Realities, Facts, Theories, and Practices
pp. 133–149

INTRODUCTION

On Saturday, May 25, 1907, the two surviving daughters of John B. Gordon stood before a crowd of 5,000 onlookers on the Georgia statehouse grounds. They were there to honor their father, the former Confederate general, United States Senator, and Georgia Governor, who had died three years prior. The two women pulled a rope that removed a silk covering, revealing an equestrian statue, rising twenty-five feet high. That was the cue for the band to play Dixie and, reportedly, the crowd let out a spontaneous rebel yell ("Statue of General John B. Gordon will be unveiled on Saturday," 1907; "As in battle Gordon sits his charge: Equestrian statue of Georgia's dauntless leader disclosed to the public view yesterday," 1907; "Gordon statue was unveiled before crowd," 1907). This ceremony honored the first statue to be placed on the current grounds of Georgia's capital, and it remains there today, overlooking downtown Atlanta to the northwest.

At the base of the statue is a bronze relief, depicting a rather obscure moment of the Civil War. The bronze relief represents a scene from May 12, 1864, when General Gordon found himself at the center of the fighting at Spotsylvania Courthouse in Virginia. Ulysses S. Grant's army, as the story goes, was about to break through the Confederate lines. Just as Gordon was rallying his soldiers for a counterattack, Robert E. Lee appeared. The bronze relief depicts this moment, when Gordon grabbed hold of Lee's reigns and chivalrously ordered his commanding officer to the rear of the fighting. Gordon, therefore, saved Lee's life while rallying his own soldiers to save the Army of Northern Virginia. Gordon was later given the nickname of "The Man of the 12th of May" (Freeman, 1934, p. 385). According to one newspaper report, the 12th of May was "an act which has figured in poetry, song and story" ("Statue of General John B. Gordon will be unveiled on Saturday," 1907).

The 12th of May story was retold at the ceremony in 1907. The keynote speaker, General Clement Evans, did not mention slavery or race. Nor did he refer to the Atlanta race riots that had broken out the previous September ("Gordon statue was unveiled before crowd," 1907). During the three days of the race riots, White mobs murdered over twenty African Americans because of the unsubstantiated allegations that Black men had been assaulting White women. The murders occurred on Atlanta's downtown streets just to the northwest of the capital, the same direction that the Gordon statue faces (Bauerlein, 2002). The statue, the riots, and the story of the 12th of May all embody the Lost Cause myth. According to the Lost Cause narrative, the Civil War was a conflict over state's rights, not slavery, and one punctuated by romantic acts of individual heroism (Gallagher, 1997; Gallagher &

Nolan, 2000; Korda, 2014; Nolan, 1991; Ransom, 2005). Virginia had Robert E. Lee and Stonewall Jackson. Georgia needed its hero, and Gordon's actions on the 12th of May helped fill that void.

Speeches and statues were not the only tools through which Southern Whites constructed the Lost Cause. Education played an important role, as well, and textbooks from the era give current historians insight into how the Civil War was portrayed in Southern classrooms in the early 20th century. Therefore, an examination of local Georgia history textbooks advances our understanding of the ubiquity of the Lost Cause narrative. The romanticizing of the Civil War not only filled public spaces with statues. It also filled Georgia's classrooms. How did statues and textbooks complement each other during the creation of the Lost Cause myth? Did textbooks reinforce the supposed grandeur and heroism of the conflict?

This study traces the evolution of Georgia's local history textbooks from 1884 to 1968. It is part of a larger study on "mint julep textbooks," a phrase coined by a New York publisher to describe history textbooks created for a specifically Southern audience (Bohan et al., 2020). Here, we focus on the wartime depiction of John B. Gordon, in particular, as a case study for broader trends of romanticizing the Civil War. The story of the 12th of May is the litmus test for the degree of nostalgia in each textbook. In this study we employ content analysis to measure the emphasis placed on the 12th of May and on Gordon generally. The emphasis on 12th of May is then compared to the overall number of words dedicated to the issue of slavery during the war and the Emancipation Proclamation in particular. Our hypothesis is that the more relative weight given to Gordon and the 12th of May would reflect a higher degree of Lost Cause nostalgia. We were also curious as to whether the ratio of words dealing with Gordon and the 12th of May relative to slavery and the Emancipation Proclamation changed over time.

The findings were surprising. The emphasis on Gordon and the 12th of May did not reach its peak until the 1910s, a decade after the unveiling of Gordon's statue. Nonetheless, until the late 1960s, the story of the 12th of May remained a presence in Georgia. Even in the second half of the 20th century, Gordon's reported heroism received a greater emphasis than the issue of slavery. Considering the length and resiliency of Lost Cause stories such as Gordon's, it comes as little surprise that his statue still overlooks downtown Atlanta. Understanding Lost Cause textbooks, we argue, is one key to understanding the power and resiliency of the Lost Cause among Southern Whites still today.

LITERATURE REVIEW

As historian David Blight (2001) discussed in *Race and Reunion: The Civil War in American Memory*, Southerners utilized monuments to the Confederacy as a means to declare their "victory over Reconstruction" (p. 265). So too, Southern textbooks offered another Confederate victory over the invading Northerners. As the Lost Cause became the "tonic against a fear of social change," Southern historians, writers, and politicians worked to ensure their children received an "appropriate" view of Southern culture and history through textbooks (Blight, 2001, p. 266; Cox, 2003; Moreau, 2004; Zinth, 2005). These views included depictions of contented slaves and of a war being fought over states' rights (Springston, 2018). Pro-South advocates even counted the textbook lines to make sure authors had provided balanced perspectives. Thus, Jefferson Davis should be mentioned as many times as Abraham Lincoln, and Robert E. Lee should be portrayed as often as Ulysses S. Grant (Cox, 2003; Rutherford, 1919).

With the growth of public schooling in the South as a result of Reconstruction, a sectional textbook industry emerged and Southern educational leaders advocated for the adoption of school materials that met the unique "circumstances of the South" (Moreau, 2004, p. 60). Rather than print their own books, however, most Southern states selected state adoption as the route to safeguard against Northern monopolies. Thus, the Southern textbook publishing industry was born in the late 19th century. Today, the majority of the approximately 20 states with statewide textbook adoption policies are still located in the South (Association of American Publishers, 2015; Webb, 2016). Because authoring, printing, and distributing textbooks could be difficult and expensive, the Southern state textbook committees could control content by demanding changes to narratives, wording, and images, or by threatening to cancel book contracts, which could close down smaller publishing firms (Zimmerman, 2004).

Why do we focus on textbooks in our larger study of mint julep textbooks (Bohan et al., 2020)? As Woyshner and Schocker (2015) noted, "textbooks remain the primary source of instruction in secondary classrooms, even though problems with them are well documented" (p. 443). Textbooks have long dominated the educational landscape (Black, 1967) and especially so in the 19th and early 20th centuries, which was long before the advent of standards-based education and multimedia resources. Furthermore, textbooks have provided a basic roadmap of the curriculum (Dagbovie, 2014). Although textbooks were not the only medium for conveying historical information, they were certainly an important component of early 20th century teaching and learning.

Several scholars have examined the role of textbooks in the history curriculum. David Blight (2001), James Loewen (2010), Jonathan Zimmerman (2002, 2004, 2017), and Joseph Moreau (2004) provided considerable insight with respect to the influence of textbooks on history education and memory. Zimmerman's research introduced us to the concept of Lost Cause textbooks. Diane Ravitch's *The Language Police* (2003) demonstrated how special interest groups influenced textbook publishers from both the right and left. James V. Wertsch (1998) provided a framework for understanding the construction of historical narratives in Southern Georgia textbooks, including "being temporally organized, having a central subject, plot, and narrative voice, and achieving closure around a conclusion" (p. 80). In the wake of the more recent debates over the Confederate legacy, current textbook literature included representations of race and racism in Southern Black schools from 1865–1876 (Brosnan, 2016), fighting the Lost Cause (Bausum, 2017), and the teaching of Black history to White Southern students in the 1930s (Woyshner, 2018). A gap exists, however, in the analysis of late 19th and early to mid 20th century Southern history textbooks. Our research helps to fill this gap.

Peter Novick's (1988/2005) *That Noble Dream: The "Objectivity Question" and the American Historical Profession* documented the professionalization of the historian in the late 19th century. Preprofessional historians did not primarily earn their living through the creation of history texts; the "gentleman amateurs" led the discipline in the preprofessional era (p. 50). Preprofessional historians—apt to insert flowery language, opinion, and controversy into their writings—were not restrained by the obsession for objectivity that later dominated professional historians. Many of these preprofessionals also saw the purpose of their work as moral instruction, not a scientific and objective search for truth. Reich and Corning (2015) explained another purpose of the preprofessional textbooks: the building of "collective memory" in order to facilitate "people's orientation in time and place" (p. 500). At the turn of the century, professor of history at Columbia University William Dunning led the professional historical dialog regarding the Reconstruction era. Dunning's strict and often bigoted analysis of Reconstruction promulgated the reconciliation approach to post-war historiography and the Dunning school remained dominant for 2 decades (Grob & Billias, 1992). His attitudes were reflected in so many scholars and writers at the time, such as James Ford Rhodes and Thomas Dixon, that it was difficult to find anyone to critique let alone contradict the reconciliation dogma (Franklin, 1980). Dixon wrote *The Clansman*, upon which the film *Birth of a Nation* was based. When African American historians Carter G. Woodson and W. E. B. Du Bois spoke out against the racist "objectivity" put forth by the professional historians, the Dunning school dismissed their research as being overtly biased—due to the supposed limitations of their race (Novick, 1986/2005, p. 231). The Dunning school and the racial tensions it reflected provide the broader context of the local Georgia history textbooks that we examined.

RESEARCH DESIGN AND METHODS

Content analysis provided data-driven information to complement the historical narrative. Klaus Krippendorff (2004) defined content analysis as the "research technique for making replicable and valid inferences from texts to the contexts of their use" (p. 18). According to Krippendorff, replicability is the idea that multiple researchers working at different times should obtain the same results using the same techniques. Words were our units of measurement in our content analysis (Krippendorff, 2004). Similar to the methodology employed by Woyshner and Shocker in their analysis of Black women in American history textbooks (Woyshner & Shocker, 2015), the effect of this method is to equalize the units for quantitative comparison.

We coded references to four concepts: two more general ideas and two more specific. First, we counted the number of words dedicated to describing the military career of John B. Gordon. We decided to separate Gordon's actions during the war from his postwar political career because, we believed, his combat experiences would better reflect each textbook's glorification of Confederate heroism. Second, we counted each textbook's discussion of slavery or the perspective of the enslaved during the war. Again, we focused solely on references to slavery from the textbook's sections covering events from 1861 to 1865. We omitted references to slavery as a cause of the war, events such as the Compromise of 1850, the Kansas-Nebraska Act, and John Brown's Raid in 1859. We did this because we thought it would provide a clearer comparison to the combat experiences of Gordon. We wanted to find the degree to which textbooks emphasized Southern generals at the expense of the perspectives of enslaved Georgians.

We also analyzed each textbook's emphasis on more specific events: the 12th of May and Lincoln's Emancipation Proclamation. We counted the words dedicated to describing Gordon's actions on May 12, 1864, an event that was far from historically significant, either militarily or politically. Presumably, the main purpose of retelling a story such as the 12th of May would be to provide evidence of Gordon's heroism, thus justifying his reputation as Georgia's greatest Confederate general. The Emancipation Proclamation, on the other hand, is considered a turning point in United States history. Granted there were limitations to Lincoln's executive order, for example, freeing only the enslaved in areas of open rebellion. The document, however, ultimately led to the 13th Amendment and it critically sent a message to the world that the Civil War was a conflict over the institution of slavery. We coded references to the Emancipation Proclamation and abolition of slavery in Georgia because this reflected the inverse of another aspect of the Lost Cause myth: a deemphasis on the importance of slavery's role in the Civil War. A lack of emphasis on the Emancipation Proclamation might provide a clear barometer to gauge the Lost Cause mentality within a textbook, especially in comparison to the words spent discussing the 12th of May.

There are flaws in this process, of course. The role of the editors, for one, might have changed word counts and therefore the original intent of the authors. Nonetheless, we hypothesized that the content analysis would reaffirm the patterns that we found in the narrative analysis. A further limitation, as Jörn Rüsen (2005) explained, was the problematic nature of comparing two different ideals of historiography especially since both hold inherent biases. We recognized that we have our own biases in interpreting the sources, and the sources selected for examination could be problematic. Furthermore, our own regional biases may have influenced our understandings, although we hail from both the North and the South. A final limitation rests with the challenge of comprehending sources written 50–130 years ago without being able to experience first-hand the Gilded Age, Progressive Era, or mid-20th century context. Such is the challenge all historians encounter.

THE MAN OF THE 12TH OF MAY

Modern military historians, even those working to debunk the Lost Cause, recognize John B. Gordon as an effective commander. James M. McPherson (1988), whose *Battle Cry of Freedom* is considered the definitive single-volume history of the war, referred to Gordon as the Army of Northern Virginia's "rising star" in 1864 (p. 726). Gordon C. Rhea (1997), an expert on Grant's 1864 Overland Campaign, wrote of Gordon:

> The lanky thirty-two-year-old Georgian lacked formal military training, but he was a fighting general in every respect and ranked among Lee's most aggressive subordinates. He had an intuitive grasp of military matters and a temperament suited to audacious maneuvers. Above all, he knew how to inspire men to bold action. (p. 246)

Robert K. Krick (1998), former chief historian of the Spotsylvania Courthouse battlefield, seems to agree with Rhea. He described Gordon as a "superb soldier" (p. 89). Like Krick, Joseph Wheelan (2014), an Associated Press journalist and historian, admired Gordon's lack of formal military training, which added to the mystique of the tough Confederate from the North Georgia mountains who, by the end of the war, was considered Lee's most trusted lieutenant.

Not only is there consensus among historians that Gordon was a capable division general, historians also agree that Gordon's actions on May 12, 1864, were pivotal at the Battle of Spotsylvania Courthouse. Gordon commanded the division at the center of the fighting that day, later known as the "Mule Shoe" or "Bloody Angle" (Freeman, 1944, pp. 402–405). Shelby Foote (1986) details the story in the third volume of his popular history of the war. Historian Ralph Lowell Eckert (1989) cites 13 first-hand accounts when he retold the "Lee to the rear" story. "Despite minor discrepancies between all these accounts," Eckert wrote in his footnotes, "the differences are not that important, for all agree on the basic storyline" (pp. 77–78). Douglas Southall Freeman (1934), albeit a great perpetuator of Lost Cause mythology, relied on the account of eyewitness W.W. Smith, a Confederate soldier writing contemporaneously, for his retelling. Another contemporary account that chronicles the story of Gordon and Lee's interaction on May 12, 1864 was an article in Richmond's *Dispatch*, appearing just a month after the event (Krick, 1998, p. 89). Other recordings of Gordon's actions on the 12th of May followed over the decades, primarily as letters written among Confederate veterans. Gordon himself recorded his first version of the event in 1878, when he described the scene in a letter to Charles S. Venable. Venable was one of Lee's aide-de-camps and claimed to have witnessed Gordon pleading with Lee to return to safety (Rhea, 1997).

The story, nevertheless, appears not to have entered the popular consciousness until Gordon published his memoirs, *Reminiscences of the Civil War*, in 1903. The memoir, though, lacks credibility for multiple reasons. Gary Gallagher of the University of Virginia calls Gordon's narrative "self-serving" (Gallagher, 1998, p. 14). Krick (1998) argues that Gordon's memoir was "so compromised by romantic viewpoints and purple prose that historians often do him the disservice of discounting his wartime experiences on that basis" (p. 89). However, Gordon's death in 1904 appears to be the moment when the 12th of May entered the popular consciousness of the White South. Throughout 1904 and 1905, the story appeared in eulogies and obituaries across the South (Krick, 1998). By the time that the Georgia state legislature established a commission to design and construct the Gordon statue, the romantic version of Gordon on May 12th had solidified in White Southerners' memories. The commission even interviewed Confederate veterans who claimed to have witnessed Gordon and Lee at Spotsylvania (Rhea, 1997). Their memories, however, deserve a degree of skepticism as they were recorded decades after the war and may have been influenced by published accounts of the story.

FINDINGS AND DISCUSSION

The truth of what happened on May 12, 1864 is less important to this study than how it was retold to Georgia's children for generations. Steven Terry's article, "Depiction of the Reconstruction Period in Georgia History Textbooks," provided a helpful list of Georgia textbooks approved by the state textbook adoption committee throughout the twentieth century. His article led us to study six Georgia history textbooks. Lawton B. Evans wrote the earliest textbook in this study, publishing it in 1884. At the time, Evans was a schoolteacher in his mid-20s, living in Augusta. He rose to the rank of superintendent of Richmond County schools, a position that he held until the 1930s. Evans published a second textbook in 1913 that we also coded, revealing an interesting evolution in Evans' writing. Katherine B. Massey and Laura Glenn Wood wrote the next textbook in 1904. Their book was published in Boston by D.C. Heath, a national (not Southern) publishing company. In 1933, four Georgia women and classroom teachers—Mary Savage Anderson, Elfrida de Renne Barrow, Elizabeth MacKay Screven, and Martha Galladet Warring—published *Georgia: A Pageant of Years*. Twenty-five years later, James C. Bonner published *The Georgia Story* (1958). Bonner was an academic historian who taught at the Georgia State College for Women in Milledgeville; he was also a member of the Georgia Historical Commission. Finally, in 1968, Bernice McCullar published *This is Your Georgia*. McCullar had a long career as a college professor, journalist, and the Information Director of the Georgia Department of Education.

Our first task was to count the words dedicated to John B. Gordon's military career in each textbook. Prior to the unveiling of Gordon's statue in 1907, Georgia history textbooks placed little emphasis on the Confederate general. While both the first Evans textbook (1884) and Massey/Wood (1904) mention Gordon in military contexts, the descriptions are minimal: just 27 words and 63 words, respectively. However, the data shows that the peak emphasis on Gordon's military career came in Evans' second book (1913), in the decade after the construction of the Gordon memorial. For the next 50 years, Gordon remained a feature of Georgia's history textbooks. Anderson et al. (1933), Bonner (1958), and McCullar (1968) all described Gordon's military record in some detail by mentioning not only his actions at specific battles but also his lack of military training. In the early 20th century, Georgia needed its Civil War hero. Subsequent textbook authors provided that hero in the form of John B. Gordon.

After coding for references to John B. Gordon's military career, we coded for references to slavery within each textbook's discussion of the Civil War. We decided not to count the references to slavery in the buildup to the war, which included events like the Compromise of 1850, the Kansas-Nebraska Act, and John Brown's Raid in 1859. We wanted a contrast by which to compare the emphasis on the wartime actions of Gordon against the wartime experiences of the enslaved. Furthermore, Gordon was not a prominent leader prior to the war. So, the most balanced comparison, in our view, was to focus on 1861 through 1865 for both Gordon and the enslaved. The limited coverage of the experiences of the enslaved, we hypothesized, would also reflect a deemphasis on slavery, in general, in Lost Cause lore.

Prior to the construction of the Gordon statue, Georgia history textbooks dedicated more words to the issue of slavery during the war than they dedicated to Gordon's wartime experiences. That trend ended in the 1910s, after the construction of the statue. For over 50 years, Georgia's textbooks dedicated more words to Gordon than to wartime slavery, as depicted in Figure 7.1. Evans (1913) wrote ten times more words on Gordon than on the enslaved population during the war; Anderson et al. (1933) wrote more than double the number of words on Gordon than on wartime slavery; for Bonner (1958) it was more than triple; finally, McCullar wrote 258 words about Gordon's military experiences and 156 words on slavery during the war.

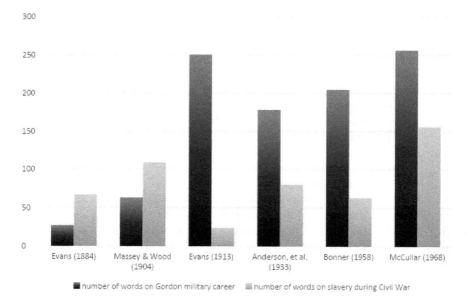

Figure 7.1.   Words dedicated to Wartime Gordon versus words dedicated to wartime slavery.

Perhaps it should come as no surprise that Lost Cause textbooks defended wartime slavery. Instead of writing from the perspective of the enslaved or attempting to describe their experiences during the war, both of Evans' textbooks (1884, 1913) focused on the diminishing value of slaves and how Georgia lost hundreds of billions of dollars of wealth as a result of the Civil War (p. 283, p. 297). Massey and Wood (1904) emphasized the myth of the loyal slave, stating that "slaves behaved remarkably well" during Sherman's march through Georgia (p. 109). "Well," in this context, refers to the enslaved who did not flee to Sherman's army. As late as the 1960s, McCullar (1968) argued that slaves remained loyal to Whites during the war, implying that slavery was therefore far from as cruel as Northerners believed (p. 511). Ultimately, an examination of context reveals flaws in the method of content analysis. The fact that a textbook contains a relatively high number of words on the topic of wartime slavery does not mean that the book minimizes the Lost Cause perspective. The meaning of the words is more important than the count.

Since the publication of these textbooks, historians have done considerable work on the wartime experiences of the enslaved. According to the 1860 census, on the eve of the war there were 462,198 people enslaved in Georgia, or 43.72% of the total population (MacKay, 2019). The responses of these hundreds of thousands of people to the events of the war was obviously a complicated one that varied by region. Joseph P. Reidy (1992) and David E. Patterson (2009) focused on the experiences of the enslaved in central Georgia. Julia Floyd Smith (1985) and Charles Joyner (1989) studied the experiences of those enslaved on coastal rice plantations. Anthony Gene Carey (2011) recently wrote a microhistory of slavery in southwest Georgia and Paul D. Lack (1989) covered slavery in Atlanta and the upcountry. W.E.B. Du Bois (1935) may have best synthesized their work decades earlier when he described a "general strike" by the enslaved that crippled the Confederacy (p. 49). In Georgia, this phenomenon played out in unique ways, particularly because of Sherman's famous "March to the Sea" when slaves "continued to employ the skills of caution, calculation, and concealment of emotions which they had developed in bondage" (Escott, 1974, p. 101). Sherman's march culminated in Savannah and his meeting with twenty representatives and leaders of the local enslaved population. Prophetically, the chief spokesman of the group of African Americans, the Reverend Garrison Frasier, warned Sherman that freedom for the formerly enslaved could only be achieved through the ownership of land (Foner, 1998). Nowhere, though, did Georgia's history textbooks grapple with the complex and varied experiences of the enslaved.

Finally, we wanted to trace the evolution of how Gordon's 12th of May moment was depicted in Georgia's history textbooks. By way of comparison, we counted the number of words dedicated to describing Gordon at Spotsylvania Courthouse to the number of words dedicated to describing the Emancipation Proclamation. One event was an obscure combat anecdote; the other is considered by modern historians as a turning point in the history of the United States. Our hypothesis was that a Lost Cause textbook would dedicate more space to the obscure anecdote than to the Emancipation Proclamation. The results of the comparison reveal a glorification of Southern bravery with a deemphasis on slavery. These are hallmarks of Lost Cause mythology.

As shown in Figure 7.2, two of the six Georgia textbooks dedicated more words to the 12th of May than to the Emancipation Proclamation. Three of the textbooks do not mention the Emancipation Proclamation at all. Notably, the earlier two textbooks, written before Gordon's memoirs and before the popularization of the story about the 12th of May, did not refer to the story despite lengthy descriptions of Gordon. The first reference to the 12th of May in a textbook came six years after the construction of Gordon's statue. Evans (1913) provided the most detailed description of the event with 177 words. Both Anderson et al. (1933) and McCullar (1968) described the "Lee to the rear" event at Spotsylvania

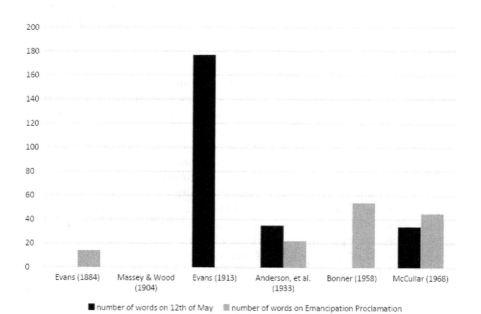

Figure 7.2.   Words dedicated to the 12th of May versus words dedicated to the Emancipation Proclamation.

Courthouse in short paragraphs of 34-35 words; Bonner (1958) did not mention the story. After a peak in the 1910s—which, incidentally, corresponds with the height of the Lost Cause movement—the 12th of May remained an anecdote, but one that still influenced generations of Georgia school children.

The impact of the Emancipation Proclamation on the enslaved peoples of Georgia was mentioned in several textbooks but was rarely emphasized. In 1884, Evans mentioned the Emancipation Proclamation, but he did so in a way that emphasized Georgia Governor Joseph E. Brown's willingness and efforts to cooperate with abolition in the closing months of the war (p. 298). Massey/Wood (1904) did not mention abolition or the Emancipation Proclamation. In 1913, Evans also ignored the topic. Anderson et al. (1933) mentioned Lincoln and the Emancipation Proclamation in passing with only 22 words. Her description did not deal at all with its impact on Georgia. Bonner (1958), on the other hand, referenced the Emancipation Proclamation in the following context:

> Houses were pillaged and their contents stolen or given to negroes who followed [Sherman's] army. These plantation negroes, enjoying for the first time the freedom granted by Lincoln's emancipation proclamation of the previous year, proved a great hinderance to Sherman's movements. Sherman's officers frequently used drastic measures to discourage them from following the army. (p. 299)

Thus, according to Bonner, emancipation led to lawlessness and the burdening of the Union army. Finally, McCullar (1968) dedicated 45 words to the topic of emancipation but, he also did not elaborate on how abolition impacted the lives of the enslaved. Ultimately, three of the textbooks dedicate more words to the Emancipation Proclamation than to the 12th of May. This belies, however, how the textbooks characterized emancipation and abolition. All but one of the textbooks ignored the social impact of the event. Only Bonner (1958) discussed the lives of enslaved Georgians, but he did so with a quintessentially Lost Cause spin.

CONCLUSION

On Friday, April 26, 2019, Georgia governor Brian Kemp signed legislation that bans local governments from removing Confederate memorials (Jett, 2019). Kemp signed the law 112 years after the state government unveiled the Gordon memorial. During those 112 years, the statehouse grounds became a shrine to the Lost Cause. After Gordon's statue, the state capitol memorialized the Confederacy's Vice President and Secretary of State, Georgia's two Confederate Senators and Governor, five more

Confederate generals in addition to Gordon, a Confederate colonel, a Confederate major, a Confederate naval commander, and even a Confederate lieutenant (Joyner, 2015). The most notorious of Georgia's memorials to the Confederacy, however, is not on the statehouse grounds; it is Stone Mountain's carving of Jefferson Davis, Stonewall Jackson, and Robert E. Lee, which is located less than fifteen miles east of the capital. The idea for the Stone Mountain carving was originally conceived in 1909 but was not completed until 1970 (Foody, 2015). Stone Mountain, not the Gordon statehouse equestrian statue, became the focus of protests in the wake of the 2015 murders at Charleston's Emmanuel A.M.E. Church and it reemerged as a topic of public debate during the 2018 governor's race (Ellis, 2019).

White support for Confederate statues in Georgia remains strong. The bill that Governor Kemp signed into law in April 2019 was first proposed years earlier by State Representative Tommy Benton, who stated, "I'm proud of my heritage... [Removing Confederate statues] is an attempt to have a cleansing of the Confederacy" (Joyner, 2015). According to a poll from Winthrop University, 80% of White Southerners believe that Confederate statues should remain as they are or remain with additional markers for contextualization. Meanwhile, 55% of Black Southerners said that the statues should be removed altogether (Bently, 2018). Southerners are deeply divided. The debate over what to do with Lost Cause memorials is far from over.

The John B. Gordon statue is not presently at the center of the controversy regarding Confederate statues. In this paper we argue, however, that examining the memory of Gordon can help 21st century readers understand the depth and intensity of the Lost Cause mythology. Governor Kemp, Representative Benton, and the millions of White Southerners who defend Confederate monuments have inherited generations of propaganda and not just in the form of public statues. For generations, White Southerners studied a version of the Civil War that all but ignored the experiences of the enslaved and that glorified the actions of men like John B. Gordon. Changing that mindset, a deeply held set of beliefs that transcends generations, will not be easy.

REFERENCES

Anderson, M. S., Elfrida, D. R. B., Screven, E. M., & Waring, G. W. (1933). *Georgia: A Pageant of Years.* Garrett & Massie.
As in battle Gordon sits his charge: Equestrian statue of Georgia's dauntless leader disclosed to the public view yesterday. (1907, May 26). *The Atlanta Constitution.* ProQuestHistoricalNewspapers.com

Association of American Publishers. (2015). *Instructional materials adoption.* http://publishers.org/our-markets/prek-12-learning/instructional-materials-adoption.

Bauerlein, M. (2002). *Negrophobia: A race riot in Atlanta, 1906.* Encounter Books.

Bausman, A. (2017, November/December). Fighting the lost cause. *The Horn Book Magazine.*

Bently, R. (2018, December 18). Southerners less supportive of Confederate flag, new poll finds. *The Atlanta Journal-Constitution.*

Black, H. (1967, October 7). What our children read. *Saturday Evening Post.*

Blight, D. (2001). *Race and reunion, the Civil War in American memory.* The Belknap Press of Harvard University Press.

Bohan, C. H., Bradshaw, L. Y., & Morris, W. H. (2020). The mint julep consensus: An analysis of late 19th century Southern and Northern textbooks and their impact on the history curriculum. *The Journal of Social Studies Research, 44,* 139–149.

Bonner, J. C. (1958). *The Georgia story.* Harlow.

Brosnan, A. (2016). Representations of race and racism in the textbooks used in Southern Black schools during the American Civil War and Reconstruction Era, 1861–1876. *Paedagogica Historica: International Journal of the History of Education, 52*(6), 718–733.

Carey, A. G. (2011). *Sold down the river: Slavery in the lower Chattahoochee Valley of Alabama and Georgia.* The University of Alabama Press.

Cox, K. (2003). *Dixie's daughters: The United Daughters of the Confederacy and the preservation of Confederate culture.* University Press of Florida.

Dagbovie, P. G. (2014). Reflections on conventional portrayals of the African American experience during the Progressive Era or "the nadir." *The Journal of the Gilded Age and Progressive Era, 13*(1), 4–27.

Du Bois, W. E. B. (1935). *Black reconstruction in America: Toward a history of the part which Black folk played in the attempt to reconstruct democracy in America, 1860–1880.* Hardcourt, Brace and Co.

Eckert, R. L. (1989). *John Brown Gordon: Soldier, southerner, American.* Louisiana State University Press.

Ellis, R. (2019, March 12). Blocked from taking Confederate statues down, Atlanta, Birmingham, and Memphis try other ideas. *USA Today.* https://www.usatoday.com/story/news/nation/2019/02/12/confederate-monuments-leaders-cities-removal-alternatives-civil-rights-groups/2525178002/

Escott, P. D. (1974). The context of freedom: Georgia's slaves during the Civil War. *The Georgia Historical Quarterly, 58*(1), 79–104.

Evans, L. B. (1884). *The student's history of Georgia.* University Publishing Company.

Evans, L. B. (1913). *First lessons in Georgia history.* American Book Company.

Foner, E. (1998). *The story of American freedom.* Norton & Company.

Foody, K. (2015, July 25). Georgia Debates Confederate carving set in stone and state law. Associated Press.

Foote, S. (1986). *The Civil War: From Red River to Appomattox.* Vintage Books.

Franklin, J. H. (1980, February). Mirror for Americans: A century of Reconstruction history. *American Historical Review, 85*(1), 1–14.

Freeman, D. S. (1934). *R. E. Lee,* (Vol. III). Charles Scribner's Sons.

Freeman, D. S. (1944). *Lee's lieutenants: A study in command* (Vol. 3). Charles Scribner's Sons.

Gallagher, G. W. (1997). *The Confederate War*. Harvard University Press.

Gallagher, G. W. (Ed.). (1998). *The Spotsylvania Campaign*. The University of North Carolina Press.

Gallagher, G. W., & Nolan, A. T. (2000). *The myth of the lost cause and Civil War history*. Indiana University Press.

Gordon, J.B. (1904). *Reminiscences of the Civil War*. Charles Scribner's Sons

Gordon statue was unveiled before crowd. (1907, May 25). The Atlanta Georgian. DigitalLibraryofGeorgia.edu.

Grob, G. N., & Billias, G. A. (1992). Black history since 1865: Representative of racist? In G. N. Grob & G. A. Billias (Eds.), *Interpretations of American history: Patterns and perspectives* (6th ed., pp. 116–142). The Free Press.

Jett, T. (2019, April 26). *Without once mentioning the Civil War, Georgia governor Brian Kemp signs bill protecting Confederate monuments, other memorials*. Times Free Press.

Joyner, C. (1989). *Remember me: Slave life in coastal Georgia*. University of Georgia Press.

Joyner, C. (2015, September 5). *Georgia capital heavy with Confederate symbols*. TCA Regional News.

Korda, M. (2014). *Clouds of Glory: The life and legend of Robert E. Lee*. HarperCollins.

Krick, R. K. (1998). An insurmountable barrier between the army and rain: The confederate experience at Spotsylvania's bloody angle. In G. Gallagher (Ed.), *The Spotsylvania campaign*. The University of North Carolina Press.

Krippendorff, K. (2004). *Content analysis: An introduction to its methodology*. SAGE.

Lack, P. D. (1982). Law and disorder in Confederate Atlanta. *The Georgia Historical Quarterly 66*(2), 171–195.

Loewen, J. (2010). *Teaching what really happened: How to avoid the tyranny of textbooks and get students excited about doing history*. Teachers College Press.

MacKay, K. L. (2019). *Statistics on slavery*. Weber State University. https://faculty.weber.edu/kmackay/statistics_on_slavery.htm

Massey, K. R. & Wood, L. G. (1904). *The story of Georgia for Georgia boys and girls*. D.C. Heath & Co.

McCullar, B. (1968). *This is your Georgia*. Viewpoint.

McPherson, J. M. (1988). *Battle cry of freedom: The Civil War era*. Oxford University Press.

Moreau, J. (2004). *Schoolbook nation*. The University of Michigan Press.

Nolan, M. T. (1991). *Lee considered: General Robert E. Lee and Civil War history*. The University of North Carolina Press.

Novick, P. (2005). *That noble dream: The "objectivity question" and the American Historical profession*. Cambridge University Press. (Original published 1988)

Patterson, D. E. (2009). "Slavery, slaves, and cash in a Georgia village, 1825–1865." *Journal of Southern History, 75*(4), 879–930.

Randsom, R. L. (2005). *The Confederate States of America: What might have been*. W.W. Norton.

Ravitch, D. (2003). *The language police*. Knopf.

Reich, G. A., & Corning, A. (2017). Anatomy of a belief. The collective memory of African American Confederate soldiers. *Historical encounters: A journal of historical consciousness, historical cultures, and history education, 4*(2), 11–49.

Reidy, J. P. (1992). *From slavery to agrarian capitalism in the cotton plantation South: Central Georgia*. The University of North Carolina Press.

Rhea, G. C. (1997). *The battles for Spotsylvania Courthouse and the road to Yellow Tavern*. Louisiana State University Press.

Rüsen, J. (2005). How to compare cultures? The case of historical thinking. *Koers, 70*(2), 265–285.

Rutherford, M. L. (1919). *Measuring rod to text books, and reference books in schools, colleges and libraries*. Mildred Lewis Rutherford at the request of United Confederate Veterans.

Smith, J. F. (1985). *Slavery and rice culture in low country Georgia, 1750–1860*. The University of Tennessee Press.

Springston, R. (2018, April 14). *Happy slaves? The peculiar story of three Virginia school textbooks*. Richmond Times Dispatch. https://www.richmond.com/discoverrichmond/happy-slaves-the-peculiar-story-of-three-virginia-school-textbooks/article_47e79d49-eac8-575d-ac9d-1c6fce52328f.html

Statue of General John B. Gordon will be unveiled on Saturday (1907, May 19). *The Atlanta Constitution.* ProQuestHistoricalNewspapers.com.

Terry, S. (1983). Depiction of the Reconstruction period in Georgia history textbooks. *Georgia's Social Science Journal, 14*(2), 5–10.

Webb, R. (2016). Red, white and black: The meaning of loyalty in Georgia education (Doctoral dissertation). Georgia State University.

Wertsch, J. V. (1998). *Mind as action*. Oxford University Press.

Wheelan, J. (2014). *Bloody spring: forty days that sealed the Confederacy's fate*. D. A. Capo Press.

Woyshner, C. (2018). 'I feel I am really pleading the cause of my own people': U.S. Southern

White students' study of African-American history and culture in the 1930s through art and senses. *History of Education, 47*(2), 190–208.

Woyshner, C., & Schocker, J. (2015). Cultural parallax and content analysis: Images of Black women in high school history textbooks. *Theory and Research in Social Education, 43*(4), 441–468.

Zimmerman, J. (2004). Brown-ing the American textbook: History, psychology, and the origins of modern multiculturalism. *History of Education Quarterly, 44*(1), 46–69.

Zimmerman, J. (2002). *Whose America?: Culture wars in public schools*. Cambridge: MA: Harvard University Press.

Zimmerman, J. (2017, November 06). A confederate curriculum: How Miss Millie taught the Civil War. *Lapham's Quarterly*. https://www.laphamsquarterly.org/millie_rutherford

Zinth, K. (2005). *State textbook adoption*. Education Commission of the States. http://www.esc.org/clearinghouse/5775/5775.htm

CHAPTER 8

BRIDGING THE GAP

One School's Attempt to Build Community Through Service-Learning

Amy Allen
University of Oklahoma

ABSTRACT

This qualitative case study documents one school's attempt to bridge the gap between 2 very diverse factions of society by engaging students in service-learning in communities unlike their own. Specifically, it investigates how administrators and faculty at a private high school understand the goals and intentions of a community service program. Data collected and analyzed includes interviews with staff members at the high school where the program takes place as well as existing artifacts surrounding the program. Initial findings indicate that the intention of the program is to build relationships within the community. Assisting with science instruction is a secondary goal. However, in attempting to achieve this goal, there is a divide between theory and practice. Without engaging in critical reflection, what sounds good in theory can have unintended side effects and raises questions about how and why community service is done in a high school environment. Ideally, other schools will be able to use the findings to make decisions about how to implement community service programs in their schools in a way that is sensitive to all those involved and does not further "othering" or the White savior narrative.

The Divide Within: Intersections of Realities, Facts, Theories, and Practices
pp. 151–169

A primary goal of social studies is citizenship education. As educators attempt to achieve this end, some form of community service is often required or encouraged (National Council for the Social Studies, 2001). This behavior appears to be especially encouraged at the schools of privileged[1] students as a report from the U.S. Department of Education (2003) noted that students from households of high socioeconomic status (SES) were significantly more likely to volunteer during high school than students from either low or middle SES.

Many schools choose to incorporate this community service requirement because these acts offer a source of personal development for the students taking action as well as an increased sense of civic responsibility and political engagement (Waldstein & Reiher, 2005), although this idea has been disputed (Reich, 2005). The goals of personal growth and increased action on the part of the student also appear in service-learning programs (Mitchell, 2008). Some service-learning studies demonstrate the underlying intentions of volunteer programs both toward the community at large as well as attempting to describe how such programs influence the actions or beliefs of those involved (Kajner et al., 2013). This study considers the goals of a school mandated community service program, as well as how the theory behind the program manifested in actual practice. It is important to note that although the school identifies the program as traditional community service, throughout the study it became clear that the program was planned and developed as a service-learning initiative. While traditional community service has the potential to lead to transformative education, service-learning explicitly makes that connection.

Considering how and why administrators and faculty members choose to enact community service programs and whether the reality of implementing them matches up with the goals is important for several reasons. Although school mandated community service and service-learning programs mean well, their design can risk furthering stereotypes of those considered underprivileged (Cowhey, 2006), oversimplifying the problems at hand (Cowhey, 2006), taking away the agency of those they wish to help (Freire, 1970), or extending false generosity (Freire, 1970). This risk is especially apparent when considering that a majority of students who volunteer come from high SES households (U.S. Department of Education, 2003). Furthermore, dominant culture bombards students with the message that the underprivileged can be saved by a single, White, privileged individual (Cammarota, 2011). The effect of this pervasive message can be seen in both domestic and international adoptions (Patton, 2018), the development of volunteer tourism (Hogan, 2015), urban classrooms (Castro, 2012), and popular Hollywood movies (Cammarota, 2011). Without adequately preparing students to serve in underprivileged areas, there is potential they may engage in false generosity or develop a savior complex, and as a result, participate in othering or dehumanizing those less fortunate than themselves (Freire, 1970).

On the opposite side, when done well, community service programs can assist in equipping underprivileged groups with the skills and connections needed to develop their sense of agency. Teachers and administrators can help students challenge stereotypes, understand the complexity of poverty and help reduce the stigma surrounding it, and empower them to impact their community beyond the scope of the program by preparing students to enter communities unlike their own and helping them understand the goals and intentions of the community service program in question (Cowhey, 2006). Given the potential benefits and inherent challenges present in community service, it is essential to consider the goals and intentions of this service, along with how the reality of practice matches those goals.

RESEARCH PURPOSE AND QUESTIONS

This study investigates how administrators and faculty members involved in developing a community service program at a privileged high school describe the goals or intentions of the program. At Community High School (CHS),[2] a primarily White, private, Christian school located in the Midwest United States, all high school students are required to participate in community service together at Jackie Robinson Elementary School (JRES), an underprivileged elementary school where the population is 78% Black and 100% of the students receive free and reduced lunches. Once a week, as a group, all high school students assist in teaching science lessons in two third-grade classrooms. Students are also involved in various projects to raise money to fund this program. In relation to this community service program, this study asks how administrators and faculty members at CHS explain the goals and intentions of the mandatory high school community service program and analyzes whether their practice matches their goals.

LITERATURE REVIEW

The Savior Complex

Significantly, volunteer service can negatively impact those it is designed to help. Freire (1970) says the oppressor attempts "to transform everything surrounding it into an object of its domination. The earth, property, production, the creations of people, people themselves, time - everything is reduced to the status of objects at its disposal" (p. 58). If those of the oppressing class tend to dominate all those things around them, why would we expect something different within the realm of community service? The "idea that it is the role of the White outsider to 'lift' the poor and oppressed in developing countries seems universal in the Western world" (Straubhaar, 2105, p. 384). Indeed, the idea of the White savior, or the savior complex, appears over and over in popular movies such as *Avatar*, *The Blind Side*, *Dances With Wolves*, and *The Last Samurai* (Cammarota, 2011). While this false generosity (Freire, 1970) may temporarily help some who are oppressed, it is unlikely to result in long-term systematic change. Rather, what they need is an ally who will help transform their circumstances rather than try to save them (Cammarota, 2011). Since young White adults are more likely to volunteer than Black or Hispanic young adults (U.S. Department of Education, 2003), critical reflection of service activities that attempt to help those who are oppressed is crucial.

Since recognizing a need for critical reflection is essential to designing community service programs that will positively impact those they are designed to help, Cowhey (2006) suggests finding ways to prepare students to enter communities unlike their own by helping them challenge stereotypes, explaining the systemic underpinnings of poverty, and pointing out the importance of retaining agency. The first step in this process is to help students understand the goal and intentions of a volunteer program. Critically considering the goals of the volunteer work will also decrease the chance of participating in activities that other or dehumanize the oppressed and marginalized (Freire, 1970).

Service-Learning

While service-learning traditionally refers to the idea of students participating in acts of service intended to help them make connections between course themes and community experiences (Jacoby, 1996), a second cohort of service-learning practitioners argue that the traditional approach focuses on service without addressing ideas of social justice (Westheimer & Kahne, 2004). This group suggests a critical approach to service-learning that combines the traditional definition with an explicit aim to "dismantle structures of injustice" (Mitchell, 2008, p. 50). These two approaches differ in the way students are asked to consider and reflect upon not only their service opportunities but, in a critical/social awareness approach, also the hidden complexities that allow these circumstances to exist. "Unlike 'service-learning,' where youth learn through participation in community service projects, social awareness places an emphasis on community problem solving through critical thinking that raises questions about the roots of social inequality" (Ginwright & Cammarota, 2002, p. 90). In traditional service-learning, the critical thinking piece that helps students ask questions and grapple with notions of structural norms is absent.

However, even critically based service-learning opportunities are subject to the same pitfalls as traditional volunteer work, and students must be adequately prepared for the work. Mitchell (2008) asserts, "Preparation for the service experience and the varied roles students and community members will be challenged to fill must be clearly conveyed in a critical service-learning pedagogy" (p. 60). However, Cipolle (2004) suggests that students are often unprepared and, specifically, lack knowledge about the people being served. Preparation is crucial for helping students build authentic relationships with those being served (Mitchell, 2008). Developing relationships may also help mitigate the appearance of the White savior complex. Ideally, through the development of relationships, students will choose to participate in additional opportunities that are not mandatory and pursue additional action on issues that they find most compelling (Mitchell, 2008).

THEORETICAL FRAMEWORK

The Nazareth Manifesto

The Nazareth Manifesto (Wells, 2008) offers three styles of engagement which categorize interactions present in our daily lives and how those interactions affect those involved when they take place between those who could be labeled privileged and underprivileged.

The first, which other scholars might label as the savior complex, is *working for* (Wells, 2008). *Working for* is characterized by doing things on behalf of others, regardless of whether they have asked for your help. One person has a need, the other has a skill, and so the first does that work for the person in need. Many of our daily interactions exemplify this idea, like someone carrying your groceries to your car despite the fact you did not ask for help or holding the door open for someone. While these are straightforward examples, this type of interaction can be very satisfying for the person filling the need but can leave the person who was helped feeling that they lack agency, especially in situations where the players are clearly unequal. *Working for* also prohibits the development of relationships as the interactions lack either empowerment for those in need or the building of trust.

The second style of engagement is *working with* (Wells, 2008). In this paradigm, the issue of empowerment is addressed. Those being helped define what their needs are and invite others in to work in partnership to address those needs. *Working with* brings different groups together to unite varying skills and experience and work toward a common goal. In this style, everyone is on an equal playing field. The views of all involved are considered and respected.

The final style of engagement is *being with* (Wells, 2008). *Being with* means precisely what it seems to suggest: Rather than taking away the agency of those you wish to help or engaging with them to solve a problem, *being with* begins to develop a relationship of trust between the two parties involved. While you are interacting with someone in this style of engagement, there is no underlying goal involved, no problem to be solved. You are simply spending time with each other for the sake of developing a relationship or building up community. While Wells (2008) does not present these three styles of engagement as a hierarchy, he seemed to indicate *being with* was preferable to the other two styles.

In this paper, I will use *The Nazareth Manifesto* as a lens when analyzing the community service project at CHS and will make connections between these styles of engagement with more familiar ideas such as the savior complex, false generosity, and the oppressor/oppressed relationship.

RESEARCH DESIGN

This qualitative case study (Creswell, 1998) considers the goals and intentions of a mandatory community service program that all Community High School students participate in together. This high school is unique and was chosen for the study because, although many high schools require community service to graduate, few (if any) mandate that all students participate in that community service simultaneously as a school. Because the school is only about 5 years old, the high school is still in growth mode and is fairly small. During this study, the total enrollment at the high school was approximately 40 students.

Two collection strategies were used for this study, document analysis and interviews. To select participants for this study, I chose to use purposive criterion sampling (Creswell, 2012). All administrators and faculty at CHS who are involved in the mandatory community service program were invited via email to participate in the study. Although the three respondents (see Table 8.1) were not a diverse sample, they were representative of the school administration and faculty and were all highly involved with and passionate about the program. The first participant, Mr. Woodsen, has been the principal of CHS for 5 years after working as a classroom teacher for 15 years. He was responsible for coordinating and implementing the mandatory community service program. The second participant, Mr. Hastam, has taught religion and logic classes at CHS for

Table 8.1.   Participant Information

Pseudonym	Position	Years Taught
Mr. Woodsen	High school principal/teacher	15
Mr. Hastam	Theology department head/religion and logic teacher	12
Mr. Green	History and literature teacher	5

12 years and is the Theology Department Head. Most often, any reflection of the experience is done in his classes. The final participant, Mr. Green, has taught history and literature classes at CHS for 5 years. It was in his class, in response to a lecture about race riots, that students developed the idea for this community service program. All of the participants attend and participate in the program each week, are familiar with the goals and intentions of the program, and can observe student actions or discuss beliefs with students daily. Each semi-structured interview lasted about 30 minutes. To add to the data collected via interview, I was also able to utilize documents and media posted online, which contributed additional information to support the findings. These documents included a video and two school newsletters.

Data analysis was conducted using an inductive thematic analysis approach (LeCompte & Preissle, 1993; Shank, 2002) utilizing ATLAS.ti to allow themes to emerge from the data rather than looking for specific ideas. Initially, I conducted line by line coding of these text sources (Morse, 1994) and, from these codes, looked for ways to cluster the codes together based on their similarities (Shank, 2002). These clusters were then separated into explicit themes regarding both the origins of the program and the goals and intentions of the program. Other implicit themes also emerged, such as preparation and reflection of the volunteer work, challenging or reinforcing stereotypes, the appearance of a savior complex, and development of agency for the marginalized. During data analysis, I also relied heavily on memoing (Saldaña, 2016, p. 57) to organize themes and help me make sense of the data.

FINDINGS

Background Information: Student Initiated and Situated in Mutual Need

The high school senior class initiated the community service program after learning about local race riots that happened about 100 years ago.

According to Mr. Woodsen, in their history class, they discussed "how many of those tensions are still just realities especially even in the Midwest." Many of the students were surprised to learn of the riots, and in the conversation that ensued, Mr. Green pointed out "It's not your responsibility in the sense that you are to blame for it" but "you are responsible for fixing the effects of the past or at least trying to." In this conversation, Mr. Green challenged the students, "What can we do?" and the students came up with the idea behind the program:

> We actually took several other class periods, 'cause I teach some other classes as well, and we were just talking like we'll have to brainstorm some general ideas.... They found themselves interested in education, in vocation, and a lot of other different things, but we sort of narrowed it down to things they might actually be able to do and that they could get the school to agree with.

The students came up with an idea to partner with an elementary school in some way. Initially, the seniors planned to do this program on their own, but when Mr. Woodsen found out, he felt the whole school should be involved and suggested JRES as a possible location because of connections he had there. This idea speaks to the CHS's mission because it emphasizes learning to love your neighbor with a focus on those who are marginalized. Mr. Woodsen reaffirmed this when he mentioned that one goal of the program was to "have our students interact with children in a demographic that most of us would never experience just naturally."

Participants also indicated that the program was situated in mutual need as a partnership between CHS and JRES. Specifically, Mr. Green said, "While the students don't realize it, this is just as much for their benefit as it is for the students at Jackie." Mr. Hastam elaborated on this further:

> We want to develop relationships, because we want to develop friendships, we want to develop real, genuine community. We can't go in there with some sort of savior complex, we can't go in there with some sort of, we're the fixers and you're the fixed. It actually ends up going the other direction. We realize how we need fixing and their gifts and abilities are the ones that fix us in that way.

From an administrative perspective, it was clear that those involved in facilitating the program felt the CHS students would be able to learn something from their interactions with JRES students, although what they would take away from the experience was never clearly articulated.

Explicit Goals and Intentions

The answer to the research question, how do administrators and faculty members at CHS describe and explain the goals and intentions of the mandatory high school community service program, emerged through the appearance of four themes explaining the explicit goals and intentions of the programs.

While the program started as student-initiated, those students have now graduated, and currently, participation in the program is mandatory for all students. According to Mr. Hastam, the school now considers it an integral part of their curriculum, critical in bringing the ideas taught about in the classroom to life:

> I think this is as much a part of the curriculum as geometry. This is not, what we desperately don't want is to think of this as, is something we add extra to our actual, real curriculum. This has to be our curriculum. Our curriculum must exceed what we find in a textbook, to touch real, live, actual human beings. If the goal of education is to make humans more human then you have to actually have contact with actual humans.

It is helpful to have that perspective in mind as we consider the explicit goals and intentions as stated by the participants. These explicit goals included themes of providing science programming, building community, helping the marginalized, and transforming the students at CHS.

Providing Science Programming and Building Community

On the surface, the "why" of the program is that the students at JRES lack the funds and time needed for a quality science program. For example, Mr. Woodsen said:

> Most of our goal in being there, um, we go to do science there with third graders, which one, meets a need that science is one of the things that is most quickly cut by school budgets as ... and just as teachers get busy, so on one element, we're helping with [academics].

Every Friday during an extended lunchtime, all of the students at CHS travel to JRES and spend time in the third-grade classrooms, one on one with JRES students, teaching a hands-on science lesson prepared in advance by Mr. Woodsen. However, Mr. Woodsen indicates that, while this does help fulfill a need present at JRES, it is not the real purpose of CHS being there: "In another sense, that's just our 'in' to the school. The goal is really to have our students interact with children in a demographic that most of us would never experience just naturally."

Overwhelmingly, through all of the interviews I conducted and the documentation I looked at, the most common theme was that of building relationships within the community and having CHS students interact with others who are unlike themselves. All three of those interviewed cited building relationships within the community as the main goal of the program. As mentioned earlier, Mr. Hastam articulates, "We want to develop relationships, because we want to develop friendships, we want to develop real, genuine community." According to Mr. Green, this result is visible in the students. He says, "They do start caring for these people that are different than them…. It's really easy for us not to care about nameless faceless people but once you're there and once you see these people." This experience, he says, normalizes those who are different and helps the students see them as someone they have can a friendship with.

Seemingly supporting these ideas is the fact that all three interviewees also prioritized building relationships over seeing visible improvements in science. When asked about helping students understand the goals and intentions of the program, Mr. Green said:

> Part of it is really just framing expectations like we are here to build relationships. We would love for things like science scores to go up or all these measureables … we would love that. [But] it's not the goal and if it doesn't happen, it doesn't mean we failed.

Helping the Marginalized and Transforming CHS Students

As a result of the program, administrators and staff see two things that primarily happen. One, underprivileged or "marginalized" students, like those at JRES, are helped, and two, students at CHS are transformed through their education. Throughout this section, I use the word marginalized interchangeably with my previous description of underprivileged (those of low SES) because that is how those interviewed referred to the students at JRES, presumably because "helping the marginalized" is part of the school's explicitly stated goals.

Although the faculty and staff see the primary goal as building community, Mr. Green says "I think a lot of them are still going in as like we need to go in and help these people, which I don't think is a terrible thing for them to do." However, that attitude seems to be more reminiscent of the White savior complex the Mr. Hastam says they are trying to avoid, "We don't want these sort of short term one-offs, where we go in and make ourselves feel better because we dealt with poor kids or whatever."

Instead, they want to help students transform their idea of what it means to help others, which they have also seen happening. As Mr. Woodsen describes:

> For many of them, even from a very early time, in our time there, it began to change the way that they see themselves, the way that they see social dynamics and interactions, the way they see questions of justice and mercy in the gospel. Many of them formed very deep relationships with students ... even within 2 or 3 weeks, they identified kids and they got to work with them throughout the year, they saw what was going on in those kids lives and then, because of that, felt a certain calling on their life not only to love that child but to say that we as Christians should seek to act in ways to undo the injustices which are just systemic.

The three interviewees also mention helping the "marginalized" students at JRES through a yearly fundraiser called the CHS Awards. The students create short films, unrelated to the work they do at JRES, and the school produces one film, usually around 10 minutes long, that describes the community service program at JRES. The students and faculty then host a "screening" of these movies for friends and family members at CHS. The audience at the awards must purchase tickets to attend and are then asked to donate an additional but optional amount after learning about the program. Although the money raised is for the students at JRES, they are not involved in the fundraiser in any way. According to Mr. Woodsen, to be able to provide the sort of science experiments they would like to offer, they need additional funds, and this allows them that opportunity. He said:

> [The awards] wasn't just here's this fun thing we are doing, that would have been a great excuse for them, but it was here's this fun thing we are doing and as you are doing these videos, be thinking about [how] this is to help our friends at Jackie Robinson, and so it became this great experience.

In the end, the school sees this fundraiser as a stepping stone in helping CHS students receive and even initiate the sort of transformative education Mr. Woodsen thinks is necessary:

> To have our students catch the vision, and then sort of repeat your mission statement back to you as a way to convince you to do something, is really nice ... I think if our school can get that right, and that's the measure of getting it right, is when a student actually catches that vision, I think that's when we are doing transformative education. And I think that's what I would hope for other schools, that they could catch that vision that this is something that is so important to what goes on that you are not losing class time. This matters so much and will actually enliven the rest of your classes

because there is this life giving impulse in what you do that I think it just transforms everything about what the students do educationally.

DISCUSSION

It is interesting that, despite the fact that I never mentioned the idea of a White savior mentality, all three of the participants, as well as the advertising video, expressly denied the idea that a savior complex was at play in the volunteer work. Alternatively, they offered the Nazareth Manifesto as a specific lens through which to view the work done by CHS at JRES. Throughout all three interviews, the participants shared that the explicit goal of the program which was *being with*. However, in analyzing the actions they engaged in, I would argue that through various aspects of the program, they engaged in all three styles of engagement.

Working For: CHS Movie Night

The CHS Movie Night was developed by an administrator and faculty members, so this is one aspect of the program that is not student driven. In this case, it seems the principal was spending his discretionary allotment on the program and was frustrated by the quality of science curriculum CHS was able to provide. He explicitly presented the CHS Awards as a way to raise the funds necessary to not only continue but also improve the science programming.

The students at JRES were not involved in the creation of this program, nor were they invited to attend. This example seems to be a way in which CHS students and staff are *working for* those they seek to help. Rather than ask the students at JRES for ideas on how they could raise money or asking the school for funds through its school budget, the CHS staff decided not only the need the school had but also how to rectify that need. First, they decided the students needed more funding for better science programming, and second, they put a plan into place that allowed them to achieve this goal. This activity, which Freire (1970) would call false generosity, seems to unintentionally place the students in the role of the oppressor, taking away the agency of those they seek to help, the oppressed. Furthermore, this reinforces the idea of the White savior seen by students in many Hollywood films today (Cammarota, 2011) by placing students in the position to make decisions on behalf of others whose voices are not represented.

Mr. Green said, "I think a lot of them are still going in as like we need to go in and help these people, which I don't think is a terrible thing for them to do." However, I would argue that the attitude Mr. Green is describing here could be a terrible thing. Volunteer service has the potential to negatively impact those it is designed to help. As mentioned in the literature review, Freire (1970) said the oppressor attempts "to transform everything surrounding it into an object of its domination." He indicates that those of the oppressing class tend to dominate all those things around them. *Working for* is characterized by doing things on behalf of others, regardless of whether they have asked for your help. This description from Freire clearly seems to align with what *working for* is: when a group of people in power (the oppressing class) consciously decides and enacts what they feel is best for a group which is not only statistically less privileged based on their SES but also considered by the group in power to be "marginalized" without consulting them (dominating them). However, those in positions of power here do not seem to see that it is at play even while they are consciously trying to avoid it. For this reason, critical reflection is crucial. Without critical reflection, we return to Straubhaar's (2015) "idea that it is the role of the White outsider to 'lift' the poor and oppressed in developing countries seems universal in the Western world" (p. 384). That universal feeling of acceptance may be what Mr. Green is referring to when he says, "which I don't think is a terrible thing for them to do."

As a result of this attitude, CHS students may be getting the message that it is okay to "need to go in and help these people" solve their problems from administrators and faculty directing the program. While verbally suggesting to the students that the goal is not for them to play the role of savior, when school staff make comments like this, they are demonstrating the opposite idea. By making choices about how to raise money and deciding what that money will be used for without consulting the group they are attempting to help, staff members show that it is ok for others to make decisions that affect the lives of those less fortunate as long as they are trying to help. As discussed in the findings, if the school sees this fundraiser as a stepping stone in helping CHS students receive a transformative education, we must ask how this fundraiser, this act of *working for*, helps achieve that goal. False generosity (Freire, 1970) has the potential to help some who are oppressed or marginalized temporarily, but it is unlikely to result in long-term systematic change. As Cammarota (2011) notes, what the oppressed or marginalized need is an ally who will help transform their circumstances instead of saving them.

Working With: Development of a Science Curriculum

In one of CHS's second goals, however, they seem to be more of the ally Cammarota (2011) suggests is necessary. In multiple interviews, the idea that the science curriculum was just seen as an "in" to gain access to the students at JRES was present. However, this portion of the program does fulfill a need expressed by the administrators and faculty at JRES. While Mr. Woodsen and the students did initially engage with JRES because of a connection he had with that school, the administration and faculty there were the ones who articulated a need for science instruction. Mr. Woodsen says, "We go to do science there with third graders, which one, meets a need that science is one of the things that is most quickly cut by school budgets." Additionally, I have seen evidence from JRES teachers that indicates they do invite and appreciate the science instruction from CHS as JRES administrators prioritized neither time or money for science programming. In this case, it seems that CHS is *working with* JRES. CHS came in to work alongside teachers to help fill a need the school expressed.

Wells (2008) suggests that *working with* acknowledges the issue of empowerment in that those being helped define their needs and invite others in to work in partnership to address them. Cowhey (2006) further supports this idea when she says, when helping others, students should see the need to allow those being served to retain agency. In the science situation, because JRES articulated their needs and how they would like to work in partnership with CHS, those at JRES were able to retain some agency while still receiving the support they needed.

Being With: Developing Relationships

Despite the fact that implicit instances of *working for* and *working with* were visible in a critical analysis of the program, the overarching explicit goal of *being with* was also visible. Each of the three interviewees expressed this goal of *being with* in different but conciliatory ways.

Mr. Hastam said, "If the goal of education is to make humans more human then you have to actually have contact with actual humans." According to Freire (1998), schooling should be "ethical" (p. 57) and should be a "human act of intervening in the world" (p. 6). So not only should the process of education not just churn out a reproduction of the current social order, it should upend it. This view of what schooling should look like in a democratic society is present in the action of *being with* those who are unlike you in order to foster a sense of community and build deep relationships. This view aligns with Mr. Woodsen's articulation, "The goal is really to have our students interact with children in a demographic that most of us would never experience just naturally." Mr. Green furthers this idea and affirms that it is happening when he says, "They do start caring for these people that are different than them.... It's really easy for us not to care about nameless faceless people but once you're there and once you see these people."

However, ideas such as these can also be problematic. As mentioned earlier, one of the goals of the school is to teach students to graciously love their neighbor, especially the most broken and marginalized. Demonstrating this, Mr. Hastam says, "The goal of this volunteer work is to introduce our students, who come from a very different kind of background, to students who come from a very different type of background.... We think it's valuable for our students to get to know people who aren't exactly like them." Later, he continues, "we wanna develop relationships, because we wanna develop friendships, we wanna develop real, genuine community." In response to these goals he articulates, I think there are a couple of things to consider. First of all, I would ask why: Why is it important to introduce students to people who are different? Why is that the primary goal of the volunteer work? If the mission says that students should love their neighbor, does just introducing them to people unlike themselves achieve that goal? How do we measure whether that is accomplished, and how does that produce a change in students? Rhoads (1997) suggests a service-learning program which brings students into significant relationships with others helps students, maybe from both sides, consider many important issues about themselves and the codes they live by. That may be the goal here, but more reflection on this point is undoubtedly warranted.

Second, I think it is important to think about the setting in which these meetings are taking place. If students from CHS are always traveling to meet students from JRES at their school, is that truly going to be an avenue where genuine relationships, friendships, or communities will be able to develop and flourish? It seems that some consideration should also be given to bringing JRES students to CHS to spend time in their natural environment, or even in a neutral location. In many ways, it seems this relationship development still hinges on the primarily White, private, Christian school students being in a position of power, coming into the environment of the underprivileged elementary school students. Because the CHS students remain in control of the situation by visiting the students where they are at and never inviting or including them in their own space, they are able to maintain some distance and a power position in the relationship. I would argue that this distance may prevent or hinder students from developing the deep change the school hopes to produce.

Having the opportunity to *be with* does allow students the chance to receive an education which recognizes systemic injustices. It reminds students, as Mr. Green says "It's not your responsibility in the sense that you are to blame for it" but "you are responsible for fixing the effects of the past or at least trying to." Cowhey (2006) suggests that participation in this type of volunteer work helps students challenge stereotypes along with helping them understand the systematic underpinnings of poverty and the stigma surrounding it. This realization is critical to designing community service programs which positively impact all parties involved. But, while recognizing the existence of systematic injustice, this specific goal, *being with*, does little to address the root causes of social injustice or "fixing the effects of the past" as Mr. Green suggests they are responsible for doing. In this sense, participation in the community service program seems to fall into the category of traditional service-learning as it does not approach from a critical perspective. Mitchell (2008) suggests, "while beneficial for the students in service roles and providing much needed service in the communities," these sort of programs "do not lead to any transformation in the community and certainly do not tap into the revolutionary potential" (p. 52) of service-learning. However, Mitchell does agree with Cowhey that participation in service-learning programs (although particularly referencing critical service-learning), enhanced by the creation of authentic relationships, "challenges students to confront stereotypes and generalizations and leads to the development of a more caring self" (Mitchell, 2008, p. 62). In this case, the lack of critical reflection may be connected to the appearance of the White savior complex, and the absence of this component seems to be a barrier to more social justice-oriented service-learning.

IMPLICATIONS

While it is hard to generalize data from a unique situation such as the one considered here, this study does have implications for how and why community service is done in a high school environment. First, it is important to administrators and those involved in facilitating a community service program or service-learning initiative to have a clear understanding of what they hope to achieve. However, as we see here, an explicit objective is not always enough as there are always implicit effects as well. For this reason, it is also critical for those involved to think through both the explicit goals and implicit effects, especially when an oppressing class is working with those from an oppressed class. Some questions to consider include:

- What is the goal of this community service program? How will we measure whether this goal is met?
- Are students adequately prepared for the work they will engage in?
- Does this program encourage students to engage in false generosity?

- Does this program "other" students unlike those initiating the project in any way?
- Are there any ways in which students are taking on the role of savior or "working for" those they intend to help?
- Are those being helped allowed to retain agency and included in the decision-making process?
- Does this program replicate the oppressor/oppressed relationship or create/maintain an imbalance of power?
- Does this program require administrators and students to reflect on the ways in which they are interacting with others?

In spite of good intentions, there are many risks involved with this type of work and, because there is the potential to cause harm, critical reflection is essential. I hope that others will be able to use this study to make decisions about how to implement community service programs in their schools in a way that is sensitive to everyone involved.

CONCLUSION

The research question investigates one school's attempt to utilize service-learning to bridge the gap between two diverse factions of society by helping students develop relationships in communities unlike their own. Specifically, it asked how administrators and faculty members at CHS describe and explain the goals and intentions of the mandatory high school community service program. Findings show four explicit goals behind the program: providing science programming, building community, helping the marginalized, and transforming the students at CHS. Ultimately, the primary goal for the program was to teach CHS students how to "be with" others unlike themselves. Implications of this study show that even when the explicit goal of the program is focusing on building relationships within a community, those involved need to be careful to consider whether the reality of enacting a program matches the theory and goals behind it. If they do not, those involved also need to investigate the implicit effects and whether they are acceptable.

NOTES

1.   While I know used of the terms privileged/underprivileged can be defined in different ways, throughout this study, I use privileged to mean students from families with a high socioeconomic status and underprivileged to mean students from families with a low socioeconomic background.

2.   All names have been changed to pseudonyms

REFERENCES

Cammarota, J. (2011). Blindsided by the avatar: White saviors and allies out of Hollywood and in education. *The Review of Education, Pedagogy, and Cultural Studies, 33*, 242–259.

Castro, A. (2012). Visionaries, reformers, saviors, and opportunists: Visions and metaphors for teaching in the urban schools. *Education and Urban Society, 46*(1), 135–160.

Cipolle, S. (2004). Service-learning as counter-hegemonic practice: Evidence pro and con. *Multicultural Education, 11*(3), 12–23.

Cowhey, M. (2006). *Black ants and Buddhists*. Stenhouse.

Creswell, J. W. (2012). *Qualitative inquiry and research design*. SAGE.

Freire, P. (1970). *Pedagogy of the oppressed*. Bloomsbury Academic.

Freire, P. (1998) *Pedagogy of freedom: Ethics, democracy, and civic courage*. Rowman & Littlefield.

Ginwright, S., & Cammarota, J. (2002). New terrain in youth development: The promise of a social justice approach. *Social Justice, 29*(4), 82–95.

Hogan, J. (2015). Gap year saviours—An analysis of the role of race in an advertisement for development volunteering. *Irish Journal of Applied Social Studies, 1*(15), 15–22.

Jacoby, B. (1996). *Service-learning in higher education: Concepts and practices*. Jossey-Boss.

Kajner, T., Chovanec, D., Underwood, M., & Mian, A. (2013). Critical community service learning: Combining critical classroom pedagogy with activist community placements. *Michigan Journal of Community Service Learning, 19*(2), 36–48.

LeCompte, M. D., & & Preissle, J. (1993). *Ethnography and qualitative design in educational research*. Academic Press.

Mitchell, T. (2008). Traditional vs. critical service-learning: Engaging the literature to differentiate two models. *Michigan Journal of Community Service Learning, 14*(2), 50–65.

Morse, J. (Ed.). (1994). Emerging from the data: The cognitive processes of analysis in qualitative inquiry. In *Critical issues in qualitative research methods* (pp. 230–243). SAGE.

National Council for the Social Studies. (2001). Creating effective citizens. *Social Education, 65*(5). http://www.socialstudies.org/sites/default/files/publications/se/6505/650511.html

Patton, S. (2018, April 6). We can't ignore race in the tragic story of Devonte Hart and his White adoptive mothers. *The Washington Post*. https://www.washingtonpost.com/news/post-nation/wp/2018/04/06/we-cant-ignore-race-in-the-tragic-story-of-devonte-hart-and-his-white-adoptive-mothers/?noredirect=on&utm_term=.6550aca987bc

Reich, R. (2005). Service learning and multiple models of engaged citizenship. *The Journal of Education, 186*(1), 23–27.

Rhoads, R. A. (1997). *Community service and higher learning: Explorations of the caring self.* State University of New York Press.

Saldaña, J. (2013). *The coding manual for qualitative researchers.* SAGE.

Shank, G. D. (2002). *Qualitative research: A personal skills approach.* Merrill Prentice Hall.

Straubhaar, R. (2015). The stark reality of the 'White saviour' complex and the need for critical consciousness: a document analysis of the early journals of a Freirean educator. *Compare, 45*(3), 381–400.

U.S. Department of Education. (2003). *Volunteer service by young people from high school through early adulthood.* https://nces.ed.gov/pubs2004/2004365.pdf

Waldstein, F. A., & Reiher, T. C. (2005). Service learning and students' personal and civic development. *The Journal of Experiential Education, 24*(1), 7–13.

Wells, S. (2008). *The Nazareth manifesto.* https://web.duke.edu/kenanethics/NazarethManifesto_SamWells.pdf

Westheimer, J., & Kahne, J. (2004). Educating the "good" citizen: Political choices and pedagogical goals. *Political Science and Politics, 37*(2), 241–247.

CHAPTER 9

EVALUATING THE EFFECTS OF DISCIPLINE LITERACY VERSUS GENERAL LITERACY IN ADOLESCENT READERS

Antoinette M. L. Rochester, Tina L. Heafner, and Kristen Beach
University of North Carolina at Charlotte

ABSTRACT

Instructional exposure to literacy and content knowledge in social studies is not equal for all students furthering educational differences in rural and urban education as well as exacerbating racial and socioeconomic divides within schooling structures. As low student reading proficiency continues to increase, educators are in dire need to find and include the necessary reading support for all students, especially in urban and rural school districts. General literacy support (GLS) and discipline literacy support (DLS) are 2 approaches to supporting literacy skills within content areas. Within this pilot study, GLS and DLS strategies were implemented in middle school U.S. history classes to determine the impact on content knowledge and reading comprehension. Results suggested that students in all conditions experienced growth in content knowledge, and students in both treatment conditions experienced more growth in reading comprehension compared to the comparison condition. Findings examine the promise of teaching

The Divide Within: Intersections of Realities, Facts, Theories, and Practices
pp. 171–188
Copyright © 2021 by Information Age Publishing

middle school students both general and discipline-specific reading strategies within history, along successfully applying theory to practice to promote lasting outcomes for all students including struggling and reluctant readers.

INTRODUCTION

From 1992 to 2019, research has shown minimal growth in adolescent reading proficiency. For example, in 1992 only 29% of adolescents were at or above the eighth-grade reading level (Hussar et al., 2020). Likewise, in 2015, only 34% of adolescents were at or above the eighth-grade reading level (The Nation's Report Card, 2019), only an overall 5% increase within 27 years. Furthermore, as of 2019, the lowest performing students (those in the bottom 10th percentile), did not improve as compared to 1992 and declined when compared to 2017. An even more alarming finding is 92% of students with disabilities (SWD) are below-grade level reading proficiency (The Nation's Report Card, 2015) and scores for students with disabilities on average declined in 2019 (The Nation's Report Card, 2019). While there are a variety of reasons as to why students struggle with reading and acquiring adequate reading comprehension skills, it is clear adolescents are not reading proficiently. Poor reading skills heavily impact students' academic performance across all general education courses.

There are similar trends of poor performance in social studies. In civic courses, only 23% of eighth graders are at or above knowledge and skills proficiency, 27% are at or above knowledge and skills proficiency in Geography, and 18% are at or above knowledge and skills proficiency in U.S. history (The Nation's Report Card, 2014). Scores from the 2018 administration of National Assessment of Educational Progress eighth-grade social studies indicate that less than a quarter of students are at or above proficient levels as measured by National Assessment of Educational Progress for civics and geography while only 15% of eighth-grade students score at or above proficient in U.S. history (The Nation's Report Card, 2020). National Assessment of Educational Progress 2018 eighth-grade exam outcomes suggest that for every four students, three eighth graders will not have proficient or advanced knowledge and skills in civics and geography and six of seven eighth graders cannot demonstrate proficient or advanced knowledge the foundational knowledge and skills about our country's history.

To be academically successful in social studies, a significant deal of reading comprehension and inquiry skills are necessary (Monte-Sano, 2010; Shanahan & Shanahan, 2008; Willingham, 2010). Meaning, if students are to unpack and understand various aspects of geography (i.e., state lines changes), or events within U.S. history (i.e., what led up to Revolutionary War), or the various levels of bureaucracy that is taught in civics (i.e., understanding the U.S. government), students must be able to comprehend and analyze the various pieces found within each topic. Thus, reading proficiency and reading comprehension significantly impact eighth graders' learning ability in social studies courses (Toste et al., 2013; Vaughn et al., 2009).

Unfortunately, once students arrive in middle school, reading expectations increase, but teachers provide little opportunity for students to practice reading (Swanson et al., 2009; Toste et al., 2019). Due to this, scholars encourage the incorporation of general literacy support (GLS) into teacher curriculum (Vaughn et al., 2009; Vaughn et al., 2013). With the use of GLS, reading comprehension increases and knowledge-based skills become further developed (McKenna & Robinson, 1990). Furthermore, GLS skills enable students to read more fluently, understand background knowledge, acquire beneficial reading information, expand student vocabulary, and comprehend overarching reading ideas (Barber et al., 2015; Vaughn et al., 2009; Vaughn et al., 2013).

While GLS has considerable benefits, some scholars believe discipline literacy support (DLS) presents more promise than GLS for promoting content understanding (De La Paz et al., 2013; Nokes, 2010; Reisman, 2012; Shanahan & Shanahan, 2009, 2012). Similar to GLS, DLS assists students' reading fluency and comprehension level, but focuses on disciplinary specific aspects of comprehension to increase these needs (Annenberg Learner, n.d). The areas of interest in DLS in history include a focus on experiences found within a text, authorships of readings, the influence authorship has on the perspective of the text, sourcing, how sourcing impacts a text, and argumentation (Moje, 2007; Wineburg, 2001; Wineburg et al., 2013; Wineburg & Reisman, 2015). Because DLS approaches are specifically tailored to the discipline, they are often preferred to GLS strategies by upper grade content area teachers.

Research has demonstrated some promise for each of GLS and DLS for improving students' reading skills and content knowledge. Specifically, research suggests positive effects of teaching GLS to average and struggling readers (Alvermann, 2002; Faggella-Luby et al., 2012). However, the impact of DLS without the prior support of GLS on content knowledge and reading comprehension for average and struggling readers is unclear. Therefore, the main purpose of this study is to describe trends in content knowledge and reading comprehension outcomes for students in eighth-grade general education U.S. history classes who received instruction in DLS Only, DLS Plus GLS (i.e., "DLS Plus"), or typical instruction and to apply educational research theory to practice to evaluate it effectiveness.

This chapter begins with a review of the literature of reading comprehension and the incorporation of GLS and DLS within the classroom. Next, it presents the descriptive pilot study design, method, and results. Few studies have examined the effect of combined GLS and DLS instruction on content knowledge and reading comprehension. Moreover, today in the United States and elsewhere we see the troubling effects of increasingly polarized educational discourse and disparities in instructional practice based on where a student attends school. Variables such as racial composite of schools, the percentage of students receiving free and reduced lunch, and the urbanity of schools are associated with the frequency of disciplinary literacy practices and content knowledge gains of students on National Assessment of Educational Progress U.S. history (Heafner & Fitchett, 2015). Instructional exposure to literacy and content knowledge in social studies is not equal for all students furthering educational differences in rural and urban education as well as exacerbating racial and socioeconomic divides within schooling structures. Ultimately, this research seeks to further the discussion and research as it relates to supporting literacy skills that are necessary for adolescents to perform at or above grade level in general education courses, the application of theory to practice, and, more specifically social studies. This study seeks to provide empirical evidence to support literacy and content instruction in social studies to address the educative inequalities and to level learning access to conceptual knowledge and comprehension skills needed to understand U.S. history.

LITERATURE REVIEW

Literacy consists of three levels: basic, intermediate, and disciplinary (Shanahan & Shanahan, 2008). Basic literacy consists of decoding and knowledge of highly frequency words that are used within all reading tasks; intermediate literacy entails reading skills to common task, basic comprehension strategies, basic word meanings, and level of fluency; and disciplinary literacy involves specific literacy skills for history, science, social studies, math, and English (Shanahan & Shanahan, 2008). Literacy gains for young students have been connected to future literacy advancements, but unfortunately, once students reach the eighth grade these gains plateau (Shanahan & Shanahan, 2008).

Understanding how to effectively incorporate intermediate reading skills into the content area classroom can be challenging especially for content area teachers in the middle grades who may not have been trained in how to support literacy development (Swanson et al., 2009; Toste et al., 2019).Thus, literacy training for teachers is needed, since students need strong intermediate reading skills to be successful in academic courses. Students may have difficulty understanding concepts in social studies if they do not perform at intermediate levels of reading proficiency; thus, it may be particularly advantageous to support students' literacy within this content area.

Reading Comprehension

In order to understand the importance of reading comprehension skills, it is first vital to recognize the difference between reading skills and reading strategies. While these terms are many times used interchangeably within education and/or literacy, their meanings are distinct. According to Afflerbach et al. (2008), the standard definition for reading skills is "an acquired ability to perform well; proficiency; refers to parts of acts that are primarily intellectual, as those involved in comprehension or thinking" (p. 365). In contrast, reading strategies are commonly defined as, "in education, a systematic plan, consciously adapted and monitored, to improve one's performance in learning" (Afflerbach et al. 2008, p. 365). Although reading skills and strategies are distinct, both are needed to support reading comprehension.

Daniel Willingham (2006) has done extensive research on the impact of reading comprehension on students' classroom experiences. His research indicates that reading comprehension is more than students solely reading and comprehending a text. He states, "reading strategies do not build reading skills, but rather are a bag of tricks that can indirectly improve comprehension" (Willingham, 2006, p. 36). Students experience many challenges when trying to learn the strategies necessary to gain strong reading comprehension skills. Reading comprehension requires students to have a particular level of awareness as to whether or not he or she understands the readings and then how to know what skills must be applied to grasp the main arguments of the reading (Willingham, 2006). Riener and Willingham (2010) identified that students struggle in reading for four key reasons. First, students have different learning capacities based on the content. Second, students' ability to learn is dependent on their interests. Third, students have different background knowledge, which impacts their learning experience, and lastly, some students have learning disabilities that impact their learning. Hence, what allows students to have strong reading comprehension skills outside of what has been previously discussed, is their ability to derive meaning from text, which is influenced by text itself and the student's background knowledge (Willingham, 2006; Wineburg et al., 2013). The more substantial students' background knowledge, the more likely they are to have strong reading comprehension of the particular text.

The research literature details multiple ways to support students' comprehension of content area text. Some of these techniques include the use of graphic organizers, cooperative learning, listening activities, keyword mnemonic, distributed practice, self-explanation, mental imagery, and vocabulary-comprehension relationships (Dunlosky et al., 2013; Willingham, 2006). The effectiveness of using these skills varies due to the development of these techniques, resulting in the need for further exploration to occur to determine the overall effectiveness of each strategy. One recommendation involves gaining a better understanding of the value of providing general literacy strategies or disciplinary literacy strategies.

Content Area and General Literacy

Content-area literacy is an area of classroom literacy practices that focus on teaching students foundational reading strategies that enable students to read and respond to text regardless of the subject (Faggella-Luby et al., 2012; McKenna & Robinson, 1990). A core feature of content-area literacy is application of general literacy skills and strategies to read and understand content area texts (e.g., generating main ideas and summaries). Other features include content-specific literacy skills (e.g., interpreting a timeline in social studies text) and application of prior content knowledge. Having prior knowledge of text in particular, facilitates application of general and content specific literacy strategies to enable learning from text. Though having some content knowledge facilitates content literacy content-area literacy, and specifically application of general literacy skills, supports learning for adolescents who have reading difficulties. Indeed, general literacy activities, such as prereading documents, monitoring comprehension, making predictions, questioning, generating main ideas, and writing in response to text, support text comprehension and development of content area knowledge, especially for students who experience reading difficulties (Fisher & Frey, 2009; Swanson et al., 2015; Vaughn et al., 2009: Vaughn et al., 2013).

Disciplinary Literacy

In comparison to content-area and general literacy, disciplinary literacy focuses on teaching students the literacy skills that are required to read and understand discipline-specific text (Annenberg Learner, n.d.). In social studies, teachers instruct their students to think like historians

(Wineburg, 2001), which will ideally in turn allow students to appropriately infer meaning from the material (Moje, 2007; Shanahan & Shanahan, 2008). Disciplinary literacy skills within the social studies classroom include evaluation of text, contextualization, corroboration inquiry, and analysis and critique of texts (Chauvin & Theodore, 2015).

Researchers developed inquiry pedagogies in order to create effective social studies instruction (Grant, 2018; Levstik & Barton, 2005; Saye, 2017). The steps of inquiry include asking questions, pursuing answers with teacher support, articulating findings/conclusions, acting on understandings, evaluating problems, and retaining interest. Within the use of inquiry pedagogies, project-based learning is incorporated. Project-based learning involves creating a curriculum that is based on real-life concerns of students and also includes the inclusion of content-area literacy (Halvorsen et al., 2012; Parker et al., 2013). Although inquiry pedagogies have shown promising results to students regardless of age, grade, or academical level, very few social studies courses fail to merge inquiry into their classroom (Saye & the SSIRC, 2013). A key reason for why teachers are unable to include inquiry pedagogies within their classroom is primarily because many instructors lack the necessary support along with examples of how to successfully embrace inquiry-based pedagogy (Thacker et al., 2017).

PURPOSE OF THE PRESENT STUDY

Research suggests that content area and general literacy strategies are important for supporting students' comprehension of text, and disciplinary literacy strategies are important for supporting students' discipline-specific comprehension of text. Literacy support as a combination of general literacy and disciplinary strategies may help level the achievement and opportunity gaps many students experience in reading complex social studies texts. However, little research has investigated whether there are relative benefits to a combined approach that involves both general and discipline specific supports for understanding social studies text. The aim of this research was to investigate the impact of two treatments, one involving DLS Only and the other involving DLS plus GLS on content knowledge and reading comprehension outcomes for eighth-grade general education students who demonstrated average or below-average reading ability, compared to a no-treatment comparison (i.e., business as usual, or BAU) to better understand theory to practice. We hypothesized that students receiving DLS and DLS Plus would have stronger content knowledge outcomes compared to BAU, and students receiving DLS Plus would demonstrate stronger improvement in general reading comprehension compared to DLS Only and BAU.

METHOD

Participants and Setting

Two eighth-grade U.S. history teachers and 151 students participated in the study. The research team recruited one teacher who had received in-service professional development in teaching disciplinary literacy within social studies to participate as the intervention teacher. The rationale for this decision was tied to the study purpose and training considerations. First, a major goal of the study was to determine the added benefit of teaching GLS in addition to DLS. Working with a teacher who was already trained to implement DLS increased the likelihood that DLS implementation would be strong, which was important when investigating added benefit of GLS. Second, having a teacher experienced in teaching DLS allowed for the training to be focused on incorporating GLS, which was expected to be relatively novel for the teacher. The comparison teacher was recruited from the same school as the intervention teacher to enable control over school-level factors that might influence outcomes (e.g., scope and sequence of curriculum). Both teachers self-reported teaching disciplinary literacy strategies in their history classes, but only the intervention teacher had self-reported prior training in teaching DLS. Student participants were all students within the recruited teachers' classrooms who had returned signed parent consent forms and who had assented to participation. Students attended a Title I school located in the southeastern United States.

Design

A quasi-experimental, pretest/posttest comparison group design was used to evaluate the effect of DLS Plus and DLS Only on generalized reading comprehension and content knowledge, compared to a business as usual (BAU) condition. The intervention teacher taught both DLS Plus and DLS conditions (two sections each), and the comparison teacher at the same school taught two sections of BAU.

Procedures

DLS Plus and DLS Only instructional units were codesigned in summer by the research team in collaboration with the treatment teacher.

Units were designed to be taught within 2–3 weeks, and addressed four elements of disciplinary literacy instruction in history: (1) questioning literacies, (2) contextualization, (3) sourcing and perspective, and (4) corroboration. The DLS Plus condition also included instruction on general literacy strategies, including previewing text, finding the main idea, click and clunk, and answering literal and inferential questions from text.

Researchers trained the treatment teacher to implement each approach across two 6-hour training sessions that occurred in the beginning of the 2018–2019 school year. Training on the disciplinary literacy strategies involved reviewing the core definitions and concepts for each strategy, review of materials for implementation, and discussion of logistics around implementation. Training on general literacy strategies involved the same features, in addition to sample modeling of instruction by the research team.

MEASURES

Benchmark scores from the state mandated test of history knowledge were used to estimate history content knowledge of students in before (December) and after (May) intervention. The research team administered the Gates MacGinitie Reading Test before and after intervention as a measure of generalized reading comprehension. In addition, the research team conducted observations of instruction across conditions two to three times per unit. The observation protocol included a rubric with items for evaluating the extent to which instruction followed the unit plan materials and student engagement. The data collection period spanned one school year and included data from the beginning of the academic year to summative state administered evaluations at the end of the grade.

RESULTS

Table 9.1 shows the average December and May benchmark scores (in percentages) by period and intervention type. The two classes with DLS Only were first and fifth period for the intervention teacher. First period's benchmark score was 49% in December; this score rose to 64% (a 15% point increase) in May. The December gradebook average for fifth period was initially 51%, and rose to 55% in May. Both periods demonstrated growth, yet at different rates (4 to 15 percentage points).

For DLS Plus class period 3, the average December benchmark percentage was 48%; May's benchmark average increased to 56% (8 percent-

**Table 9.1. December and May Benchmark Percentages
by Intervention Type and Class Period**

Intervention Type	Class Period	December Benchmark Gradebook Average	May Benchmark Gradebook Average	Raw Percentage Increase From December to May
DLS Only	1st	49	64	15
DLS Only	5th	51	55	4
DLS Plus	3rd	48	56	8
DLS Plus	4th	55	55	0
BAU	4th	51	64	13
BAU	5th	43	56	13

Source: Data originally gathered from pilot study.

age points). For fourth period, the December benchmark average was 55%, and the May average was 55%, indicating limited growth.

In the BAU group, the December benchmark average for fourth period was 51% and the May average was 64%. For BAU fifth period, the December benchmark average was 43% and the May average was 56%. Each class experienced growth of about 13 percentage points from December to May.

Overall, results suggest that students in all conditions improved in history content knowledge, though to varying degrees. While the first period DLS Only class experienced the most growth, this growth was not mirrored in the fifth period DLS Only group. Students in the DLS Plus group experienced low growth in content knowledge overall, relative to other classes. Finally, students in BAU experienced among the strongest and most consistent growth in content knowledge at about thirteen percentage points for each class.

Table 9.2 shows raw scores and grade equivalents on Gates MacGinitie Reading Test pre- and postintervention for each condition. Trends in averages by condition suggest that students in the DLS Plus and DLS Only conditions experienced stronger growth in reading comprehension compared to students in BAU. Specifically, students in either treatment condition answered correctly between four and nine more reading comprehension questions correctly at posttest, compared to students in BAU who answered between one and two more reading comprehensions correctly at posttest. Additionally, the grade equivalent in reading comprehension for each of the treatment conditions improved by at least one grade level by posttest, but this was true for only one of the two BAU

Table 9.2. 2. Gates Pre- and Posttest Assessment Raw Total and Grade Equivalent Averages

Intervention Type	Class Period	Gates Pretest Raw Total Average	Gates Pretest Grade Equivalent Average	Gates Posttest Raw Total Average	Gates Posttest Grade Equivalent Average
DLS Only	1st	57	7th	66	9th
DLS Only	5th	58	7th	63	8th
DLS Plus	3rd	55	7th	59	8th
DLS Plus	4th	56	7th	60	8th
BAU	4th	60	8th	62	8th
BAU	5th	51	6th	52	7th

Source: Data originally gathered from pilot study.

classes. Overall, descriptive results suggest potentially stronger growth in reading comprehension for students who received either version of the intervention. While exposure to DLS in either DLS Only or DLS Plus did not produce consistent differences in content knowledge growth, these interventions seem to offer great supports in generalized comprehension skills than BAU.

DISCUSSION

Analyzing the benchmark averages within the intervention group, the only period that did not experience any growth was the fourth period, which maintained an average of 55%. Amongst the four intervention groups, the first period, DLS Only experienced the most substantial benchmark average growth of fifteen percentage points. The remaining intervention classes improved in content area knowledge, but at minimal levels. Both BAU periods experienced content knowledge growth of thirteen percentage points, despite disparate initial scores. For reading comprehension, most intervention periods improved scores from December to May, with largest growth in the first period DLS Only class. Students in each of the BAU classes demonstrated minimal growth in reading comprehension overall.

We hypothesized that students receiving DLS and DLS Plus would have stronger content knowledge outcomes compared to BAU. This hypothesis was generally not supported by the data. Though period one (DLS Only) demonstrated the strongest growth, this growth was not mirrored by the other DLS Only class, nor either DLS Plus classes. Interestingly, the BAU classes demonstrated the most consistent and strongest growth overall in content knowledge in U.S. history. One potential reason for this finding has to do with the methods by which students can acquire content knowledge. Acquiring content knowledge does not have to occur solely or even primarily through text-based reading and discussion.

It is possible that students in BAU spent proportionally more time learning content from teacher led or student collaborative discussion and multimedia, compared to text-based activities. Students in both intervention conditions, however, spent considerable time reading and analyzing text as part of the intervention. If students had difficulty accessing these texts, their ability to acquire content knowledge from the text could have been impacted. Another potential reason is that the intervention teacher was tasked with teaching content in addition to content-area and disciplinary skills. Time spent to teach content-area literacy skills, in particular, detracted from time spent teaching content during class instructional time. The BAU teacher did not provide explicit strategy instruction and consistently offered more teacher directed discussion of readings during class time. Though there is evidence that learning and applying content-area literacy skills to content text can improve content area knowledge (Fisher & Frey, 2009; Swanson et al., 2015; Vaughn et al., 2009; Vaughn et al., 2013), it is possible that the quality of instruction, or uptake by the students, was not strong enough to facilitate this relationship. It is also possible that students did not receive enough practice in either DLS or GLS to improve content knowledge, and that more time learning to apply both types of strategies was needed. This possibility is supported by our class observations and unit tracking, which revealed that the intervention classes received less content instruction than BAU due to teacher absences (see Limitations).

Regarding reading comprehension gains, we hypothesized that DLS Plus would experience the most significant growth in reading comprehension since these students were exposed to both GLS and DLS instruction. However, means presented in Table 9.2 suggest that Period 1, which received DLS only, experienced the strongest growth. This trend was not sustained with the other DLS Only class period, so the finding should be interpreted with caution. Nevertheless, there are a few potential explanations for this finding. First, DLS Plus condition involved instruction in eight key areas: four GLS strategies and four DLS strategies. It is possible that students in the DLS Plus condition were overwhelmed with the amount of new strategy information and had a harder time retaining new knowledge. Students may have needed more time to master GLS, which in turn could have had an impact on their content comprehension. The task of teaching both GLS and DLS may have also overwhelmed the

**Table 9.2.   Gates Pre- and Posttest Assessment
Raw Total and Grade Equivalent Averages**

Intervention Type	Class Period	Gates Pretest Raw Total Average	Gates Pretest Grade Equivalent Average	Gates Posttest Raw Total Average	Gates Posttest Grade Equivalent Average
DLS Only	1st	57	7th	66	9th
DLS Only	5th	58	7th	63	8th
DLS Plus	3rd	55	7th	59	8th
DLS Plus	4th	56	7th	60	8th
BAU	4th	60	8th	62	8th
BAU	5th	51	6th	52	7th

Source: Data originally gathered from pilot study.

teacher, which could have influenced the quality of instruction. The influence of cognitive overload theory (Sweller, 1994) might be a contributing factor for lower observed content knowledge gains for DLS intervention students. The difficulties students face when learning new intellectual tasks can fluctuate dramatically depending on variations in amount of information. In other cases, two tasks may appear to have roughly similar amounts of information but differ enormously in the effort required to achieve mastery. The focus on DLS skills may have created a situation for students of cognitive overload of skills focus or skills effort which could have distracted from content learning.

A third plausible explanation is the staggered, layered approach designed for teaching DLS strategies. The intervention teacher taught GLS strategies in the first unit to all students in the DLS Plus condition. From that point forward, she taught one DLS strategy (e.g., author's purpose/perspective, contextualization, questioning and argumentation, and corroboration) over the course of four units. It was not until the fifth unit that students applied all four DLS strategies to a document. The purpose for this approach was to allow students to distribute student practice with skills to develop confidence and accuracy in the use of one attribute of DLS before adding a new component of historical thinking skills. This instructional delivery decision was based on the cognitive theory of distributing verses massing students' practice time and the positive association of the former with long-term retention (Willingham, 2010). This graduated method of adding on a new skill of DLS may have enabled students to become more consistent and effective in their use of each DLS strategy but might have hindered overall content comprehension. The combined findings of limited content knowledge growth for intervention students as well as the higher gains in general comprehension strategies for intervention students suggest a need to consider the focus of students attention in each condition: text comprehension strategies, even if these were discipline specific, as compared to content of the texts.

Analyzing written text, as is required when engaging in DLS, can be a change from the passive acceptance of textbook information, and is partly why experiencing high reading comprehension in history is difficult (De La Paz, 2005, 2013; Willingham, 2006, 2010). The DLS Only classes had more time to practice these disciplinary ways of thinking than the DLS Plus classes, which split time between GLS and DLS activities. The emphasis on one set of comprehension skills could have been more beneficial in short-term evaluation of student learning and skills. Interviews with the intervention teacher throughout the study indicated a teacher observed difference in students' confidence and willingness to approach complex text previously avoided by struggling and reluctant readers. These findings suggest that attention to disciplinary skills can have positive effects on student generalized comprehension and affirm the overall value of instructional time allocated to this practice (Toste et al, 2019). What cannot be discerned is the long-term value of the combined DLS and GLS skill development. While attention to GLS and/or DLS skills was associated with stronger general reading comprehension compared to BAU, neither intervention provided higher content knowledge outcomes.

LIMITATIONS

This study was conducted during an academic school year with intact history classes in a single school. As typical in any school, some students were admitted to school late, and therefore did not participate in this study. Some students who began the study did not complete posttests due to moving schools or classrooms. Results should not be generalized beyond the local sample of students who remained at the school during the intervention period and participated in all testing sessions.

Another limitation involves restriction of intervention dosage for the intervention classes. The intervention teacher was unexpectedly unavailable to teach during one of the intervention units, and so students in neither treatment condition received the full dose of instruction as prescribed. In contrast, the nonintervention classes were taught all the units in their entirety. Therefore, the effects of the intervention on student outcomes may have been attenuated.

Lastly, the research team did not control for levels of student engagement or discussion of strategies by students or teachers across condition.

Although teachers were trained to avoid contamination of treatment by maintaining confidentiality of treatment materials, there was no way to ensure that contamination was completely prevented. Further, students in treatment conditions may have shared skills learned within their classroom with one another. Therefore, it is possible that students' reading comprehension and content knowledge scores were impacted by information gained outside of the prescribed condition.

CONCLUSION

In conclusion, researchers have demonstrated the value of teaching both general and disciplinary literacy skills to students learning history; however, results of the present study suggest that students may not experience increased benefits with combined instruction. Students in the present study improved overall in their content knowledge from winter to spring, and students in the treatment conditions improved more in reading comprehension compared to students in BAU. The value of teaching DLS and GLS for improving reading comprehension in social studies affirms the overall merit of using instructional time to teaching comprehension strategies (Swanson et al, 2015; Toste et al., 2019; Vaughn et al., 2013; Wanzek et al., 2019). The increase in content comprehension of first period (DLS Only) over all classes suggests the possible positive value of discipline literacy supports in improving content knowledge (Monte-Sano, 2010; Nokes, 2010; Wineburg, 2001; Wineburg et al., 2013). However, it is concerning that this trend did not hold up across all classes that learned DLS, and this suggests the need for further investigation.

Results of this study called into question the notion that providing instruction in GLS is required for students to benefit from DLS instruction. Future research might explore whether teaching DLS to students with disabilities and/or students who are below grade-level reading proficiency leads to strong comprehension and content knowledge, and whether supplementing DLS with GLS improves outcomes. Finally, given that combining DLS and GLS instruction involves teaching additional, potentially complex, approaches to reading, future research might explore whether it is possible or necessary to combine the approaches to support content knowledge and comprehension outcomes for students who experience reading difficulties. Given the significance of reading as a critical skill for learning social studies, in particular U.S. history, this study offers insights into process that might attended to the comprehension needs of struggling and reluctant readers who often receive fewer opportunities to engage with texts (Miller et al., 2009).

REFERENCES

Afflerbach, P., Pearson, P., & Paris, S. (2008). Clarifying differences between reading skills and reading strategies. *The Reading Teacher*, *61*(5), 364–373. https://doi.org/10.1598/rt.61.5.1

Alvermann, D. (2002). Effective literacy instruction for adolescents. *Journal of Literacy Research*, *34*(2), 189–208. https://doi.org/10.1207/s15548430jlr3402_4

Annenberg Learner, (n.d.) *What is discipline literacy?* https://www.learner.org/courses/readwrite/disciplinary-literacy/what-is-disciplinary-literacy/4.html

Barber, A. T., Buehl, M. M., Kidd, J. K., Sturtevant, E. G., Nuland, L. R., & Beck, J. (2015). Reading engagement in social studies: Exploring the role of a social studies literacy intervention on reading comprehension, reading self-efficacy, and engagement in middle school students with different language backgrounds. *Reading Psychology*, *36*(1), 31–85.

Chauvin, R., & Theodore, K. (2015). *Teaching content-area literacy and disciplinary literacy.* http://www.sedl.org/insights/3-1/.

De La Paz, S. (2005). Effects of historical reasoning instruction and writing strategy mastery in culturally and academically diverse middle school classrooms. *Journal of Educational Psychology*, *97*(2), 139–156.

De La Paz, S. (2013). Teaching and learning in history: Effective and reform-based practices for students with learning disabilities. *Learning Disabilities: A Contemporary Journal*, *11*(1), 89–105.

Dunlosky, J., Rawson, K., Marsh, E., Nathan, M., & Willingham, D. (2013). Improving students' learning with effective learning techniques. *Psychological Science in the Public Interest*, *14*(1), 4–58. https://doi.org/10.1177/1529100612453266

Faggella-Luby, M., Graner, P., Deshler, D., & Drew, S. (2012). Building a house on sand—Why disciplinary literacy is not sufficient to replace general strategies for adolescent learners who struggle. *Topics in Language Disorders*, *32*(1), 69–84. https://doi.org/10.1097/tld.0b013e318245618e

Fisher, D., & Frey, N. (2009). *Background knowledge: The missing piece of the comprehension puzzle.* Heinemann.

Grant, S. G. (2018). Teaching history practices. In S. Metzger & L. Harris, (Eds.), *The Wiley international handbook of history teaching and learning* (pp. 419–448). Wiley-Blackwell.

Halvorsen, A., Duke, N. K., Brugar, K. A., Block, M. K., Strachan, S. L., Berka, M. B., & Brown, J. M. (2012). Narrowing the achievement gap in second-grade social studies and content area literacy: The promise of a project-based approach. *Theory & Research in Social Education*, *40*(3), 198–229.

Heafner, T. L., & Fitchett, P. G. (2015). An opportunity to learn US history: What NAEP data suggest regarding the opportunity gap. *The High School Journal*, *98*(3), 226–249.

Hussar, B., Zhang, J., Hein, S., Wang, K., Roberts, A., Cui, J., Smith, M., Bullock Mann, F., Barmer, A., & Dilig, R. (2020). *The Condition of Education 2020* (NCES 2020-144). U.S. Department of Education, National Center for Education Statistics. https://nces.ed.gov/pubsearch/pubsinfo. asp?pubid=2020144

Levstik, L. S., & Barton, K. C. (2005). *Doing history: Investigations with children in elementary and middle schools.* Lawrence Erlbaum Associates.

McKenna, M., & Robinson, R. (1990). *Content literacy: A definition and implications.* https://www.jstor.org/stable/40014518.

Miller, S., Heafner, T., & Massey, D. (2009). High-school teachers' attempts to promote self-regulated learning: I may learn from you, yet how do I do it? *The Urban Review, 41*, 121–140.

Monte-Sano, C. (2010) Disciplinary literacy in history: An exploration of the historical nature of adolescents' writing. *Journal of the Learning Sciences, 19*(4), 539–568. https://doi.org/10.1080/10508406.2010.481014

Moje, E. (2007). Developing socially just subject-matter instruction: A review of the literature on disciplinary literacy teaching. *Review of Research in Education, 31*(1), 1–44. https://doi.org/10.3102/0091732x07300046

The Nation's Report Card. (2014). *U.S. History, geography, and civics assessment Grade 8.* U.S. Department of Education: Institute of Education Sciences. https://www.nationsreportcard.gov/hgc_2014/#

The Nation's Report Card. (2019). *Reading Grades 4 and 8.* U.S. Department of Education: Institute of Education Sciences. https://nces.ed.gov/nationsreportcard/reading/

The Nation's Report Card. (2020). *Civics, Geography and U.S. History Grade 8.* U.S. Department of Education: Institute of Education Sciences. https://www.nationsreportcard.gov/highlights/ushistory/2018/

Nokes, J. D. (2010). Observing literacy practices in history education classrooms. *Theory & Research in Social Education, 38*(4), 515–544.

Parker, W. C., Lo, J., Yeo, A. J., Valencia, S. W., Nguyen, D., Abbott, R. D., Nolen, S. B., Bransford, J. D., & Vye, N. J. (2013). Beyond breadth-speed-test: Toward deeper knowing and engagement in an advanced placement course. *American Educational Research Journal, 50*(6), 1424–1459. https://doi.org/10.3102/0002831213504237

Reisman, A. (2012). Reading like a historian: Document-based history curriculum intervention in urban high schools. *Cognition and Instruction, 30*(1), 86–112.

Riener, C., & Willingham, D. (2010). The myth of learning styles. *Change: The Magazine of Higher Learning, 42*(5), 32–35. https://doi.org/10.1080/00091383.2010.503139

Saye, J. W. (2017). Disciplined inquiry in social studies classrooms. In M. M. Manfra & C. M. Bolick (Eds.), *The Wiley handbook of social studies research* (pp. 336–359). Wiley Blackwell.

Saye, J., & the SSIRC. (2013). Authentic pedagogy: Its presence in social studies classrooms and relationship to student performance on state-mandated tests. *Theory & Research in Social Education, 41*(1), 89–132.

Shanahan, C. (2009). Disciplinary comprehension. In S. Israel & G. Duffy (Eds.), *Handbook of research on reading comprehension* (pp. 240–260). Routledge. https://www.academia.edu/37378134/Handbook_of_Research_on_Reading_Comprehension_Duffy_and_Israel_Taylor_Francis_2014_pdf

Shanahan, T., & Shanahan, C. (2008). Teaching disciplinary literacy to adolescents: Rethinking content-area literacy. *Harvard Educational Review, 78*(1), 40–59. https://doi.org/10.17763/haer.78.1.v62444321p602101

Shanahan, T., & Shanahan, C. (2012). What is disciplinary literacy and why does it matter? *Topics in Language Disorders, 32*(1), 7–18. https://doi.org/10.1097/TLD.0b013e318244557a

Swanson, E. A., Wexler, J., & Vaughn, S. (2009). *Text reading and students with learning disabilities.* In. E. H. Hiebert (Ed.), *Reading more, reading better* (pp. 210–230). Guilford.

Swanson, E., Wanzek, J., Vaughn, S., Roberts, G., & Fall, A.-M. (2015). Improving reading comprehension and social studies knowledge among middle school students with disabilities. *Exceptional Children, 81*(4), 426–442. https://doi.org/10.1177/0014563704

Sweller, J. (1994). Cognitive load theory, learning difficulty, and instructional design. *Learning and Instruction, 4*, 295–312.

Thacker, E. S., Lee, J. K., & Friedman, A. M. (2017). Teaching with the C3 framework: Surveying teachers' beliefs and practices. *Journal of Social Studies Research, 41*(2), 89–100.

Toste, J. R., Fuchs, D., & Fuchs, L. S. (2013). Supporting struggling readers in high school. In R. T. Boon & V. G. Spencer (Eds.), *Adolescent literacy* (pp. 79–91). Brookes.

Toste, J. R., Vaughn, S., Martinez, L. R., & Bustillos-SoRelle, D. A. (2019). Content-area reading comprehension and teachers' use of instructional time: Effects on middle school students' social studies knowledge. *Reading and Writing, 32*(7), 1705–1722.

Vaughn, S., Martinez, L. R., Linan-Thompson, S., Reutebuch, C. K., Carlson, C. D., & Francis, D. J. (2009). Enhancing social studies vocabulary and comprehension for seventh-grade English language learners: Findings from two experimental studies. *Journal of Research on Educational Effectiveness, 2*(4), 297–324. https://doi.org/10.1002/rrq.039

Vaughn, S., Swanson, E., Roberts, G.,Wanzek, J., Stillman-Spisak, S. J., Solis, M., & Simmons, D. (2013). Improving reading comprehension and social studies knowledge in middle school. *Reading Research Quarterly, 48*(1), 77–93. http://doi:10.1002/rrq.039

Wanzek, J., Petscher, Y., Otailba, S., & Donegan, R. (2019). Retention of reading intervention effects from fourth to fifth grade for students with reading difficulties. *Reading & Writing Quarterly, 35*(3), 277–288. https://doi.org./10.1080/10573569.2018.1560379

Willingham, D. T. (2006). The usefulness of brief instruction in reading comprehension strategies. *American Educator, 30*(4), 39–50.

Wineburg, S. (2001). *Historical thinking and other unnatural acts: charting the future of teaching the past.* Temple University Press.

Wineburg, S., Martin, D., & Monte-Sano, C. (2013). *Reading like a historian: Teaching literacy in middle & high school classrooms.* Teachers College Press.

Wineburg, S., & Reinsman, A. (2015) Disciplinary literacy in history. *Journal of Adolescent & Adult History, 58*(8), 636–639. https://doi.org/10.1002/jaal.410

CHAPTER 10

RESPONDING TO AN ERA OF GLOBALIZATION WITH MULTICULTURAL EDUCATION

Amanda R. Casto
Southern Oregon University

Greg Wiggan
University of North Carolina at Charlotte

ABSTRACT

This chapter presents a recently conducted critical analysis (2019) of the current multicultural education policies and practices in the Republic of Korea (South Korea) to subsequently evaluate similar social science education policies and practices in the United States (Chang, 2017; Eden & Kang, 2016; Park & Watson, 2011). In response to the social and economic divisions created by globalization, South Korea has made significant strides during the 21st century to prioritize multicultural education in their educational system's policies and practices. Since 2007, many South Korean schools added new cultural education and language education programs to their core curricula, schools have also created "multicultural teacher" faculty positions, and South Korean teachers have increasingly employed multicultural textbooks to engage students in discussions on topics related to tolerance and global matters (Chang, 2017; Eden & Kang, 2016). These findings

The Divide Within: Intersections of Realities, Facts, Theories, and Practices
pp. 189–206

suggest that academically high-performing capitalist nations have experienced success in implementing multicultural social science educational policies and practices during the globalization era. In examining their progress, suggestions for how the United States can begin to improve social science education to achieve similar educational goals are presented.

On October 5, 2010, educational leaders from six nations, including Australia, China, Denmark, Singapore, the United Kingdom, and the United States, arrived in Singapore for the fourth annual meeting of the International Alliance of Leading Education Institutes (IALEI; Kumaravadivelu, 2012; Mehlsen, 2010). The primary goals of this international alliance included transforming the widely held assumptions and systems in education to better prepare teachers for an era of unprecedented globalization, the rapid development of technology dependency and global connections. The annual meetings have covered an array of pertinent topics such as climate change, sustainable development, knowledge mobilization, and the eradication of educational disadvantages. The IALEI research theme of the 2010 annual conference was *multicultural education*.

The fact that multicultural education was selected as a conference research theme during IALEI's infancy demonstrates the significance of this educational phenomenon and its perceived ability to transform education and unify a divided society. This theme was chosen specifically because of the IALEI's growing concerns that many Western democracies (e.g., the United States) had pulled away from making multicultural education a priority in their schools (Mehlsen, 2010). Instead, these nations have embraced neoliberal education policies focused on improving student achievement on standardized-tested subjects (i.e., reading, mathematics, and science), thus marginalizing the humanities and social sciences (Stromquist & Monkman, 2014). Despite this trend, one academically high performing democratic nation stands out due to their relatively recent efforts to integrate multiculturalism into their educational policies and practices: the Republic of Korea (South Korea). Since 2007, South Korea's multicultural education initiatives have made them an exemplar of high academic performance with a sound commitment to implementing multicultural policies to drive societal change.

Multicultural education is viewed as the reform movement that can build a unified and pluralistic society, closing the divides that have emerged during an era of globalization. The purpose of this paper is to analyze the multicultural education policies and practices in South Korea to subsequently evaluate current education policies and practices in one of her closest allies since the Korean War (1950–1953), the United States. After a brief introduction to multicultural education in the globalization era, a critical analysis of each country's education system and multicultural education policy is discussed. To conclude, the authors make suggestions for improving U.S. multicultural education policies and practices based on the critical analysis and the national standards for social studies teachers outlined by the National Council for the Social Studies (NCSS).

LITERATURE REVIEW

Defining Multicultural Education

Multicultural education emerged in the United States as part of the Civil Rights movement of the 1960s and 1970s, yet faded from the national spotlight around the time *A Nation At Risk* (National Commission on Excellence in Education, 1983) was published and the national "back to basics" conversation began (Darling-Hammond et al., 2017; Gay, 2000; Sleeter & McLaren, 2000). During the 21st century, however, discussions about multicultural education, in the United States and abroad, have slowly reemerged as populations have transformed into more pluralistic societies.

According to Gorski (2011), "At its core, multicultural education attempts to institutionalize inclusivity, to engage a broader set of worldviews that, woven together, provide all of us with a deeper understanding of the world and ourselves" (p. 83). There are many goals of multicultural education. Some of the goals agreed upon by prominent scholars in the field include: (1) to help all students acquire the skills, attitudes, and knowledge necessary to live in a more democratic and socially just nation; (2) to help students view themselves from perspectives of other cultures; (3) to promote democracy; (4) to transform the curriculum; and (5) to eliminate education inequities (Banks, 1999; Gay, 2000; Gorski, 2011; Nieto & Bode, 2008). Educational policies and practices that incorporate these goals vary around the world. However, multicultural education is an institutional matter; for these goals to make an observable impact on students, they must be comprehensively embedded into the educational system with fidelity (Gorski, 2011).

Multicultural Education in a Global Context

Globalization, which is defined as the "social and economic process that is identifiable by growing levels of financial and technological integrations and interconnections in the world system" (Wiggan & Hutchinson, 2009, p. 2), has had a trickle-down effect from economic to education systems in the 21st century. The growth of information communication technologies has accelerated the pace of global interaction between cultures, languages, and identities (International Network of Educational Institutes, n.d.). Secondly, it has spurred more social inequities between the dominant culture groups and their underrepresented minority counterparts (e.g., immigrants; underrepresented racial, ethnic, and religious groups; and economically disadvantaged). Finally, the spread of globalization during the 21st century has created a new sense of urgency amongst many developed nations, including South Korea (Park & Watson, 2011), causing them to reevaluate their education systems.

The effects of globalization vary across jurisdictions. However, the IALEI identified one unique symptom of globalization, the social inequities created by the influx of migration, as a severe issue facing all education systems at their 2010 conference. The dramatic increase of international student enrollment in South Korean schools serves as one such example; the enrollment of foreign-born students (largely from refugee and migrant working-class families) increased more than 30% from 2000 to 2010 (Park & Watson, 2011). According to the South Korean Ministry of Gender Equity and Family (n.d.), more than 212,000 children identified as belonging to a *multicultural* family (a family consisting of multiple races, ethnicities, or cultures; Chang, 2017) across South Korea in 2017 (2.7 million students were enrolled in primary schools in 2017 [UNESCO Institute for Statistics, 2020]). To improve educational equity for students such as these around the globe, the alliance made a call for prioritizing multicultural education in schools and raising it to the top of the list of societies' needs (International Network of Educational Institutes, n.d.).

South Korea is not the only nation that has made efforts to address multiculturalism in the 21st century. Several other countries around the globe have also made great strides in prioritizing multicultural education in their educational systems' policies or practices. Belgium, for instance, has been attempting to meet the needs of a growing Muslim student population with an additive approach to multicultural curriculum reform by altering their textbooks to reflect more cultural variance (Agirdag et al., 2016). Multicultural education has also become a significant aspect of educational policymaking in Malaysia, where they are reforming their curricula to integrate "different groups until the divisive aspects of each group have been whittled away and a new culture has been created" (Stromquist & Monkman, 2014, p. 239). Additionally, some of the most successful educational systems in the world (i.e., Finland, Australia, Canada, Singapore, and the Shanghai province of China) have made similar noteworthy efforts to embed multicultural education in their teaching policies (Darling-Hammond et al., 2017). Although they have made many efforts collectively, there is a dearth of literature capturing their multicultural curriculum reform in comparison to South Korea's. South Korea may not have been represented at the IALEI conference; however, their multicultural education reform movement over the past decade arguably serves as an exemplary model of boosting equity and academic excellence through multicultural education.

DISCUSSION

Multicultural education has only been a part of South Korea's educational system for a brief time. Therefore, to better understand how and why multiculturalism emerged as part of this exemplary educational system, it is important to first examine other contributing factors such as historical, economic, and educational contexts. The purpose of this paper is to analyze the current multicultural education policy and practices in South Korea to further evaluate multicultural education policies and practices in the United States. Based upon that evaluation, the authors turn to the NCSS's National Standards for Social Studies Teachers to suggest multiple prescriptions for multicultural education reform in the United States.

South Korea in Context

South Korea is located in the southern half of the Korean peninsula which jets out into three seas in East Asia. According to WorldAtlas (2018), it is approximately 37,901 square miles in total land area and has an estimated population of 51 million people.

History

The people of South Korea have endured a turbulent history as a young nation. For centuries, South Korea was invaded and ruled by other world powers, including China and Japan, their neighbor across the East Sea. They were granted independence from Japan after World War II and, instead of being unified with the north, were declared a separate and sovereign nation and an ally of the United States. Later, in 1950, they were invaded by a Soviet-backed North Korea, which initiated the Korean War. Although the war only lasted 3 years, the devastating political and economic effects were long lasting. To this day, South Korea endures an intense relationship with their hostile neighbor to the north. The two nations, who share one ancestry, are separated by a 2.5-mile wide and 160-mile long demilitarized zone.

Economics

Globalization took off in South Korea after the 1988 Seoul Olympic Games. In response to a labor shortage crisis at that time, South Korea introduced an industrial training program that recruited a large number of international workers throughout the 1990s (Chang, 2017). Many trainees in the program became permanent residents and married foreign-born women, which resulted in dense urbanization and the growth of multiethnic communities (Eden & Kang, 2016). Although they were gaining an experienced and diverse workforce, they still suffered from a significant lack of natural resources at their disposal. South Korea had to turn to other sources of income so it began investing heavily in its people. According to Ripley (2013), South Korea's strong economic standing today is solely contributed to one thing: a national emphasis placed on quality education.

Education in South Korea

South Korea is well known for its ambitious and rigorous education system governed by a centralized ministry of education. The South Korean Ministry of Education oversees more than 20,300 schools that serve approximately 11.6 million K–16 students (Ministry of Education, n.d.). They are continuously ranked near the top of the Program for International Student Assessment (PISA) performance standings in reading, math, and science (see Table 10.1). Program for International Student Assessment, an international assessment developed by the Organization for Economic Co-operation and Development, was created to test students' critical thinking skills and is used to evaluate "which countries were teaching kids to think for themselves" (Ripley, 2013, p. 15). It comes as no

Table 10.1.   Program for International Student Assessment 2015 Data

Education System	Average Reading Literacy Score	Average Math Literacy Score	Average Science Literacy Score
Singapore (#1)	535	564	556
Republic of Korea (#11)	517	524	516
United States (#25)	497	470	496
OECD average	493	490	493

Source: Organization for Economic Cooperation and Development, Program for International Student Assessment (2015).

surprise that South Korean students have mastered these skills; they devote 10 to 14 hours per day for approximately 220 days each year in formal and informal education settings (Diem et al., n.d.; Ripley, 2013). Although students express dissatisfaction with their long school days, they are also notoriously driven to succeed by their education-focused South Korean culture.

Multicultural Education in South Korea

Following the Korean War, South Korea made numerous efforts to strengthen their Korean identity. According to Chang (2017), one way they promoted their ethnic pride was through their schools' textbooks. Textbooks featuring a dominant Korean heritage were introduced in the 1960s and were favorably utilized in public schools into the 21st century (Chang, 2017). At the turn of the century, it appeared unlikely that South Korean schools would ever veer away from the traditionally monocultural curriculum. However, that changed when the Ministry of Education was petitioned by a National Football League Korean American *hero* to make a dramatic change (Lee, 2013).

After winning the Super Bowl (and Super Bowl Most Valuable Player award) in 2006, Hines Ward, a biracial Korean American, returned to his birthplace in South Korea's capital city, Seoul, as a champion and a new spokesperson for multiculturalism (Chang, 2017; Lee, 2013). During his visit in April of that year, he visited with President Moo-hyun Roh, appeared on numerous talk shows, and spoke at national events about his interest in amending laws to support multicultural families (Lee, 2013). According to Lee (2013), Ward's vision was well-received and considered a huge turning point for multicultural education policy in South Korea. During that same month, the government proposed new antidiscrimination laws against non-Koreans; and during the following year, the Ministry of Education published a new multicultural education curriculum that omitted any reference to monoculturalism or "one blood" (Lee, 2013, p. 17).

South Korean Multicultural Education Policies

Since 2007, multiple governmental agencies have stepped up to support the Ministry of Education in developing and enforcing multicultural education policies. According to Chang (2017), 11 of the 17 South Korean ministries are involved with multicultural education to some extent. The policy goals in South Korea are simple and twofold. First, the nation is focused on creating a better understanding of all cultures for the majority of the population. Additionally, through the creation of mentorship programs (i.e., Korean language programs, online courses for multicultural parents, family programs for learning Korean culture), they aim to gently assimilate multicultural (non-Korean born) individuals into Korean culture instead of expecting non-Korean students and their families to abandon their own cultures (Chang, 2017). According to Chang (2017), scholars have criticized these goals as being too broad, lacking definition, and creating ambiguity for the implementation standards of multicultural practices in schools. Despite these weaknesses, South Korea's multicultural education policies are still guiding schools toward educational and social equity for their students.

South Korean Multicultural Education Practices

There is a considerable range of multicultural education practices in South Korea. According to Lee (2013), many schools added new cultural education and language education programs to their core curriculums immediately following the announcement of the new multicultural education policies. Some programs were intentionally designed for students while others were for teachers to increase their awareness of multiculturalism. The teachers in Lee's (2013) study who had not participated in inservice training programs tend to hold deficit views of the non-South Korean students in their classes. However, the teachers who attended multicultural education training held beliefs that closely aligned with the Ministry of Education's intent.

South Korean schools have also created the role of a multicultural teacher, and in some cases, a multicultural teacher aide (Eden & Kang, 2016). Multicultural teachers work primarily with classroom teachers to meet the needs of their multicultural students who are primarily from migrant families and North Korean refugees (Park & Wilson, 2011). They are responsible for adding "the culture of multicultural students to the class" and contribute significantly to South Korean schools' equity pedagogy (Eden & Kang, 2016, p. 300). They also support classroom teachers in engaging with parents. This is significant in helping schools meet their mission of creating empowering and inclusive school climates for all learners.

Finally, it should be mentioned that South Korean teachers have increased their attempts at multicultural education in their instruction by employing the Ministry of Education's multicultural textbooks and engaging students in discussions on topics related to tolerance and global matters (Chang, 2017; Eden & Kang, 2016; Lee, 2013). While these are not transformative approaches to multicultural education, they are critical first steps in paving the way for more sophisticated efforts of improving educational equity in the future.

Multicultural Education in the United States

The concept of multicultural education was introduced during the Civil Rights era and has weaved in and out of the U.S. national debate ever since. The goals of multicultural education discussed in the United States are similar to the goals in South Korea: to improve educational equity, tolerance, and students' worldviews (Gorski, 2011). However, the educational policies and practices guiding those goals in South Korea and the United States are quite different.

To better understand the needs of students sitting in U.S. classrooms, it is important to analyze this population at large. Unlike South Korea, the United States has historically been regarded as a melting pot of cultures. Yet, it has been historically dominated by the ancestors of the White European settlers who began colonizing the eastern seaboard in the early 17th century. The demographics of the United States have shifted significantly in the era of globalization and are expected to continually do so (see Figure 10.1). According to the U.S. Census Bureau, more than 50% of all Americans are projected to belong to minority groups other than those classified as non-Latino White by 2044 (Colby & Ortman, 2014). By 2060, nearly 20% of the nation's total population is projected to be foreign born. If U.S. classrooms are actual microcosms reflecting society at large, these assumptions can be delicately carried over into the context of educational settings.

To illustrate how this population shift impacts schools, consider Latinx students, who are the fastest-growing ethnic group in U.S. schools (Gay, 2000). Current educational policies and practices in the United States are not meeting the academic, social, or language needs of this group, which has resulted in serious gaps in access, opportunity, and academic performance. Table 10.2 illustrates the change in Grade 8 Reading and Math scores on the National Assessment of Educational Progress since 2000/ 2002 for all six subgroups in the U.S. Latinx students perform similarly to their Black and American Indian/Alaska Native peers, yet significantly lower than White and Asian/Pacific Islander subgroups. These gaps exemplify a significant problem within the U.S. educational system affecting millions of students; a lack of multicultural education will only continue to exacerbate the educational issues being experienced by the fastest-growing population in the era of globalization (Gay, 2000).

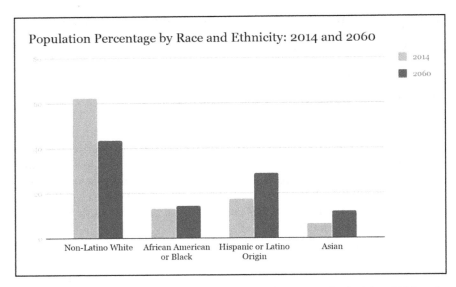

Figure 10.1.   Change in population percentage by race and ethnicity, 2014 and 2060.

Table 10.2.   National Assessment of Educational Progress Scale Scores per Race/Ethnicity Subgroup During the 21st Century

Race/Ethnicity Subgroup	Grade 8 Reading Scores		Grade 8 Math Scores	
Year	2002	2017	2000	2017
Asian/ Pacific Islander	267	282	288	310
American Indian/Alaska Native	250	253	259	267
Black	245	249	244	260
Hispanic (Latino)	247	255	253	269
Two or more races	265	272	270	287
White	272	275	284	293

Source: U.S. Department of Education, Institute of Education Sciences, National Center for Education Statistics (n.d.-a, n.d.-b).

U.S. Multicultural Education Policies

Unlike South Korea, the United States does not have a centralized education system. Each of its fifty states and U.S. territories is responsible for its students' education. While federal policies have been established to protect students' rights, such as the Family Educational Rights and Privacy Act (1974), the Individuals with Disabilities Education Act (1975), and the Every Student Succeeds Act (2015), multicultural education has not been included as part of these policies and remains missing from the federal spotlight. Consequently, it is up to each state or local education agency to determine policies related to multicultural education for its students. While some states (e.g., Nevada, Oregon) have created social studies education standards that incorporate multicultural topics or teaching standards that address multiculturalism in the classroom, these have not been adopted nor standardized nationwide.

U.S. Multicultural Education Practices

During the 21st century, many states, including the 46 states that participated in the 2015 Race to the Top initiative, have been consumed with improving standards-based curricula and instructional practices. Designing and implementing effective standards-based curricula became a top priority across the United States after the No Child Left Behind Act of 2001 was signed, holding states more accountable to boost the academic performance of all students, including English-language learners, students in special education, and underrepresented minority students (Klein, 2015). During this time, conservative critics of multicultural education have claimed that standards and multicultural education are not compatible. According to a leading scholar of multicultural education, Christine Sleeter (2011), they can be if the standards-based curriculum is intentionally multicultural and taught using culturally relevant methods.

The lack of multicultural education in standards-based teaching materials and the lack of cultural awareness training in the United States are a great concern. According to Wiggan (2012), most school curricula in the United States lack multiculturalism and represent the lives and perspectives of White, middle class America. Additionally, U.S. teachers, who are predominantly White females, are not being provided with enough training to teach an increasingly diverse student body (Alismail, 2016). Sharma (2011) writes, "Due to the lack of understanding of ethnic, racial, social, and linguistic diversity of students, teachers can engage themselves consciously or unconsciously in 'mis-education practices'" (p. 53). According to Gay (2000), U.S. teachers must be given time to develop an awareness about cultural diversity, be trained to incorporate cultural diversity in their classroom instruction, and change their attitudes about teaching diverse ethnicities. Without time and training for teachers, multicultural education reform will fail and the divisions between U.S. citizens will remain.

PRESCRIPTIONS FOR MULTICULTURAL
EDUCATION IN THE UNITED STATES

The epicenter of globalization is currently located in the continental United States. It is the home of many international organizations' headquarters (e.g., the World Bank, the International Monetary Fund, and the United Nations) as well as some of the most influential transnational corporations, like Walmart, Exxon Mobile, Berkshire Hathaway, and Apple. As an economic world leader, the United States should be leading the multicultural education reform suggested by IALEI. Instead, they are trailing behind many other nations in their education reform efforts. Federal educational policies implemented during the 21st century (e.g., No Child Left Behind, 2001) to improve standardized test scores have consequently resulted in teachers "teaching to the test," average student academic performance, and rampant educational inequity across the nation (Nieto & Bode, 2008).

To improve all students' educational experiences in the era of globalization, the United States should look at the multicultural education reform models of other nations, namely South Korea, for solution strategies. Despite their cultural differences, an analysis of multicultural education reform in a capitalist and democratic South Korea provides three solutions that can be prescribed to her economic and political ally, the United States, at a combination of federal, state, or local levels:

1. Recruit multicultural education spokesperson(s)
2. Invest in multicultural education professional development and specialized staff
3. Invest in multicultural curriculum and instructional mandates

The overall goal of these prescriptions is a combination of increasing the overall awareness of multicultural education and promoting more equitable learning for students, especially those from underrepresented minority groups who have been excluded in the past.

The Multicultural Education Spokesperson

One might question if South Korea would have ever launched their multicultural reform had Hines Ward not visited his birthplace in 2006. At the same time, it should be no surprise that a celebrity *hero* was the instigator of a huge wave of change. Celebrities—famous actors, athletes, musicians, and media personalities—have an ability to garner attention and are frequently selected as spokespersons for important causes, charities, and events. They have also demonstrated an unparalleled ability to generate societal influence. Today, this influence is desperately needed to raise awareness of multicultural education in the United States. Therefore, one of the prescriptions from this research is to recruit celebrity spokespersons who have a passion for increasing educational equity and multiculturalism. With support from the U.S. Department of Education and educational organizations such as the National Association of Multicultural Education, the multicultural education spokesperson would hold meetings similar to Ward's in South Korea: they would meet with political leaders and education policymakers, fundraise, and advocate for multicultural education using NCSS standards. Whether this work is done locally or nationally, it would be a critical initial step toward the systemic change that is desperately needed for all students to succeed.

Multicultural Education Professional Development and Specialized Staff

There is a dire need to educate U.S. teachers on topics related to multiculturalism, multicultural education, systemic oppression, and the dominant culture (Alismail, 2016; Banks, 1999; Nieto & Bode, 2008). To increase educational equity, it is common for schools to increase the number of multicultural workshops, sensitivity training, and cultural celebrations. However, according to Gorski (2011), these events do not challenge the "euro, male, Christian, heterosexual, English-speaking, upper-middle-classcentrism" (p. 85) that dominate most American public schools. To create systemic change, *critical* multicultural education professional development and preservice teacher training is needed.

First, preservice and inservice teachers need to be informed about the various definitions of multicultural education and the approaches to multicultural curriculum reform. While there is evidence that teachers are incorporating multicultural education using Banks's (1999) contributions or additive approaches (e.g., celebrating diverse heroes and holidays, discussing diverse content, concepts, and themes), these approaches are not making a significant impact on the U.S. education system when measured by the disparities in academic opportunity and achievement between White students and their non-White peers. According to Gorski (2011), "making small changes within a traditional classroom, school, or school system does not constitute multicultural education" (p. 80).

Second, teachers need to be informed about the political nature of multicultural education. When asked to define multicultural education, teachers tend to depoliticize the concept and discuss "culture" in very broad and general terms (Aragona-Young & Sawyer, 2018; Gorski, 2011).

To create educational equity for all students, multicultural education will need to become more political. According to Gorski (2011), this can be done by enlisting teachers' help in creating more equitable and socially just schools, framing multicultural education reform as a complex and transformational task, and avoiding "simplistic" changes to curriculum or programs.

In addition to training, supporting teachers and administrators in their integration of multicultural education curriculum and instruction in their schools by a multicultural education specialist. The role of a multicultural education specialist should be added to every district, and if possible, school. The role of the multicultural education specialist in the United States should resemble the "multicultural teacher" described in Eden and Kang's (2016) study. South Korean multicultural teachers are primarily responsible for working with classroom teachers to meet the needs of their multicultural students. These specialist teachers also perform other vital tasks such as communicating with multicultural students' parents and organizing multicultural events at the school. This is significant in helping schools meet their mission of creating inclusive yet empowering school climates for all learners.

The preservice teacher training, inservice teacher professional development, and additional staffing needed for this prescriptive endeavor will require a considerable investment of time, human resources, and money. Some portion of this necessary funding could be generated through the fundraising efforts of the multicultural education celebrity spokesperson. To implement this solution with fidelity, however, education budgets will require reevaluation and reallocation by local education systems and the U.S. federal government. For this solution to be enacted, the U.S. government will need to follow South Korea's path and make a commitment to become more actively involved.

Multicultural Curriculum and Instructional Mandates

The U.S. government does not require its states to adopt nor follow a nationally aligned curriculum or instructional standards (adding yet another policy and practice they do not share with South Korea). Since educational materials vary from state to state and change frequently in schools, it is difficult to measure their content for multiculturalism. In general, many education resources (including children's literature) lack diversity and feature America's dominant culture (Crisp et al., 2016). According to Wiggan (2012), "the current curriculum and cannon used in today's schools does not equally address the contributions and perspectives of all cultures and, therefore, must be critically deconstructed"

(p. 76). For multicultural education to prevail, curriculum and instructional resources found in today's schools will need to be critically adjusted or altogether replaced, while social studies education must join reading, science, technology, engineering, and math at the forefront of education policy. While states may keep their freedom in regards to their curriculum decisions, the consideration of stricter federal or state mandates requiring selected materials to reflect inclusivity, aspects of multiculturalism, and multiple perspectives should advance multicultural education in the United States.

The Role of National Standards for the Preparation of Social Studies Teachers

In addition to reforming curricula and learning materials, teaching standards across the United States must also be reformed to match the instructional expectations involved with increasing multiculturalism in classrooms. This means that teachers must be able and willing, for example, to embrace the sociocultural assets and unique identities of their students, enact culturally relevant and responsive pedagogy (and similar practices that support the multicultural education goal of educational equity), foster interdisciplinary learning environments, and promote social justice and human rights through civic engagement and informed action (NCSS, 2018). To adequately prepare inservice and preservice teachers to teach in an increasingly diverse and pluralistic society, the authors suggest that all U.S. state departments of education invest in multicultural professional educator training and evaluation using two of the National Standards for the Preparation of Social Studies Teachers (NCSS, 2018): Standards 4 and 5. NCSS Standard 4 states that all teachers "use knowledge of learners to plan and implement relevant and responsive pedagogy, create collaborative and interdisciplinary learning environments, and prepare learners to be informed advocates for an inclusive and equitable society" (NCSS, 2018, p. 22). Teachers who are trained to meet this pedagogical standard will be able to meet the multicultural education goals related to increasing educational equity and cultural tolerance in their classrooms and schools. Meanwhile, NCSS Standard 5 states that all teaching candidates "reflect and expand upon their social studies knowledge, inquiry skills, and civic dispositions to advance social justice and promote human rights through informed action in schools and/or communities" (NCSS, 2018, p. 25). By training teachers to meet this standard, state departments of education and local education agencies will help ensure teachers and schools meet the multicultural education goals related to social activism and transformation.

CONCLUSION

In 2010, the IALEI alliance produced a report indicating numerous challenges that students were facing due to deep inequalities and entrenched privileges created by an era of globalization (Mehlsen, 2010). Their solution involved equipping students with the ability to "develop intercultural capabilities of negotiating across differences of identity, social justice, multilingual skills and antiracist dispositions" (Mehlsen, 2010, p. 9). National governments must begin taking larger steps toward transforming their education systems to meet these demands and match the global characteristics of society in the 21st century. In sum, it is time for all education systems around the world to prioritize multicultural education.

While several countries, including South Korea, have already taken noteworthy steps toward this initiative, many others have yet to address this concern on a national scale, including the United States. By critically evaluating South Korea's solutions of addressing multiculturalism in their increasingly diverse society, other countries can begin the reform process using variations of the prescriptions presented in this chapter. Perhaps the greatest prescription, however, is the collective willingness to enact change, reduce the divides among us, and provide opportunities for all students to live and learn equitably in a socially just global society.

REFERENCES

Agirdag, O., Merry, M. S., & Van Houtte, M. (2016). Teachers' understanding of multicultural education and the correlates of multicultural content integration in Flanders. *Education and Urban Society, 48*(6), 556–582.

Alismail, H. A. (2016). Multicultural education: Teachers' perceptions and preparation. *Journal of Education and Practice 7*(11), 139–146.

Aragona-Young, E., & Sawyer, B. E. (2018). Elementary teachers' beliefs about multicultural education practices. *Teachers and Teaching, 24,* 465–486.

Banks, J. (1999). *An introduction to multicultural education* (2nd ed.). Allyn & Bacon.

Chang, I. (2017). Multicultural education in Korea. In W. Pink & G. Noblit (Eds.), *Second international handbook of urban education* (pp. 173–193). Springer International Handbooks of Education.

Colby, S. L., & Ortman, J. M. (2014). *Projections of the size and composition of the U.S. Population: 2014 to 2060.* Current Population Reports, P25-1143. U.S. Census Bureau.

Crisp, T., Knezek, S. M., Quinn, M., Bingham, G. E., Girardeau, K., & Starks, F. (2016). What's on our bookshelves? The diversity of children's literature in early childhood classroom libraries. *Journal of Children's Literature, 42*(2), 29–42.

Darling-Hammond, L., Burns, D., Campbell, C., Goodwin, A. L., Hammerness, K., Low, E. L., … Zeichner, K. (2017). *Empowered educators: How high-performing systems shape teaching quality around the world.* Jossey-Bass/Wiley.

Diem, R., Levy, T., & VanSickle, R. (n.d.). *South Korean education.* Asia Society. https://asiasociety.org/education/south-korean-education

Eden, D., & Kang, S. Y. (2016). Between 'homeland' and 'diaspora': Multicultural education in Israel and South Korea. *Intercultural Education, 27*(3), 292–306, https://doi.org/10.1080/14675986.2016.1152045

Every Student Succeeds Act, 20 U.S.C. § 6301 (2015).

Family Educational Rights and Privacy Act, 20 U.S.C. § 1232g; 34 CFR Part 99 (1974).

Gay, G. (2000). *Culturally responsive teaching: Theory, research & practice.* Teachers College Press.

Gorski, P. (2011). The unintentional undermining of multicultural education. In J. G. Landsman & C. W. Lewis (Eds.), *White teachers diverse classrooms: Creating inclusive schools, building on students' diversity, and providing true educational equity* (pp. 75–92). Stylus.

Individuals with Disabilities Education Act, 20 U.S.C. § 1400 (1975).

International Network of Educational Institutes. (n.d.) Multicultural education. http://inei.bnu.edu.cn/?page_id=197

Klein, A. (2015, April 10). No Child Left Behind: An overview. *Education Week.* https://www.edweek.org/ew/section/multimedia/no-child-left-behind-overview-definition-summary.html

Kumaravadivelu, B. (2012). *Language teacher education for a global society: A modular model for knowing, analyzing, recognizing, doing, and seeing.* Routledge.

Lee, J. Y. (2013). *Multicultural education in the Republic of Korea: How elementary school teachers interpret multicultural education and its practical use in classrooms* (Lee_ucla_0031D_11815.). [Doctoral dissertation, UCLA]. Proquest.

Mehlsen, C. (2010). The death of multiculturalism is an exaggeration. *Education Alliance Magazine,* pp. 8–9.

Ministry of Education. (n.d.). Schools, students, and teachers by year [Data file]. http://english.moe.go.kr/sub/info.do?m=050101&page=050101&num=1&s=english

Ministry of Gender Equity and Family. (n.d.). Major statistics of MOGEF [Data file]. http://www.mogef.go.kr/eng/lw/eng_lw_f002.do

National Commission on Excellence in Education. (1983). A nation at risk: The imperative for educational reform. *The Elementary School Journal, 84*(2), 113–130.

National Council for the Social Studies. (2018). *National standards for the preparation of social studies teachers.* https://www.socialstudies.org/sites/default/files/media/2017/Nov/ncss_teacher_standards_2017-rev9-6-17.pdf

Nieto, S., & Bode, P. (2008). *Affirming diversity: The sociopolitical context of multicultural education* (Custom ed.). Pearson Custom.

Park, G. C., & Watson, S. L. (2011). In context: Multicultural education in Korea—Lessons for American educators. *Multicultural Education, 19*(3), 2–6.

206 A. R. CASTO and G. WIGGAN

Sharma, S. (2011). Multicultural education: Teachers perceptions and preparation. *Journal of College Teaching & Learning, 2*(5). https://doi.org/10.19030/tlc.v2i5.1825

Sleeter, C. E. (2011). Are standards and multicultural education compatible? *ASCD Express, 6*(15). http://www.ascd.org/ascd-express/vol6/615-sleeter.aspx

Sleeter, C. E., & McLaren, P. (2000). Origins of multiculturalism. *Rethinking Schools, 15*(1). https://rethinkingschools.org/articles/the-origins-of-multiculturalism/

Stromquist, N. P., & Monkman, K. (2014). *Globalization and education: Integration and contestation across cultures.* Rowman and Littlefield.

UNESCO Institute for Statistics. (2020). Education: Enrolment by level of education [Data file]. http://data.uis.unesco.org/#

U.S. Department of Education, Institute of Education Sciences, National Center for Education Statistics. (n.d.-a). NAEP Mathematics Report Card: National Student Group Scores and Score Gaps. https://www.nationsreportcard.gov/math_2017/nation/gaps?grade=8

U.S. Department of Education, Institute of Education Sciences, National Center for Education Statistics. (n.d.-b). *NAEP Reading Report Card: National Student Group Scores and Score Gaps.* https://www.nationsreportcard.gov/reading_2017/nation/gaps?grade=8

Wiggan, G. (2012). *Education in a strange land: Globalization, urbanization and urban schools; The social and educational implications of the geopolitical economy.* Nova.

Wiggan, G., & Hutchison, C. (Eds.). (2009). *Global issues in education: Pedagogy, policy, practice and the minority experience.* Rowman & Littlefield.

CHAPTER 11

PROMOTING STUDENT ACHIEVEMENT

Arts Integration in Urban Schools in the United States and Canada

Portia Marie York and Greg Wiggan
University of North Carolina Charlotte

ABSTRACT

Though research has shown the numerous social emotional and cognitive benefits of arts education, in the last 2 decades of the accountability and standardization movement, data trends in the United States reflect less prioritization and time allocated toward arts-based learning. Furthermore, disparities in access to arts programs along lines of race/ethnicity and social class disproportionately exacerbate the decline for historically marginalized populations. In an effort to remediate these trends, in this chapter the authors present data and context from Canada, where decades of intentional reform have expanded arts education and supported student academic achievement. By detailing this country's curricular policies, programs, and assessments, findings offer implications and present action steps needed to move toward improving educational opportunities for underserved populations in the United States.

The Divide Within: Intersections of Realities, Facts, Theories, and Practices
pp. 207–221
Copyright © 2021 by Information Age Publishing
All rights of reproduction in any form reserved.

207

INTRODUCTION

Arts integration and arts education have been studied as valid curriculum and programming connected to academic achievement in large urban school systems (Catterall et al., 2012; Dean, 2014; Fiske, 1999; Fullan, 2014; Winner et al., 2002). Research shows that children exposed to arts in schools develop creativity and improve problem-solving skills (Fiske, 1999; Winner et al., 2002), engage at higher levels with peers and curriculum (Catterall et al., 2012), and experience higher academic success across disciplines and content areas (Fiske, 1999). Despite these documented benefits, educational reform efforts in the United States aimed at raising student achievement have impeded students' access to arts-rich curricula. Following the passage of No Child Left Behind (NCLB) and the subsequent era of standardization and accountability, teachers report that the arts have been subjected to reduced minutes of instruction, particularly at the elementary level (Farkas Duffett Research Group, 2012; Parsad et al., 2012). Perhaps more concerning, recent reports have illuminated the disparities in access to arts education by student demographics. While students of upper class families tend to receive a variety of arts education opportunities—music, visual arts, dance, and theater, for example—students from lower-income families are less likely to have such instruction offered at their school (Parsad et al., 2012). With access to arts education in decline for African Americans and Hispanics from disadvantaged backgrounds for more than three decades, this population experiences half the opportunities offered to their White counterparts (Rabkin & Hedberg, 2011). As business executives and school administrators agree on the importance of arts education to fuel creativity and innovation skills needed in the 21st century job market (Lichtenberg et al., 2008), this inequitable gap in participation in the arts holds significant implications for the life outcomes of increasing numbers of children and adults across the United States.

Not all countries are following this pattern of declining arts education and participation that is present in the United States. In Canada, for example, arts integration and arts education are widely implemented with concerted effort to insert music and arts programs in K–12 curriculum and to employ interdisciplinary arts education inclusive of preservice and in-service teacher education (Hanley et al., 2006). In particular, the Toronto District School Board in the province of Ontario has embraced the work of the Royal Conservatory of Music in Toronto, which launched Learning Through the Arts (LTTA) almost 20 years ago. Now extending across Canada, all of LTTA's programs are grounded by academic research, which demonstrates that LTTA students score considerably higher in math and literacy tests than non-LTTA students (Eger, 2011).

Interestingly, on the 2015 Program for International Assessment (PISA) examinations, students in Canada outperformed peers in the United States in both math and reading, as Canada ranked 10th in math literacy and 3rd in reading literacy, while the U.S. ranked only 31st in math literacy and 20th in reading literacy (National Center for Education Statistics [NCES], 2018). This prompts a deeper investigation to uncover additional connections to the impact of arts education on math and reading achievement.

In an effort to dispel educational inequities across demographics in the United States, this chapter aims to explicate connections between arts education and academic achievement. Thus, the first portion of the chapter presents a review of the literature outlining the benefits of arts integration, detailing empirical studies of creativity and its relationship to academic performance, along with the social and motivational factors associated with the arts. Then, using Canada as an example of educational reforms inclusive of the arts, the second part of the chapter builds the case for arts integration in public schools. A closing discussion proposes that the U.S. emphasize the importance of creativity through arts integration and arts education as it pertains to achievement across demographics to help dispel educational inequities.

LITERATURE REVIEW

Considered a component of the United States curriculum for decades, and most recently designated a valuable contribution to a "well-rounded education" in the 2015 Every Student Succeeds Act (ESSA), the arts offer numerous cognitive and affective benefits. Most typically presented in elementary schools through visual arts and music, arts education also includes drama/theatre and dance that often become electives in secondary education. The body of literature examining the opportunities for learning and associated advantages connected to the arts is detailed in the following section.

Creativity and Academic Achievement

According to Sawyer (2012), creativity is difficult to define but can be conceptualized in two ways. Through the *individualist* approach, creativity can be defined as "a new mental combination that is expressed in the world" (p. 2). Alternatively, through the sociocultural aspect, creativity can be defined as "the generation of a product that is judged to be novel and also to be appropriate, useful, or valuable by a suitably knowledgeable social group" (p. 2). Similarly aligned with this latter definition, others have conceptualized creativity as the ability to make or bring into existence something new, whether a new solution to a problem, a new method or device, or a new artistic object or form (Piirto, 2004). Torrance and Safter (1990) apply such conceptions to the way people learn, describing the process in line with a constructivist lens: "People prefer to learn creatively—by exploring, questioning, experimenting, manipulating, rearranging things, testing and modifying, listening, looking, feeling—and then thinking about it—incubating" (p. 13).

Creativity is often overlooked as a cognitive process associated with academic achievement, as evidenced by the gaps in the current literature. Some researchers propose creativity is needed to generate new ideas to solve problems, suggesting a somewhat indirect link between creativity and academic performance (Coate & Boulos, 2012; Lau, 2011; Madej et al., 2015). Dishke Hondzel and colleagues (2014), using the Torrance Test of Creative Thinking (TTCT) as one instrument of research, compared the results of Canadian, Norwegian, and Finnish students to explore the influence of various levels of learning environments shaping the development of creativity. The Canadian and Norwegian students performed significantly better than Finnish students on the TTCT, prompting further investigation of the linkages among individuals, schools, communities, and culture. With 72% of business leaders stating creativity the number one skill they look for when hiring for their companies (Catterall et al., 2012), these connections—even if still ambiguous—carry important implications for the youth of our world.

Social and Motivational Benefits of Arts Education

For many youth, the arts provide natural personal and interpersonal connections to school and education. Through the arts, students often experience opportunities for collaboration with peers (Catterall et al., 2012) and develop a sense of empathy for others (Winner et al., 2002). The arts increase leadership capacity for students by building confidence, equipping them to be creative, strengthening problem-solving ability and perseverance, and developing collaboration and communication skills, all of which prepare students for college or the workplace (Appel, 2006). The arts also offer a route for connecting with the curriculum (Crawford, 2004), particularly for students with different learning styles (Catterall et al., 2012). As Greene (1995) notes, to conceive the arts concerning the curriculum is to think of a deepening and expanding mode of tuning-in. Crawford (2004) recognizes the necessity of such relevance and connection, particularly amidst the current state of standardization in schools today. He states, quite artistically, "in the midst of the homogeneity of the school curriculum, the opportunity to sing your own song is a gift" (p. 10). Arts education is an outlet for students to recognize how the world views them and how they wish to be seen.

These social and emotional benefits carry strong associations with positive academic outcomes. Low-income students with high arts participation have a dropout rate that is five times lower than their peers (Parsad et al., 2012). Furthermore, low-income students who are highly engaged in the arts are twice as likely to graduate college as their peers with no arts education (Catterall et al., 2012). Not only are there benefits for low socioeconomic students who engage in the arts connected to graduating college, but there is also a strong connection to these students becoming successful members of the workforce. Essentially, engaging in the arts helps prepare students for success in life, as indicated by high rates of completing college, obtaining gainful employment, and volunteering in their communities (Catterall et. al., 2012). Given these valuable outcomes, the inequitable gap in access to arts education, as negatively experienced by students of color and students of lower-income families in the United States (Parsad et al., 2012; Rabkin & Hedberg, 2011), seems even more detrimental to their development and well-being.

CONCEPTUAL FRAMEWORK

The creativity-arts integration-critical thinking-academic achievement (CACA) model as shown in Figure 11.1 helps conceptualize the connections to the constructs thus far reviewed in the literature. It also introduces the role of critical thinking among these processes. Critical thinking is a factor of creativity that is speculated to produce increased achievement (Sawyer, 2012). It can enable people to think more deeply and clearly about what they believe, what they read, what they are told, and about what decisions they should make (Leicester & Taylor, 2010). According to Naiditch (2016), critical thinking requires a deep understanding of the topic at hand and the ability to investigate content from diverse perspectives. Critical thinkers engage with material in innovative and creative ways to analyze, synthesize and assess it to reach their own informed conclusions (Naiditch, 2016). Although Finn (2015) challenges the long-held beliefs about critical thinking, which according to him has shown to be too linear for the 21st century world, many scholars strongly believe that critical thinking is a vastly important skill for students to have when navigating education and the workforce (Appel, 2006; Leicester & Taylor, 2010; Naiditch, 2016).

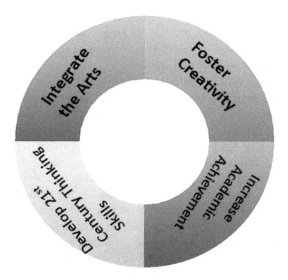

Figure 11.1.   The CACA model.

The concepts of creativity, arts integration, critical thinking, and academic achievement ultimately depend upon each other. In theory, creativity through arts integration spurs the development of critical thinking, which in turn promotes academic achievement. In understanding the relationship between these concepts, the CACA dynamic model is cyclical outlining that each concept depends upon the other for student success. In other words, when creativity is nurtured through the use of creative arts, it aids in the development of the 21st century skill of critical thinking, which ultimately increases academic achievement.

It is important to consider the definition of arts integration in order to recognize the connection between creativity and the arts. Silverstein and Layne (2010) define arts integration as "an approach to teaching in which students construct and demonstrate understanding through an art form. Students engage in a creative process that connects an art form and another subject area and meets evolving objectives in both" (p. 1). This process of creation and innovation to demonstrate knowledge and understanding implies a certain theoretical conception to teaching and learning.

Bruner's (1996) theory of constructivism is used as the framework grounding this model. It explains that learning is an active process in which learners construct new ideas or concepts based upon their current and/or past knowledge, where the learner selects and transforms information, constructs hypotheses, and makes decisions, relying on a cognitive structure. The three major principles of Bruner's constructivism theory are: (1) Instruction must be concerned with the experiences and contexts that make the student willing and able to learn; (2) Instruction must be structured by the teacher so that the student can easily grasp it; and (3) Instruction should be designed to facilitate exploration and/or fill in the gaps.

While exploring creativity's impact on achievement, students construct aspects of their learning, particularly with the use of a creative thinking process. While employing the constructivism framework, facilitation is designed so that students can explore concepts and formalize decisions to solve problems. This can happen when creativity and arts are incorporated into content to enhance the learning process. Table 11.1 depicts the parallels in creativity and constructivist learning with broad categories grounding how creativity and constructivist learning are aligned with each other.

The authors are interested in examining the equity gap concerning access to arts education between high and low-income students situated in urban schools. More specifically, the authors are interested in Canada's use of arts in education and whether arts integration may contribute to higher math and reading scores of low income urban students, and then following how this concept can be transferred to schools systems in the

Table 11.1.   Relationship Between Creativity and Constructivist Learning

Component	Characteristic of Creativity	Characteristic of Constructivist Learning
• Unique presentation	• Need for originality	• Multiple representations of reality
• Perspectives	• Ability to see different aspects of problems	• Collaborative construction of knowledge
• Knowledge construction	• New ideas for blended knowledge construction	• Context and content knowledge construction
• Real-world creation	• Imaginative solutions to real- world issues	• Real-world, case-based learning
• Reflection	• Reflection on things and experiences that hold interest	• Thoughtful reflection on experience
• Associative orientation	• Meaningful context over abstract instruction	• Transitions between fact and fiction

Sources: Bruner (1996) and Piirto (2004).

United States. The results may suggest an avenue for improved academic achievement for urban students in the United States. While retrieving data for further exploration, the authors examine the performance of Canadian students on the PISA exams and whether there is a connection to creativity and arts integration in education. Although further research is needed to support conjectures, the authors argue for increased emphasis on arts integration, calling attention to the cycle of creativity and critical thinking that may lead to increased academic achievement.

DIFFERENCES AMONG NEIGHBORS

Canada was selected as a country for this study to explore how the emphasis of the arts in curricular integration might positively impact student performance. Canada is used as an example of a country that has public school systems that intentionally integrate the arts in academics to influence achievement in core subject matter (Fullan, 2014). Findings from this analysis might provide insights for countries with lower student achievement, such as the United States (Hanley et al., 2006). Further, the inequitable access to arts education in the United States, a divide that often runs along racial and socioeconomic lines, deserves attention and remediation. A deep investigation of the international academic scores helps with the analysis of student achievement in the education systems within these countries. As an outcome of learning, academic achievement is typically measured by classroom grades, classroom assessments, and external achievement tests (Darling-Hammond, 2010). For international comparison, the PISA examinations are most often used. The results of the PISA, listed in Table 11.2, show Canadian students scoring higher than U.S. students in both math and reading.

The case of Canada depicts how creativity and arts integration may be the key to academic success through education reform (Fullan, 2014; Hanley et al., 2006), highlighting the largest school system in Canada, the Toronto District School Board spending a decade (2003–2013) devoted to

Table 11.2. PISA 2015 Results

Country	Reading Literacy	Math Literacy
Canada	527	516
United States	497	470
OECD average	493	490

Source: NCES (2018).

education reform eventually showing links to student achievement across the entire country. The Canadian education system fosters creativity and invests in the arts for their students. They insert music and arts programs in curriculum employing interdisciplinary arts education inclusive of pre-service and in-service teacher education in the arts (Hanley et al., 2006). Additionally, Learning Through the Arts (LTTA) has partnered with schools in Canada to include the use of the visual arts in lesson plans for not only the core curriculum but other subjects as well (Eger, 2011). The Royal Conservatory of Music in Toronto launched LTTA in 1994 as a simple inspiring idea to weave the arts into all learning so that students become more engaged and instruction more vivid and memorable (Learning Through the Arts, n.d.).

Furthermore, according to Fullan (2014), school reform has been successful in Canada based on a "push" and "pull" interplay that enables big school systems to improve student achievement. Key points to support this initiative are that leaders must push to challenge the status quo, convey a high sense of urgency, and have the courage needed to intervene, yet they need to also pull together to create a commonly-owned strategy, develop professional power, and attend to sustainability (Fullan, 2014). The elements of school reform in Canada focus on policies and strategies that help reduce the achievement gap for the disadvantaged in large urban schools (Fullan, 2014). In particular, a Canadian strategy that may offer success for large urban school systems in the U.S. is the use of assessment tools as a key driver in teaching and learning. As further explained, assessment played a key role in the establishment of arts programming that was developed and widely implemented across the country.

Assessing Creativity

Canada uses the TTCT for assessing creativity in students' success. This test is used to measure a person's creativity to gauge the impact of divergent thinking skills, critical thinking skills, and problem-solving skills (Kim, 2017). The TTCT consists of two components where each is expressed in two different modalities (drawn and orally). The oral test (TTCT-V) has six activities starting with a picture and the test taker responds to the picture in writing. The scoring components include fluency (measured by the number of relevant ideas to the picture), originality (measured by the unusualness of the ideas) and flexibility (measured by the variety of different types of ideas). The figural component (TTCT-F) consists of three activities of picture construction, picture completion, and repeated figures of lines. The subscales include fluency, originality, elaboration, abstractness of titles, and resistance to premature closure.

The TTCT appears to be an effective measure for discovering and encouraging everyday life processes to nurture and enhance creativity among students (Clapham, 1998; Torrance, 2008). One of the suggested uses for the test is to evaluate the effects of educational programs, materials, curricula and teaching procedures (Torrance, 1974), and it also serves as a means for emphasizing classroom experiences that stimulate creativity in students and teachers (Swartz, 1988). A main focus of the test is understanding and nurturing qualities that help people express their creativity (Kim, 2006). The TTCT appears to be the best option for creativity assessment as research has shown Canadian students fare significantly better than students in other countries indicating education environments that foster creativity are beneficial for student success (Dishke Hondzel et al., 2014).

Investing in Creativity and the Arts

Canadian education systems invest in the arts for their students (Colby, 2011; Favaro, 1999; Roberts, 1998). Additionally, multiple arts initiatives are generated through LTTA. These developments encourage lessons in science, technology, engineering, art, and math (STEAM) within the curriculum in Canadian schools. Consequently, key curriculum outcomes in Canada identify what students are expected to know and be able to do by the end of Grades 3, 6, 9, and 12 in connection to their cumulative learning experiences in arts education (Department of Education, 2001). As an International Monetary Fund (IMF) member, the level of funds managed within Canada allows governmental systems the ability to allocate funding toward education within their school system's budgets. Although the U.S. also has a strong relationship with the IMF, contributes considerably more money to the IMF than Canada, and receives more interest on its monetary contribution, Canada allocates more funding toward arts in education from their budgets. In Canada, there is not one federal government controlled or funded state school system as in the United States; therefore, state-funded provincial schools in Canada are the responsibility of individual provincial departments of education and funded mainly from local and provincial taxes, with some additional federal funds. This allows the schools in Canada to allocate more funding to the arts and adopt programs across the country like LTTA. These are some fundamental differences between arts education funding in the United States and Canada leaving an impact on academic achievement between low income and high-income students in the United States (Colby, 2011; Education Quality and Accountability Office, 2017; Favaro, 1999; NCES, 2019; Roberts, 1998).

DISCUSSION

Infusing the arts into public school curriculum offers numerous academic and affective benefits for students. Notably, arts integration increases leadership capacity for students by equipping them to be creative, strengthen problem-solving ability, and build collaboration and communication skills, all of which prepare students for life (Appel, 2006). A constructivist approach to teaching and learning allows the integration and education of the arts to provide enriched learning and teaching environments where teachers become facilitators of meaningful and engaging activities and lessons that increase student achievement. Disproportionately, students of color and students of lower-income families have even less access to arts-rich curricula and thus less opportunity to experience the advantages associated with arts education (Parsad et al., 2012; Rabkin & Hedberg, 2011). The purpose of this chapter was to examine this inequitable gap of access to arts education in the United States and to propose solutions toward its remediation.

Canada provides an example of educational success by linking creativity and the arts to student performance. Though the United States and Canada are both economically robust nations, and both encompass large urban school systems, there are great differences in their undertakings of educational reform and, consequently, student achievement. Creativity is nurtured in Canadian students with intentional curricular decisions to support arts integration from K–12 education all the way to preservice and in-service teacher education. The country has embraced the LTTA program throughout its schools that has proven success in academic areas. Additionally, students take the TTCT to explore further creativity development. This creativity test is widely used in Canadian schools to foster the idea of creativity as a tool that can be used in problem solving. Finally, Canada has intentionally invested in arts integration programs, positioning itself with the ability to continuously allocate funding toward the arts and education. Such decisions and structures create longevity for quality arts education for all students.

In an effort to remain solution focused, the U.S. can learn a great deal from the example that Canada has set. As an attempt to analyze arts integration and education in U.S. schools, North Carolina implemented the A+ Schools Program in 1995, as a school reform movement, and has maintained an active network of 40 schools and is continuing to grow annually (Whiteman, 2014). The program is a successful arts-based school reform program that started in schools in North Carolina and became a movement across the country (Robelen, 2012). Although there are core essentials at the foundation of the program, including a heavy dose of the arts, teacher collaboration, experiential learning, and exploration of multiple intelligences among students (Robelen, 2012), the requirements for A+ schools are not uniform, and the approach does not prescribe a specific curriculum, methodology or process of implementation (Whiteman, 2014). Thus, lamentably, this approach fails to provide a consistent approach to arts education in all U.S. schools.

Given these contexts, it is worth exploring these questions: Would it be beneficial for the U.S. to study what Canada is doing with arts education? Would it be beneficial for U.S. schools to focus more on fostering creativity? Would it be beneficial for U.S. schools to embrace the use of the TTCT for its students? Could the use of consistent arts-based program across the country impact achievement and standardized test scores? This chapter highlights a relationship among creativity, critical thinking, arts integration, and academic achievement. Could this focus on student creativity and arts integration help boost academic achievement? Could an arts-rich curriculum, which allows students to draw on the 21st century skills of problem-solving and critical thinking, lead to improved life outcomes such as employment and community engagement?

Most critically, these questions should be posed in relation to the already existing disparities in student achievement in the United States. Certainly this inequitable exposure to the arts is among the numerous opportunities afforded disproportionately to White, upper-class students, particularly among the segregated contexts of schools. Thus, the authors prudently urge: how could enhanced educational opportunities with the arts help narrow the divide between low-achieving and high-achieving schools in the United States? Perhaps more significantly, how could the schooling experiences and educational outcomes of students of color and students from lower-income families be improved with increased access to the arts?

The findings of this analysis suggest that there is a relationship between creativity and the arts with achievement of students in Canada, which also shows that arts integration is used as a technique in Canada to help students succeed academically. These decisions and curricular reform did not occur overnight. In order to see this creativity/achievement relationship in the United States, numerous changes must occur. Implications of this analysis point toward increased funding for the arts in education—reversing the cuts that have come with recent legislation. Thus, implications also suggest the need for policy development across various levels of government bodies to elevate the value of the arts in schools. A redesign of curriculum to infuse the arts along with changes to assessments would need to be made. Finally, teacher education and continued professional development needs to include the arts as integral components of pedagogy and practice.

Future research should include robust studies that examine potential correlations between arts education and integration with low-income urban students in the U.S. with achievement scores. Additionally, future research should include longitudinal studies tracking strategic arts education with low-income urban students and their career success. Supplementary research will also help with these efforts to propel the arts in schools in the United States. Case studies that provide detailed examination of successful arts integration programs in certain countries, such as Canada, and explicate the curricular development in particular districts would be beneficial. Lastly, the implementation and use of the CACA model for students in large, urban school systems is another research focus to examine the implication that the use of the model has on the achievement of low-income urban students in the United States. Overall, the findings in this paper indicate that learning through the arts can be an effective strategy for countries to broadly research, create policy, design, and implement curriculum to support improving the achievement scores of urban students in the United States to help close the divide within.

REFERENCES

Appel, M. (2006). Arts integration across the curriculum. *Leadership, 36*(2), 14–17.

Bruner, J. (1996). *The culture of education.* Harvard University Press.

Catterall, J., Dumais, S., & Hampden-Thompson, G. (2012). *The arts and achievement in at-risk youth: Findings from four longitudinal studies* (Research Report #5). National Endowment for the Arts. https://www.arts.gov/sites/default/files/Arts-At-Risk-Youth.pdf

Clapham, M. (1998). Structure of figural forms A and B of the Torrance Tests of Creative Thinking. *Educational and Psychological Measurement, 58*(2), 275–283. https://doi.org/10.1177/0013164498058002010

Coate, K., & Boulos, A. (2012). Creativity in education: Challenging the assumptions. *London Review of Education, 10*(2), 129–132. https://doi.org/10.1080/14748460.2012.691278

Colby, S. (2011). Multicultural arts education in the post-secondary context?: Creating installation and performance art in Surrey, Canada. *International Journal of Multicultural Education, 13*(1), 11. https://doi.org/10.18251/ijme.v13i1.328

Crawford, L. (2004). *Lively learning: Using the arts to teach the K–8 curriculum.* Northeast Foundation for Children.

Darling-Hammond, L. (2010). *The flat world and education: How America's commitment to equity will determine our future.* Teachers College Press.

Dean, D. (2014). *Comparing standardized test scores among arts-integrated and non-arts integrated schools in Central Mississippi* (Publication No. 3583303) [Doctoral dissertation, University of Phoenix]. ProQuest.

Department of Education. (2001). *Arts education foundation.* https://www2.gnb.ca/content/dam/gnb/Departments/ed/pdf/K12/curric/Arts/ArtsEducation.pdf

Dishke Hondzel, C., Hansen, R., Guilliksen, M., & Lindfors, E. (2014). *Creativity and the environment: Looking at differences between Canadian, Norwegian and Finnish Students on the TTCT*. https://www.edu.uwo.ca/HIRG/documents/CSSE%20May%202014.pdf

Education Quality and Accountability Office (EQAO). (2017). *Highlights of the provincial results*. http://www.eqao.com/en/assessments/results/communication-docs/provincial-report-highlights-elementary-2017.pdf

Eger, J. (2011, May 25). Arts integration in Canada: America's wake up call. *Huffington Post*. https://www.huffpost.com/entry/if-you-want-to-reinvent-t_b_821086

Farkas Duffett Research Group. (2012). *Learning less: Public school teachers describe a narrowing curriculum: A report for common core*. Common Core.

Favaro, E. (1999). A vision for arts education in Canada: A report from the national symposium on arts education. *A Fine FACTA, 1*(2), 48–49. http://search.proquest.com/docview/224714698/

Finn, P. (2015). *Critical condition: Replacing critical thinking with creativity*. Wilfrid Laurier University Press.

Fiske, E. (1999). *Champions of change: The impact of the arts on learning*. Arts Education Partnership.

Fullan, M. (2014). *Big-city school reforms: Lessons from New York, Toronto, and London*. Teachers College Press.

Greene, M. (1995). *Releasing the imagination: Essays on education, the arts, and social change*. Jossey-Bass.

Hanley, B., Favaro, E., & Pearse, H. (2006). Principal themes: Coalition for arts education in Canada (CAEC)—Report on arts education for the Canadian commission for UNESCO: Consultation on arts and learning, June 22, 2005. *Canadian Music Educator, 47*(4), 40–43. http://search.proquest.com/docview/1029591/

Kim, K. (2006). Can we trust creativity tests? A Review of the Torrance Tests of Creative Thinking (TTCT). *Creativity Research Journal, 18*(1), 3–14. https://doi.org/10.1207/s15326934crj1801_2

Kim, K. (2017). The Torrance Tests of Creative Thinking - figural or verbal: Which one should we use? *Creativity. Theories–Research–Applications, 4*(2), 302–321. https://doi.org/10.1515/ctra-2017-0015

Lau, J. (2011). *An introduction to critical thinking and creativity: Think more, think better*. Wiley.

Learning Through the Arts. (2019, May 5). http://www.indigenousartists.ca/ltta/

Leicester, M., & Taylor, D. (2010). *Critical thinking across the curriculum: Developing critical thinking skills, literacy and philosophy in the primary classroom*. Open University Press.

Lichtenberg, J., Woock, C., & Wright, M. (2008). *Ready to innovate: Are educators and executives aligned on the creative readiness of the U.S. workforce?* (Research Report 1424). The Conference Board.

Madej, K., Judson, G., & Egan, K. (2015). *Engaging imagination and developing creativity in education* (2nd ed.). Cambridge Scholars Publishing.

Naiditch, F. (2016). *Developing critical thinking: From theory to classroom practice*. Rowman & Littlefield.

National Center for Education Statistics (NCES). (2018, December 12). https://nces.ed.gov/surveys/pisa/pisa2015/index.asp

National Center for Educational Statistics (NCES), *Nation's Report Card*. (2019, February 3). https://nces.ed.gov/nationsreportcard/subject/publications/dst2017/pdf/2018040xn8.pdf

Parsad, B., Spiegelman, M., & Coopersmith, J. (2012). *Arts education in public elementary and secondary schools, 1999-2000 and 2009-10*. National Center for Education Statistics. https://nces.ed.gov/pubs2012/2012014rev.pdf

Piirto, J. (2004). *Understanding creativity*. Great Potential Press.

Rabkin, N., & Hedberg, E. (2011). *Arts education in America: What the declines mean for arts participation*. National Endowment for the Arts.https://permanent.access.gpo.gov/gpo34263/2008-SPPA-ArtsLearning.pdf

Robelen, E. W. (2012). A+ schools infuse arts and other essentials. *Education Week*. https://www.edweek.org/ew/articles/2012/11/27/13arts_ep.h31.html

Roberts, B. (1998). *Connect, combine, communicate: Revitalizing the arts in Canadian schools*. University College of Cape Breton Press.

Sawyer, R. (2012). *Explaining creativity the science of human innovation* (2nd ed.). Oxford University Press.

Silverstein, L., B., & Layne, S. (2010). *Defining arts integration*. http://www.artsintegrationpd.org/wp-content/uploads/2017/07/What-is-Arts-Integration.pdf

Swartz, J. D. (1988). Torrance Tests of Creative Thinking. In D. J. Keyser & R. C. Sweetland (Eds.), *Test critique* (Vol. 7, pp. 619–622). Test Corporation of America.

Torrance, E. P. (1974). *The Torrance Tests of Creative Thinking-norms-technical manual research edition-verbal tests, forms A and B- figural tests, forms A and B*. Personnel Press.

Torrance, E. P. (2008). *The Torrance Tests of Creative Thinking norms-technical manual figural (Streamlined) forms A & B*. Scholastic Testing Services.

Torrance, E., & Safter, H. (1990). The *incubation model of teaching Getting beyond the aha!*. Bearly.

Whiteman, W. B. (2014). *Arts-based school reform: Adaptations of the A+ schools program in three unique contexts*. https://files.nc.gov/ncaplus/pdf/AplusCaseStudies-Final.pdf

Winner, E., Hetland, L., Catterall, J., Deasy, R., & Arts Education Partnership. (2002). *Critical links: Learning in the arts and student academic and social development*. http://hdl.handle.net/2027/mdp.39015064205522

CHAPTER 12

UNDERSTANDING UNITED STATES ECONOMIC INEQUALITY AND THE STRAIN ON OUR DEMOCRACY

James E. Davis
Former Executive Director
of the Social Science Education Consortium

ABSTRACT

This chapter addresses a continuing problem of injustice in the United States—income and wealth inequality and the impact of this inequality on our democracy. The chapter introduces the reader to macroeconomic analysis and the basics of fiscal and monetary policy. Using current available information, the unequal distribution of income is addressed and the more serious matter of wealth inequality is examined. The impact of these 2 issues of economic inequality on our democracy is discussed in some detail, particularly the matter of current extensive poverty in the United States. Seven proposals are presented with associated discussion.

The Divide Within: Intersections of Realities, Facts, Theories, and Practices
pp. 223–249

INTRODUCTION

Kathy and Roger Duvall, brother and sister, are walking home from high school in a United States urban area. Here is some of their conversation:

Kathy: You know those rich people on the hill, the Sumpters? Have you ever seen them? One time I saw them driving home in their shiny new Mercedes.

Roger: The red one or the black one? They've got two. With that wall around their mansion and a guard at the gate, the only people allowed in and out are other rich people.

Kathy: Both our parents work—real hard, every day—and we don't have any of that. Mom cleans motel rooms, and never catches a break. She still gets dinner on the table for us every night, too.

Roger: Yeah, and Dad busts his butt hauling garbage. He's been doing that for over 20 years. He says his back hurts all the time, but he doesn't know what else he could do for a living. He says he didn't finish high school—I guess that's why he gets on us about our grades.

No doubt, something like this conversation could be heard in many places in the United States. Kathy and Roger's conversation highlights significant differences in the financial well-being (the wealth) between the two families. Keep in mind that at least four factors can be used to identify characteristics of any family: income, education, property, and spending. The purpose of this chapter is twofold: (1) to shed light on the economic divide between rich and poor in America, and (2) to explain how this economic divide contributes to the political divides (the privileged and the forgotten) that have become more acute in recent years.

Clearly, the Sumpters have more income—much more—than the Duvalls, as witnessed by the expensive cars the Sumpters drive and the mansion they own. It is reasonable to presume that the Sumpter adults have more education than the Duvalls, as Mr. Duvall did not finish high school. Clearly, the Sumpters have a mansion and many other items as their property, while the Duvalls have significantly less property. It is likely that the Duvalls spend almost all their income on food, clothing, and shelter (their basics), while the Sumpters likely spend a significantly smaller percentage of their income on these basics. And, after paying for their basics, the Sumpters have significant funds remaining. It is a certainty from their balance sheet data below that the Sumpters have much more wealth than the Duvalls.

The Balance Sheet Measure

One relatively simple way to quantify the wealth difference between the Duvalls and the Sumpters is to look at hypothetical balance sheets of the two families. A balance sheet states the monetary status of an entity (an individual, a family, a business) at some point in time. A balance sheet lists assets—what is owned, such as a car, a house or mansion, a savings account, or stocks and bonds. The balance sheet also lists liabilities—what is owed, such as a house mortgage or credit card debt. A final calculation in a balance sheet is net worth. Net worth is calculated by subtracting liabilities from assets (ASSETS – LIABILITIES = NET WORTH). Net worth is a good indicator of the wealth status of an individual, family, or business.

Hypothetical Balance Sheets

In Figure 12.1 are hypothetical balance sheets for the Sumpters and the Duvalls as of June 1, 2019. The balance sheets have been simplified to include only major assets and liabilities.

Clearly, the Sumpters have much more wealth than the Duvalls. The Sumpters are very well off. Some would say they are very rich. The Sumpters' Net Worth is $16,802,000 more than that of the Duvalls ($16,820,000 – $18,000 = $16,802,000). If the Sumpters had a health crisis, they could take care of it rather easily. However, if the Duvalls had a health crisis, they would be in financial difficulty, as they have only $1000 in savings, and they are most likely living paycheck to paycheck. This comparison is a case that wealth is clearly unequally distributed. This also happens to be the case of all wealth in the United States. In 2016, the wealthiest 20% of households in the United States owned 77% of the wealth in the country, with the wealthiest 1% owning 29% of national household wealth (Sawhill & Pulliam, 2019). The social science discipline of economics can help us explain the causes and consequences of wealth and income inequality. Now we turn to a brief study of economics to provide an analytical background to study wealth and income inequality in the United States in some depth.

INTRODUCTION TO ECONOMICS

This chapter focuses on wealth and income inequality in the United States—inequality not unlike you have just read about at the beginning of this chapter on the net worth statements of the Sumpters and the Duvalls. Economists generally agree that the increasing trend toward growing wealth and income inequality is a macroeconomic problem. This suggests

Sumpter Balance Sheet: June 1, 2019

Assets

Mansion	$10,000,000
Automobiles	120,000
Artwork	3,000,000
Stocks and Bonds	8,000,000
Total Assets	$21,120,000

Liabilities

Mansion Mortgage	$3,000,000
Credit Card Debt	300,000
Bank Loans	1,000,000
Total Liabilities	$4,300,000
Net Worth	$16,820,000

Duvall Balance Sheet: June 1, 2019

Assets

House	$40,000
Savings Account	1,000
Automobile	2,000
Total Assets	$43,000

Liabilities

Mortgage	$23,000
Credit Card Debt	2,000
Total Liabilities	$25,000
Net Worth	$18,000

Figure 12.1.

that policy measures to stem the tide of income and wealth inequality need to come from federal government policy, hopefully in collaboration with state and local governments. The federal government policy would include changes in tax policy, changes in government spending, and changes in monetary policy. The changes in monetary policy could include lowering the interest rate, which would expand the money supply. Before we analyze the two inequality situations, we turn to a brief introduction of macroeconomics to provide a background on the analytical tools and policy measures changing the current situation of wealth and income inequality in the United States.

Economics is a social science that examines the relationship between human wants and the resources available to satisfy those wants. People's wants exceed the goods and services they can purchase to satisfy those wants. This condition is called *scarcity*. We cannot have everything we want because we do not have the resources to purchase everything we want. This situation means that we must make decisions to satisfy our highest priority wants. People try to make the best economic decisions they can to satisfy their wants. Often, people think about the costs and benefits of making an economic decision. Determining costs and benefits allows people to make their own best economic decisions. This decisionmaking problem faces people and businesses everyday as they go about their economic lives.

One area of study in economics involves examination of the economic decisionmaking of individuals, businesses, and even government. This study of small economic units, such as an individual family, a business, or even a local government unit is called *microeconomics*. Microeconomics also examines individual markets, particular prices, and production of specific goods and services.

A second study of economics is called *macroeconomics*. Macroeconomics examines the economy as a whole. This includes the study of aggregates, such as households, businesses, government and governmental sectors. Of particular interest is the study of measures of the total economy. You no doubt have heard on the news such terms as gross national product, gross domestic product, inflation rate, and the unemployment rate. Our monetary system is also part of the macroeconomy. You may have heard such terms as *prime interest rate* and *money supply*. As we examine income and wealth inequality, we will refer to the policy aspects of the macroeconomy and our monetary system.

Macroeconomics: The Basics

National income analysis represents the core of macroeconomics. This analysis examines annually all consumption spending (C), gross private domestic investment (I), all government expenditures (G), and net exports—exports minus imports (E-N). The sum of these four categories of spending results in what is called *nominal gross domestic product* or GDP. Table 12.1 shows the actual nominal GDP for the years 1998, 2008, and 2018, with a projection of spending to 2028. The term "nominal" in the Table 1 title means the data are reported in current prices. That is, the figures have not been adjusted for inflation. GDP is the total value of all final goods and services produced annually within the boundaries of the United States during a given year.

Here is how to read Table 12.1. At the top of the table, the figures are stated in billions of dollars. This means that GDP in 1998 was 9,062.8 billion dollars. Another way to state this is that GDP in 1998 was 9 trillion, 62 billion, 8 million dollars. In 2018, the nominal GDP was over 20 trillion dollars ($20,494.1 billion). It is important to note the section to the right of the dollar figures. This section shows the percentage distribution

Table 12.1.   Nominal Gross Domestic Product
by Major Demand Category

Category	Billions of Current Dollars				Percent Distribution			
	1998	2008	2018	2028	1998	2008	2018	2028
Gross Domestic Product	9,062.8	14,712.8	20,494.1	30,493.1	100.0	100.0	100.0	100.0
• Personal consumption expenditures	5,877.2	9,976.3	13,948.5	20,750.4	64.8	67.8	68.1	68.0
• Gross private domestic investment	1,736.7	2,477.6	3,650.1	5,822.0	19.2	16.8	17.8	19.1
• Exports	953.0	1,837.1	2,531.3	3,891.0	10.5	12.15	12.4	12.8
• Imports	1,115.7	2,560.1	3,156.7	4,711.5	12.3	17.4	15.4	15.5
• Government consumption expenditures and gross investment	1,611.6	2,982.0	3,520.8	4,741.3	17.8	20.3	17.2	15.5
o Federal defense	368.8	750.3	778.9	945.5	4.1	5.1	3.8	3.1
o Federal nondefense	216.8	400.2	540.9	632.1	2.4	2.7	2.6	2.1
o State and local	1,026.1	1,831.4	2,201.0	3,163.7	11.3	12.4	10.7	10.4

Source: U.S. Bureau of Labor Statistics (2019).

of the GDP for each spending category. Personal consumption for 2018 was 68.1% of GDP. In the business news it is commonly reported that consumption (personal consumption by households) is about two thirds of GDP.

Table 12.1 shows the spending or expenditure approach to GDP. Personal or household consumption (C) includes durable goods, such as automobiles, nondurable goods, such as food, and services, such as health care. Gross Private Domestic Investment (I) includes business purchases of machines, buildings, and inventory that has not been sold. Government spending (G) includes the purchase of battleships, bridges, and police protection. Exports include sales of soybeans to foreign countries and U.S. banking services used by non-U.S. countries. Imports include such things as purchases of Japanese automobiles and flights on Spanish airlines. Arithmetically, the equation for nominal GDP is as follows: GDP = C + I + G + (E-N). A common term for the sum of components of GDP is called *aggregate demand*, as each component of GDP represents the demand for goods or services.

We need to complete the picture of national income analysis by looking at the income approach to GDP. This is the flip side of the demand or spending approach to GDP presented above. Briefly stated below are five categories of income in the macroeconomy:

1.   Employee compensation. This is the largest income category and includes wages and salaries paid to labor by both businesses and government.
2.   Rents. Rent is the payment made to households and businesses. Included are rent paid to landlords and lease payments by business for office space use.
3.   Interest. Interest is paid to households on their savings deposits, on their certificates of deposits, and on their corporate bonds.
4.   Profits to business owners. Both individual business owners and partnerships seek profits—money left after all business costs have been paid.
5.   Corporate profits. Corporations seek profits and they pay income taxes on their profits to both the federal and state governments. Corporations pay dividends from their profits to stockholders. Undistributed corporate profits are kept by corporations to invest in inventory, property, and equipment.

Fiscal Policy

Actions of our federal government to make changes in taxes and/or government spending is called fiscal policy. Essentially, the legislation that permits the federal government to change taxes and government spending comes from *The Employment Act of 1946*. The Act states in part that

> The Congress hereby declares that it is the continuing responsibility of the Federal Government to use all practicable means … to foster and promote free competitive enterprise and the general welfare, conditions under which there will be afforded useful employment opportunities, including self-employment, for those able, willing, and seeking to work and to promote maximum employment, production, and purchasing power. (McConnell & Brue, 1999, p. 244)

The action or actions government may take is called *fiscal policy*. If there is a recession, a downturn in economic activity, the federal government may implement expansionary fiscal policy. The federal government may implement three possible fiscal policy options: (1) increase government spending, (2) reduce taxes, or (3) some combination of the two. If there is a general increase in prices, called inflation, the federal government also has three options: (1) to decrease government spending, (2) to increase taxes, and/or (3) some combination the decreasing government spending and increasing taxes. The fiscal policy goal is to stabilize the economy.

There is much more to say on this topic, which gets into the realm of politics. Those policy makers who are considered liberal are likely to favor increased government spending and/or tax reduction case of recession. Those who are considered conservative may usually favor tax cuts in times of recession or spending reductions in times of inflation.

Money and Banking

Some folks say that money is good for nothing except to get rid of it. You can't eat it. You can't wear it. You can't live in it. For many, money is a troubling puzzle. We will unravel this puzzle by considering the essence of money and our banking system.

Money performs three major functions. Money serves as a medium of exchange. This function allows the holder of money to easily purchase goods and services. A second function of money is that it is a unit of account. This function allows sellers and buyers to state the price of goods and services in terms of dollars and cents. The third function of money is that it is a store of value. This function allows a person the convenience of ownership. It is a convenient way to store wealth, usually by putting money in a bank.

The most common use of money is as currency—coins and paper bills in the hands of individuals, who use currency to purchase goods and services. Many people also have bank checking accounts—demand deposits—in commercial banks. These deposits are debts of commercial banks or savings institutions. The debts represent what the banks or savings institutions owe people or businesses who own accounts.

Some people think a credit card is money. It is the case that a bank debit card in very close to money. That is, if you use a debit card to make a purchase, the information of the purchase reaches your bank and the amount of the purchase is deducted from your checking account. A credit card, such as a Visa or Mastercard, is a convenient way to buy things. But a credit card is not really money. It represents a short term loan from the financial institution or the store that issued you the credit card.

All money in the United States is considered debt money. The paper money you have is debt of some Federal Reserve Bank. Look at any United States paper bill. The top should read "Federal Reserve Note." In small type, also near the top of the bill, it states, "THIS NOTE IS LEGAL TENDER FOR ALL DEBTS, PUBLIC AND PRIVATE." The United States no longer has a gold standard, which allowed people who held paper notes to exchange them for gold. You can only exchange a Federal Reserve Note for another Note. Our confidence in our money supply is a matter of law, but also our currency must be accepted as a medium of exchange.

The Federal Reserve System

The Federal Reserve System, often referred to as "The Fed," is the central bank of the United States. It was founded by Congress in 1913 to provide the nation with a safer, more flexible, and more stable monetary and financial system. Accordingly, The Fed has four major duties:

- conducting the nation's monetary policy by influencing the money and credit conditions in the economy in pursuit of full employment and stable prices;
- supervising and regulating banking institutions to ensure the safety and soundness of the nation's banking and financial system and to protect the credit rights of consumers;
- maintaining the stability of the financial system and containing systemic risk that may arise in financial markets; and
- providing certain financial services to the U.S. government, to the public, to financial institutions, including playing a major role in

operating the nation's payment system. (Board of Governors of the Federal Reserve System, 2016)

Central to The Fed is the Board of Governors, which consists of seven members, serving for 14 years and staggered so that one member is replaced every 2 years. The purpose of this is to provide continuity, as well as independence from political pressures in decisionmaking. There are 12 Federal Reserve Banks, which serve a region of the United States. Look at a Federal Reserve Note and you will see four numbers close to the corners of the note. A "12" means that the note was issued by the San Francisco, CA, Federal Reserve Bank; a "5" means the note was issued by the Richmond, VA, Federal Reserve Bank.

The Fed and the Money Supply

There are seven tasks of The Fed to carry out its duties. These include the following:

1. The Fed issues currency. These are Federal Reserve Notes (paper currency).
2. The Fed sets reserve requirements. Based on a bank's money deposits, The Fed requires a percentage of deposits be set aside as reserves.
3. The Fed lends money to banks and certain thrift institutions. The rate The Fed charges is called the *discount rate*.
4. The Fed provides for collecting checks. If a check is written in Charlotte, NC, to an organization in Boston, MA, in 2 or 3 days, the check "clears" and the bank deposit in Charlotte is reduced and the bank deposit in Boston is credited.
5. The Fed acts as a fiscal agent. The federal government collects taxes and spends a lot of money. The Fed acts as the bank for the federal government.
6. The Fed supervises bank operations. Commercial banks must adhere to many regulations, and The Fed is responsible for seeing to it that banks not only fulfill the regulations, but also detect fraud.
7. The Fed controls the money supply. This is probably the most important function of The Fed. The Fed is responsible for setting interest rates and controlling the nation's money supply with a goal to support full employment and control inflation.

It is not commonly known that banks must balance their accounts daily. This is a Federal Reserve rule. If a bank is short on its required reserves, it may borrow funds to meet its reserve requirement. Usually, a bank short of required reserves may borrow funds from another bank that has excess reserves in the federal funds market. The rate of interest charged on this borrowing is called the Federal Funds Rate.

Summary: Tools of Fiscal and Monetary Policy

The fiscal policy tools of the federal government are twofold: increasing or decreasing government spending and increasing or decreasing federal taxes to maintain economic stability and predictability. Increasing government spending and/or decreasing taxes tends to stimulate the economy, while decreasing government spending or increasing taxes tends to slow down the economy.

Monetary policy tools include increasing or decreasing required bank reserves, increasing or decreasing the discount rate, increasing or decreasing the Federal Funds Rate. If bank reserves are increased, banks have less money to lend, thereby slowing down economic activity. A decrease in the bank reserve requirement allows banks to lend more money, thereby stimulating economic activity. The discount rate and the Federal Funds Rate are both interest rates, which are essentially the price of borrowing money. An increase in an interest rate discourages borrowing money, while a decrease in an interest tends to encourage borrowing.

The reader may be wondering at this point in the chapter why all the information on the macroeconomy has been presented. Knowing about government spending, taxation, and interest rates as analytical policy tools is critical to examining what may happen if certain government policies are implemented to try to change the nature of economic inequality. Almost daily government fiscal or monetary policies are reported in the news. Several policy recommendations for changing income and wealth inequality will be stated toward at the end of this chapter, and the reader has the opportunity to decide what policy or policies may be appropriate. After thinking about possible solutions to the problem below, the problems of income and wealth inequality are addressed.

INCOME AND WEALTH INEQUALITY IN THE UNITED STATES

When we talk about inequality, we are talking about how something is distributed unequally. If 50 marbles are equally distributed among ten students, each student would receive 5 marbles. This would be an equal distribution. However, if one student receives 14 marbles and the other nine students receive four marbles each from the remaining 36 marbles,

Problem

The 2019 labor force in the United States includes 163,000,000 people. In April 2019, the unemployment rate of the labor force was 3.8% or 6.2 million people. Economists view this unemployment rate as relatively full employment. Assume that by April of 2020, the unemployment rate reaches 8%, or about 13 million people. Clearly, this increase in unemployment means that the U.S. economy was in a recession, approaching a depression. It is known that a large percentage of the unemployed are African Americans and women in the fields of retail trade, construction, and food service.

Questions

To correct this situation, what fiscal policy tools would you recommend?
What monetary policy tools would you recommend? What else would you recommend?

Figure 12.2.   A problem to think about.

this would an unequal distribution of the marbles. If one student receives 41 marbles and the remaining students receive one marble each, this distribution would represent significant inequality.

Income Inequality

With respect to income, the highest earning 20% of U.S. households received more than half of the total U.S. income in 2018 (Schaeffer, 2020). Most of the growth in income inequality has been between the middle class and the top earners, with the disparity widening the farther one goes up the income distribution percentage. Fewer households now constitute the middle-income tier, with percentages dropping from 61% in 1971 to 51% in 2019. The percentage of families in the lower income tier has increased from 25% to 29% over the same time period (Schaeffer, 2020).

The Federal Reserve conducts a Survey of Consumer Finances (SCF) every 3 years. The SCF examines family incomes, net worth, balance sheet components, credit use, and other financial matters. The 2016 SCF (Bricker et al., 2017) showed gains in income and net worth between 2013 and 2016. This report showed some positive economic data. Real gross domestic product (gross domestic product adjusted for inflation) grew; civilian unemployment fell; and the consumer price index rose slightly.

Here are the major observations from the 2016 SCF report, as prepared by Bricker and colleagues (2017):

- Between 2013 and 2016, median family income grew 10%, and mean family income grew 14%.
- Families throughout the income distribution experienced gains in average real incomes between 2013 and 2016, reversing the trend from 2010 and 2013, when real incomes fell or remained stagnant *for all but the top of the income distribution* [emphasis added].
- Families at the top of the income distribution saw larger gains in income between 2013 and 2016 than other families, *consistent with widening income inequality* [emphasis added].
- Families without a high school diploma and nonwhite and Hispanic families experienced larger proportional gains in incomes than other families between 2013 and 2016, although more-educated families and white non-Hispanic families continue to have higher incomes that other families. (p. 1)

Here is another look at the situation of income inequality. How would you react to the following headline: "80% of U.S. adults face near-poverty, unemployment, survey finds"? It seems pretty frightening, doesn't it? This is a headline from the Associated Press that appeared in a CBS news article July 28, 2013, which indicated that "four out of five adults in the United States struggle with joblessness, near-poverty or a reliance on welfare for at least part of their lives, a sign of deteriorating economic security and an elusive American dream" (para 1). The article goes on to state,

While racial and ethnic minorities are more likely to live in poverty, race disparities in the poverty rate have narrowed substantially since the 1970s, census data show. Economic insecurity among whites also is more pervasive than is shown in the government poverty data, engulfing more than 76% by the time they turn age 60, according to a new economic gauge being published next year by the Oxford University Press. The gauge defines "economic insecurity" as a year or more of periodic joblessness, reliance on government aid such as food stamps or income below 150% of the poverty line. Measured across all races, the risk of economic insecurity rises to 79%. (para 8–9)

Clearly, the United States has a serious inequality situation with respect to income distribution. However, income is only one measure, albeit an important measure, on how well-off U.S. citizens are, using income as a measure of well-being. Income is something that is earned over some time period—a week, a month, a year. It does not provide a complete picture of well-being. Income does not include what people own that is of value, such as a house, automobiles, a savings account, stocks and bonds, and retirement funds. Hence, it is critical to add to this picture and address the matter of wealth inequality.

Wealth Inequality

Wealth inequality is sometimes referred in economics and business literature as the wealth gap. Wealth inequality is the unequal distribution of net assets or net worth among citizens of the United States. Reported wealth inequality in the United States substantially underestimates the actual amount of the net worth figures for the rich. In July 2012, Allen reported that the extremely wealthy have placed $21 trillion in offshore accounts, such as in Switzerland and the Cayman Islands. This amount is about what the U.S. GDP was in 2019.

Think back to the beginning of this chapter, when the net worth statements of the Duvalls and the Sumpters were compared. You were able to see the major big difference in the wealth between the two families. Net worth is considered a better measure of inequality in the United States than income, because assets, such as stocks and bonds, can easily be turned in to cash to meet troubling financial situations. Here is a reminder of how net worth is calculated: Net Worth = Total Assets – Total Liabilities. Assets are what a person or family owns—a house, automobile(s), valuables, savings account, stocks and bonds, retirement accounts, artwork. Liabilities include what a person or family owes—a home mortgage, a car loan, credit card debt, student loans, or any other form of indebtedness.

In 2017, Mark Zandi, chief economist of Moody Analytics, offered an analysis of United States wealth inequality. He looked at household wealth in trillions of dollars during two different time periods: 1980 and 2015. The top 20% of the population held $6 trillion of wealth in 1980; this percent of population held $63 trillion of wealth in 2015. The bottom 80% of the population held $4 trillion of wealth in 1980 and $22 trillion of wealth in 2015. The result is that the top 20% of the population holds close to three times more wealth than the bottom 80% of the population.

Clearly, the United States has what economists call a *wealth gap*. A wealth gap is an unequal distribution of assets. Based on Zandi's (2017) data, the wealth gap in the United States is $51 trillion! Thomas Piketty (2017), a French economist, who published a ground-breaking study of wealth inequality in 2014, has made this statement on fortunes in the United States, which are mostly inherited: "Wealth is so concentrated that a large segment of society is virtually unaware of its existence, so that

**Table 12.2.   Median Net Worth
by Race and Educational Attainment of Head of Family – 2016**

Race	Median Net Worth	
	No Bachelor's Degree	Bachelor's Degree or Higher
White	$98,100	$397,100
Black	$11,600	$68,200
Hispanic	$17,500	$77,900
Other*	$34,300	$210,000

Source: Board of Governors of the Federal Reserve System (2017, p. 3).
Note: *Includes Asians and people of mixed race.

some people imagine that it belongs to surreal or mysterious entities" (p. 545).

Wealth in the United States also is dependent on level of education and race. On September 27, 2017, the (SCF, a subgroup of the board of governors of the Federal Reserve System, issued a document which reported the median net worth holdings by race and ethnicity and by level of educational attainment (Dettling et al., 2017). The results of this investigation are shown in Table 12.2. Note that a median is the middle number in a distribution of data.

Clearly, higher education pays off for all—Whites, Blacks, and Hispanics. Whites, no matter whether they have a college degree, are better off than either Blacks or Hispanics. For those without a bachelor's degree, Whites are 8.5 times better off than Blacks and 5.6 times better off than Hispanics. For those with a bachelor's degree or higher, Whites are 5.8 times better off than Blacks and 5.1 times better off than Hispanics. Black households with higher education are about 6 times better off than Black families with no higher education. For Hispanic households, those with higher education are 4.5 times better off than Hispanics with no higher education.

Several experts have contributed their analyses to these disparities. Alan B. Krueger, Chairman of President Obama's Council of Economic Advisors, suggested some possible reasons for wealth inequality, apart from racism against Blacks and Hispanics. In a conversation with the Center for American Progress, Krueger (2012) cited several: increase in technological change that has replaced people on the job, the proliferation of very high salaries earned in the financial sector, a decline in union membership, and U.S. tax policy that has become less progressive. Jennifer Rubin (2017) claims that the GOP tax plan (the *Tax Cuts and Jobs Act of 2017*), signed into law by President Trump, "disproportionally benefits the rich at a time when income inequality is an economic, political, and social concern" (para 1). Even conservative former Chairman of the Federal Reserve Board of Governors, Alan Greenspan, comments on the Trump tax plan cited by Rubin. Egan (2017) reports Greenspan's comments: "We are premature on fiscal stimulus, whether it's tax cuts or expenditure increases. We've got to get the debt stabilized before we can even think of those terms ... economically, it's a mistake to deal with sharp reductions in taxes now" (para 3). Rubin (2017) also goes on to state,

> Understand what the GOP is up to here. In order to give enormous tax breaks to individuals and the wealthy, it will run up the debt, which effectively removes any economic benefit in the long term.... In short, the concept is fatally flawed—unless your intent is to reward rich donors. (para 6)

One feature is commonly known about wealth: wealth perpetuates itself over time. If you own stocks and bonds or real property, such as a house, you experience an annual rate of return. This annual rate could be as high as 8% in a very good year. If you are working for wages or a salary, your annual pay increase will likely not exceed 3%. Christopher Ingraham (2018) states the rate of return situation this way: "If you ... wanted to buy a representative chunk of the wealthy world's economy, you could expect a rate of return of about 6.28%" (para 14), while the "average annual economic growth works out to be just 2.87%" (para 17). This statement brings new meaning to the often heard statement, "the rich get richer, and the poor get poorer."

It is well-known that many people who are considered rich have inherited wealth. They carefully guard that wealth, and seek to increase it. It is the case that some people in the United States have become rich by sheer hard work and some good luck. Rich people have political access. They promise politicians funds for election and reelection. In return, politicians, especially in the U.S. House of Representatives and the U.S. Senate, listen to the rich about their political desires. We also know that some rich folks seek to do excellent things. Generally, they are diligent in what they do. They take initiative and they stick to their goals, usually with their own financial advantage in mind. They take risks, are competitive, and are well organized. In some cases, the rich do give (tax deductible) funds to charities. However, some of the rich think they have (own) entitlement—entitlement to the best seat in a restaurant, entitlement to entertainment events, or entitlement to access various institutions. The case study in Figure 12.3 describes how a sense of entitlement, and the desire for status crossed a legal line.

Case Study

In 2019, news broke of a college admissions scandal involving several Hollywood parents. Leonard Pitts, Jr. describes the situation (2019) in which "the wealthy, well-known and well-connected gamed the system, lying, fixing tests, and paying bribes" (p. 5A) to get their kids into top schools, including Yale, University of Southern California, and Stanford. In *Time Magazine,* Bryan Caplan (2019) states the matter this way: "Of course, the superrich parents the FBI is accusing could have just let their kids skip college and live off their trust funds, but it's not merely a matter of money. It's about youthful self-esteem—and parental bragging rights" (para 6).

Questions

How has the wealth gap infiltrated different layers of our society?
How should the justice system respond?

Figure 12.3.   Case study: Entitlements of the rich.

Nobel Laureate in economics, Joseph Stiglitz (2019), raises a hope that the United States can save our broken economic system from itself. He points out that the United States has "the highest level of inequality among advanced nations and one of the lowest levels of opportunity—with fortunes of young Americans more dependent on the income and education of their parents than elsewhere" (para 1). Stiglitz introduces the term "progressive capitalism," which means using the power of the market to serve society. He criticizes the 2017 Trump tax law, indicating that the law favors corporations and that we are now in an economy that may grow at less than 2% per year. He goes on to cite the exploitation of our economy, including abusive practices of the financial sector or the technology sector, which invades our privacy. He states, "We are now in a vicious cycle: greater economic inequality is leading, in our money-driven political system, to more political inequality, with weaker rules and deregulation causing still more economic inequality" (para 13). Under progressive capitalism, the state would be responsible for making markets serve society, with regulations ensuring strong competition without abusive exploitation, and recognizing that we must rely on the creativity and innovation of our people. Thus far, under President Trump, his brand of capitalism favors the rich. This situation is unlikely to change anytime soon. Trump's posture does not bode well for our democracy. And, under Trump there is no concern about equality of either income or wealth.

INCOME AND WEALTH INEQUALITY:
IMPACT ON OUR DEMOCRACY

In the Introduction to the United States Declaration of Independence, signed on July 4, 1776, is the following:

> We hold these truths to be self-evident, that all men are created equal, that they are endowed by their Creator with certain unalienable Rights, that among these are Life, Liberty, and the Pursuit of Happiness. That to secure these rights, Governments are instituted among Men, deriving their just powers from the consent of the governed.

The Preamble to the Constitution of the United States of America reads as follows:

> We the people of the United States, in order to form a more perfect union, establish justice, insure domestic tranquility, provide for the common defense, promote the general welfare, and secure the blessings of liberty to ourselves and our posterity, do ordain and establish this Constitution for the United States of America.

These two documents established the value foundation of the United States, and this foundation still holds today. This value foundation represents our ideals. Essentially, the two documents clearly state that citizens of the United States have the right to govern themselves! This is the most basic meaning of democracy. The citizen obligation (responsibility) is to participate in governing, even if it is just to vote.

To expand on this essential and basic meaning of democracy, U.S. citizens have many freedoms, including freedom of religion, freedom of the press, and freedom of expression. Our rights include the right to elect public officials as representatives, the right (and obligation) to influence and participate in government, the right to own property, and the right to question authority. Citizens are entitled to the equality of opportunity, equality of treatment, and the equal opportunity to learn of public decisions.

It is the obligation of citizens to work for the common good. Pursuing the common good includes, but is not limited to, supporting the education system, serving on community boards and committees, volunteering assistance for those in need, and engaging in campaigns for those running for local, state, and federal office. Acting on behalf of the common good is considered civic virtue. Our freedoms and obligations (civic responsibilities) are not to be taken for granted. We need to make commitments to our communities to assist in governing, and we need to exercise our rights.

Poverty, or near poverty, is a current major threat to our democracy. People at or near poverty are highly stressed. Many are very discouraged. They are less likely to participate in our democracy than other more well-off citizens. In short, this is a most troubling situation. We now examine briefly poverty in the United States, as people (mostly U.S. citizens) considered in poverty are at the bottom level in both income and wealth inequality.

In a study by they Pew Research Center, conducted in January 2018, the results show a distinct political bias toward the wealthy. Democrats overwhelmingly claim that the federal government does not do enough help to the poor. Close to three quarters of Democrats indicate that the federal government should do more to help the poor. In the same Pew study, more than three fourths of Democrats indicate that the federal government provides too much help to the wealthy, while fewer than half of Republicans claim the federal government provides too much help for the wealthy. Clearly, there is significant disagreement between our two major political parties. Hence, given the current make-up of the U.S. Senate, it is unlikely that the situation with respect to the poor is unlikely to change.

Poverty in the United States

The U.S. government sets what is called the *poverty threshold*. In 2016, a family of five had a poverty threshold of $29,111. If the five-member family had an annual income below this figure, they were considered "in poverty." If the same family had total annual income above this figure, they were not considered to be in poverty, and hence not eligible for any assistance, particularly from the federal government (Semega et al., 2017).

Ayres (2017) explains some of the effects of poverty. She states, "Being in poverty often leads to high levels of stress. An overwhelming desire to meet certain basic needs becomes the highest priority. Over time, if those needs cannot be met, then some individuals will commit robberies, burglaries, and other forms of crime. It can also lead to violent acts, though in the mind of the perpetrator, the actions are seen as a method of self-defense" (para 7). Ayres goes on to state, "poverty influences crime rates because at its core, it highlights and reinforces the differences between the wealthy class and those who are poor. The greater the gap happens to be, the greater the benefits are to the thief to use that wealth in some way to their own advantage" (para 17). Clearly the stress of poverty and attendant desperate, illegal behavior means serious trouble for our democracy.

Haymes and colleagues (2015) estimate that the number of Americans living "near poverty" was 100 million. This is nearly a third of the United States population! If one third of our population is near, at, or below the threshold level of poverty, our democracy is in peril. This tells us that too many—way too many—of our citizens may have lost faith in our democracy.

New York Times opinion writer, David Leonhardt, speaking at an Aspen Institute on Economic Security in 2017, shared his thoughts:

> Economic despair ... underlies a profound loss of trust in institutions, including the news media. Since the 1980s, overall confidence in the Congress, the Supreme Court, banks, public schools, and religious institutions, along with the media has tumbled ... with less than half of the population expressing confidence in any one of these institutions. When it comes to Congress, only 10% of Americans give our most powerful governing body a vote of confidence. (Kahn, 2017, para 7)

While voting is only one responsibility of all our citizens, the vote is a key indicator of the strength of our democracy. It has been reported that voter turnout in the United States is about 40% in midterm elections and 60% in presidential elections, and that richer people vote more than poor people (Simenova et al., 2018). Those who participate in elections may get their views attended to by those who are elected, as the poor vote in fewer numbers than the rich.

Democracy Must Change

Not only is our democracy in peril, it must change. Any change must be all encompassing, backed by the force of law. Civil rights legend Bayard Rustin and superb news journalist, Molly Ivins (deceased), have stated their views on democracy in the next two statements in Dionne and colleagues' (2017) book, *One Nation After Trump*. Rustin shares, "If we desire a society that is democratic, then democracy must become a means, as well as an end" (p. 245). Ivins contributes, "The thing about democracy, beloveds, is that it is not neat, orderly, or quiet. It requires a certain relish for confusion" (p. 246). Indeed, these two spokespeople are correct. We must commit to changing democracy, and we must be prepared to deal with the confusion.

E. J. Dionne, Jr. and colleagues (2017) presented the challenge this way following the election of Donald Trump to President:

> If Trump and Trumpism continue to weaken our democracy and threaten our freedoms, those who would reinvigorate democratic life must combine Ruston's aspirations with Ivins's realism. This applies not only to our attitudes—toward each other and toward the ultimate wisdom of the citizenry— but also to how we approach reform. Rustin is right that undemocratic

means should not be expected to produce democratic results. Nothing is more critical to the long-term legitimacy of a political system built on democratic values than guaranteeing that all eligible citizens are able to exercise their fundamental right to vote and have that vote matter. Getting more citizens into the democratic fray is essential to defending and repairing our republic. (pp. 245–246)

However, while voting is a good start to democratic participation, the United States needs more, much more, to repair and enhance our republic. The "much more" will likely meet with resistance, especially from the current (2020) Republican-controlled United States Senate. We need to be reminded that many members of the U.S. Senate are very well off in their own right. And, they continue to have strong relationships with rich, supportive citizens who continue to finance their reelections. Many committed and concerned citizens are hopeful that the current control of the U.S. Senate will change in the upcoming elections.

In fairness, it is reasonable to at least acknowledge the views of N. Gregory Mankiw, a conservative Harvard economist, who does not appear to be concerned about our country's income and wealth inequality. In this citation, Mankiw criticizes the work of Thomas Piketty, reflecting on inequality and democracy. Mankiw states:

A final possibility is that wealth is somehow a threat to democracy. Piketty alludes to this worry throughout his book. I am less concerned. The wealthy includes supporters of both the right (the Koch brothers, Sheldon Adelson) and the left (George Soros, Tom Steyer), and despite the high levels of inequality, in 2008 and 2012 the United States managed to elect a left-leaning president committed to increasing taxes on the rich. The fathers of American democracy, including George Washington, Thomas Jefferson, John Adams, and James Madison, were very rich men. With estimated net worth (in today's dollars) ranging from $20 million to $500 million, they were likely all in the top 0.1% of the wealth distribution, demonstrating that the accumulation of capital is perfectly compatible with democratic values. (Pippinger, 2015, p. 2)

This author could not disagree more with Mankiw. At the time of the Founding Fathers Mankiw refers to, the United States had a relatively small population of about 4 million people, compared to today's mostly urban population of over 329 million. In the late 1700s, most of the population was rural, with farming as the main industry. Washington and Jefferson held slaves, certainly an inequitable financial situation, if they were counted on a balance sheet. Today, our population is urban, with people trying to make a living in crowded cities, often in complex jobs requiring higher education. Citing the long ago past seems irrelevant to today's economic inequality problems. We have a much different and complex economy than in the 1700s, which requires more education, better work skills, and more opportunity.

Summary: Threats to Democracy

Over time, we have promulgated injustice and economic inequality throughout U.S. society. In doing so, our democracy is severely threatened. And, the threat must be taken very seriously. Here is a summary of the threats:

- income and wealth inequality;
- lack of higher education and technical training for minorities and the poor;
- inequality in the *Tax Cuts and Jobs Act of 2017*, especially the lack of tax progressiveness and the tax reductions in business profits, enhancing the rich;
- undue political influence of the rich at all levels of government;
- a general loss of faith in our democracy, especially among those near or in poverty;
- a diminishing attention to civic education in our schools;
- a lack of participation of citizens in civil society; and
- a large percentage of citizens who demonstrate a distrust in business and in law-making institutions.

PROPOSALS TO MEET THE CHALLENGES FOR DEMOCRACY

Income and wealth inequality have multiple causes. Also, the data reported on inequality vary, depending on the sources used for reporting. There is no one way to address these causes, and no quick fixes. Nor is there a magic fix to problems with our democracy. It is incumbent upon all citizens, but especially policymakers, to propose and think through what might be done to try to correct income and wealth inequality, with a major goal to meet the challenges for our democracy. Indeed, we must pursue a very strong, multifaceted mandate.

Below are seven proposals that can give us a beginning. As the reader thinks about these proposals, think back to the fiscal and monetary policy sections early in this chapter. Think about what fiscal and/or monetary policies would be needed to put these proposals in place.

Proposal 1

Replace the current federal income tax schedule with a schedule that is much more progressive, and that would include a wealth tax of at least 3% on wealth over $100 million and at least 4% on wealth over $1 billion. Reexamine the estate tax, particularly with respect to the wealthy. In addition, add to a new much more progressive tax system, a negative income tax that would pay those at or below the poverty level a living wage that would bring them at least to the poverty income level.

Discussion: A negative income tax was proposed by Milton and Rose Friedman in 1980 in their book, *Free to Choose: A Personal Statement*. One point the Friedmans made with their negative income tax proposal was that this would allow the other piecemeal income support programs to be canceled. The negative income tax received much discussion about 40 years ago, but did not result in any serious policy. It is time to bring back the negative income tax discussion.

Proposal 2

Institute a mandatory national single-payer health care reform for all citizens. This Medicare-For-All program would be based on an ability-to-pay schedule. In addition, consider nationalization of, or strict price controls on the pharmaceutical industry.

Discussion: All citizens of the United States would be covered under this health care plan. It is recognized that the rich will want options to this program, and they would be free to seek their own medical insurance provider, paying the required costs. Given what many would call outrageous and extremely unfair prices of many needed drugs, drastic action must be taken soon.

Proposal 3

Require a national mandatory school attendance program, kindergarten through Grade 14, with options to specialize in a trade or high-tech fields beginning in Grade 11.

Discussion: It is recognized that states and local cities and towns largely fund and manage their own school districts. These entities value their local control. Enforcement and any federal government support would have to be negotiated, although it is likely that school people would accept federal government funds to implement this policy.

Proposal 4

Keeping in mind that all people need a place to live, create and fund a housing/condominium/apartment building program to house those who have inadequate housing. This program may be teamed with Habitat for Humanity, which has a national infrastructure and has experience of providing housing for the poor.

Discussion: People need an adequate place to live, particularly the homeless and those close to the poverty line. Habitat for Humanity homes are not free. Like Habitat for Humanity, this program would be based on ability to pay and commitment to work on building the housing (sweat equity).

Proposal 5

Institute a national compulsory voting law which requires every citizen age 18 or older to register to vote and to show up to vote on voting day. If a person fails to show up, a fine would be imposed. Each voter must turn in a ballot.

Discussion: Over 20 countries have a similar compulsory voting law, which requires citizens to register to vote and go to their polling place to vote on election day.

Proposal 6

Plan for and conduct immediately an election reform program that (1) stops gerrymandering, (2) shortens the time for election campaigns, and (3) limits the amount of money candidates for office may raise and spend.

Discussion: States, particularly those who believe their voting laws are sacred, would likely protest this proposal. Yet, almost daily, news reports tell us that the poor and minorities are systematically excluded from voting.

Proposal 7

Enact a law stating that each potential candidate for a national office must take and pass a civics exam before that candidate is allowed to run for office.

Discussion: The purpose of this law is to try to protect our citizenry from electing fools at the federal level. The civics test would be prepared and managed by a collaboration among the National Assessment for Educational Progress, the National Council for the Social Studies, and the Social Science Education Consortium.

END NOTE

I love my country and I highly value our democracy. Yet, I am very worried that we will not act fast enough to correct our very serious problem of income and wealth inequality—truly an unjust situation. I close this chapter with the following quote from theologian Reinhold Niebuhr (1944). This quote deserves our undivided attention:

> Man's capacity for justice makes democracy possible;
> but man's inclination to injustice makes democracy necessary.

ACKNOWLEDGMENT

I wish to thank my colleague, Lewis Karstensson, emeritus associate professor of economics, University of Nevada, Las Vegas, for his advice and insight into the structure and content of the economics in this chapter.

REFERENCES

Allen, F. E. (2012, July 23). *Super rich hide $21 trillion offshore, study says*. Forbes. https://www.forbes.com/sites/frederickallen/2012/07/23/super-rich-hide-21-trillion-offshore-study-says/#1f0528396ba6

Associated Press. (2013, July 28). *80 percent of U.S. adults face near-poverty, unemployment, survey finds*. CBS News. https://www.cbsnews.com/news/80-percent-of-us-adults-face-near-poverty-unemployment-survey-finds/

Ayres, C. (2017). *How poverty influences crime rates*. https://vittana.org/how-poverty-influences-crime-rates

Board of Governors of the Federal Reserve System. (2016). *The federal reserve system: Purposes and functions* (10th ed.). https://www.federalreserve.gov/aboutthefed/files/pf_complete.pdf

Bricker, J., Dettling, L. J., Henriques, A., Hsu, J. W., Jacobs, L., Moore, K. B., Pack, S., Sabelhaus, J., Thompson, J., & Windle, R. A. (2017). Changes in U.S. family finances from 2013 to 2016: Evidence from the survey of consumer finances. *Federal Reserve Bulletin*, *103*(3). https://www.federalreserve.gov/publications/2017-September-changes-in-us-family-finances-from-2013-to-2016.htm

Dettling, L. J., Hsu, J. W., Jacobs, L., Moors, K. B., & Thompson, J. P. (2017). Recent trends in wealth-holding by race and ethnicity: Evidence from the survey of consumer finances. *FEDS Notes*. https://doi.org/10.17016/2380-7172.2083

Dionne, E. J., Jr., Ornstein, N. J., & Mann, T. E. (2017). *One nation after Trump: A guide for the perplexed, the disillusioned, the desperate, and the not-yet deported*. St. Martin's Press.

Egan, M. (2017, November 10). *Alan Greenspan: Big tax cuts a "mistake." Fix the debt first*. CNN. https://money.cnn.com/2017/11/10/investing/greenspan-tax-cuts-mistake-debt/index.html

Friedman, M. & Friedman, R. (1980). *Free to choose: A personal statement*. Harcourt Brace and Company.

Haymes, S. N., Vidal de Haymes, M., & Miller, R. J. (Eds.). (2015). *Routledge handbook of poverty in the United States*. Routledge.

Ingraham, C. (2018, January 4). Massive new data set suggests economic inequality is about to get even worse. *The Washington Post*. https://www.washingtonpost.com/news/wonk/wp/2018/01/04/massive-new-data-set-suggests-inequality-is-about-to-get-even-worse/

Kahn, K. (2017, July 26). Economic inequality and the future of democracy: Tracking the conversation. *Nonprofit Quarterly*. https://nonprofitquarterly.org/aspen-institute-explores-economic-inequality-future-democracy/

Krueger, A. B. (2012, January 12). *The rise and consequences of inequality*. Center for American Progress. https://americanprogress.org/events/2012/01/12/17181/therise-and-consequences-of-inequality/

McConnell, C. R., & Brue, S. L. (1999). *Macroeconomics: Principles, problems, and policies* (14th ed.). Irwin-McGraw-Hill.

Niebuhr, R. (1944). *Children of light and the children of darkness*. Charles Scribner's Sons.

Pew Research Center. (2018, January 30). *Majorities say government does too little for older people, the poor and the middle class*. https://www.people-press.org/2018/01/30/majorities-say-government-does-too-little-for-older-people-the-poor-and-the-middle-class/

Piketty, T. (2017). Toward a reconciliation between economics and the social sciences. In H. Boushey, J. B. DeLong, & M. Steinbaum (Eds.), *After Piketty: The agenda for economics and inequality* (pp. 543–565). Harvard University Press.

Pippinger, N. (2015, January 15). When does inequality threaten democracy? *Democracy Journal*. https://democracyjournal.org/arguments/2015/01/when-does-inequality-threaten-democracy.php.html

Rubin, J. (2017, November 13). The most compelling criticism of Trump's tax plan. *The Washington Post*. https://www.washingtonpost.com/blogs/right-turn/wp/2017/11/13/the-most-compelling-criticism-of-trump-tax-plan/

Sawhill, I. V., & Pulliam, C. (2019, June 25). Six facts about wealth in the United States. *Brookings*. https://www.brookings.edu/blog/up-front/2019/06/25/six-facts-about-wealth-in-the-united-states/

Schaeffer, R. (2020, February 7). Six facts about economic inequality in the United States. Pew Research Center. https://www.pewresearch.org/fact-tank/2020/02/07/6-facts-about-economic-inequality-in-the-u-s/

Semega, J., Fontenot, K., & Kollar, M. A. (2017). Income and poverty in the United States: 2016. https://www.census.gov/content/dam/Census/library/publications/2017/demo/P60-259.pdf

Simeonova, E., Akee, R., Holbein, J., Copeland, W. E., & Costello, E. J. (2018). This is the link between voting in elections and income. *World Economic Forum*. https://www.weforum.org/agenda/2018/07/low-voter-turnout-increasing-household-income-may-help

Stiglitz, J. E. (2019, April 19). Progressive capitalism is not an oxymoron. *The New York Times*. https://www.nytimes.com/2019/04/19/opinion/sunday/progressive-capitalism.html?smid=nytcore-ios-share

U. S. Bureau of Labor Statistics. (2019, September 4). Nominal gross domestic product by major demand category. https://www.bls.gov/emp/tables/nominal-gdp-major-demand-category.htm

Zandi, M. (2017). What does rising inequality mean for the macroeconomy? In H. Boushey, J. B. DeLong, & M. Steinbaum (Eds.), *After Piketty: The agenda for economics and inequality* (pp. 384–411). Harvard University Press.

CHAPTER 13

BRIDGING THE DIVIDE BETWEEN DATA AND SOLUTIONS

A Closer Look at a Restorative Justice Framework for School Discipline

Bettie Ray Butler
The University of North Carolina Charlotte

ABSTRACT

A long history of research has explored racial disparities in school suspension. While the data has led us to several important discoveries, it has been less helpful in identifying solutions. To achieve equity in school discipline, alternative approaches to zero tolerance discipline policies must be further explored. The purpose of this chapter is to take a closer look at restorative justice and its application in education. I introduce the most salient principles of a restorative justice framework. Then, using these principles, I differentiate theory from practice to show how schools may not fully maximize the potential of restorative justice as a viable solution to exclusionary discipline practices. I conclude with a note of caution to schools against implementing restorative justice initiatives without carefully attending to its foundational principles.

The Divide Within: Intersections of Realities, Facts, Theories, and Practices
pp. 251–264
Copyright © 2021 by Information Age Publishing

INTRODUCTION

Ten years ago, I published the first of a series of papers on school discipline (Butler et al., 2010). I was in the second year of my doctoral program and I had become increasingly agitated after hearing a litany of stories and news reports about how Black boys were disproportionately targeted and criminalized in schools. As a new mom of a Black son who would one day attend public school, there was an urgency to understand why Black boys were subject to such harsh and unfair treatment. I desperately sought answers.

Out of growing concern and, in part, frustration, I searched for resources to understand the differential treatment of Black males. I came across Carla Monroe's (2005) article, *Why Are "Bad Boys" Always Black?* To this day, one particular statement remains etched in my memory. Monroe, citing the work of Russell Skiba and colleagues (2002), stated, "African Americans receive harsher punishments than their peers, often for subjectively defined offenses" (p. 46). Monroe argued that teachers subconsciously punish Black boys more severely out of fear and as a means to control their behavior.

This article transformed my development as a school discipline scholar. Gradually, my research agenda began to take shape. At this point, I started collecting and mining data on school discipline. Every question that I could conceive, over the years, became the focus for a study. Each manuscript would yield a different conclusion. I discovered that: (1) Black girls are also disproportionality overrepresented in exclusionary discipline (Blake et al., 2011; Blake et al., 2015); (2) school discipline related absences resulted in lowered performance on standardized test (Lewis et al., 2010); (3) elementary school students had an increased risk of receiving suspensions (Butler et al., 2012); (4) the lack of diversity in the teacher workforce negatively affected discipline outcomes (Butler et al., 2014; Farinde-Wu et al., 2020; Williams et al., 2020); and 5) principals' discipline practices were likely tied to their disciplinary philosophies (Butler & Triplett, 2019).

Despite these important discoveries, in retrospect, I realized that while these studies informed and deepened my understanding of the complexities of discipline disparities; after years of researching, I still had limited knowledge about viable alternatives to school punishment. Very little research, including my own, focused on how to disrupt the pervasive inequities found in school suspension. The data tells us who was being suspended and why; but less can be discerned, with respect to, the availability of solutions.

The divide between data and solutions is longstanding in school discipline research. After decades of examining trends in discipline data, not enough attention has been devoted to identifying solutions. To achieve equity in school discipline, schools must be able to effectively translate theory into practice. In this chapter, I demonstrate how a restorative justice framework can serve as a viable alternative to overly punitive discipline policies. I conceptualize restorative justice and explain its application in education. Then, I introduce the most salient principles of a restorative justice framework for school discipline. I conclude with a caution to schools against using restorative justice without carefully attending to its foundational principles.

"RESTORATIVE JUSTICE"

The term "restorative *justice*" has become a popular catchphrase in recent years. Despite its popularity, its application in education has been met with ambivalence and mixed emotions. In schools across the country, you hear teachers talking about restorative justice. In my experience, the source of this increased discussion has generally been attributed to participation in a professional development training. Teachers leave these workshops excited to facilitate their first restorative circle—a group process where participants engage in purposive dialogue while sitting in a circle (Pranis, 2015). Once returning to their classrooms they quickly learn that circles, alone, are ineffective. This disappointment lends itself to skepticism, which then results in low teacher buy-in. Rarely is restorative justice in education practiced in a way that is true to its core values— the key practices that undergird the foundational principles of restorative justice. Absent the foundational principles, restorative justice is reduced to nothing more than a meeting or conference and its transformational potential is diluted at best; and in the worst of cases, lost altogether.

The effectiveness of restorative justice rests upon having a solid understanding of how to translate a restorative framework into practice within schools. Not having this understanding can, and often does, contribute to unsystematic planning and poor implementation. That said, there must be a clear delineation of what we really mean when we say restorative justice. Restorative justice is more than a set of strategies; it is a philosophy rooted in principled values (Sawin & Zehr, 2013). To improve understanding, educators should make a more concerted effort to read the early works of Howard Zehr (1990), who is regarded as the pioneer of restorative justice, as well as the writings of other notable restorative justice scholars. This can move them to a deeper critical consciousness of restorative justice and its application in schools. It can also create a more authentic evaluation of educational practice to determine if a school's use of restorative justice is truly aligned within a restorative framework. To be sustainable, and to achieve lasting results, practice must be guided by theory. Otherwise, as Zehr (2015) warns, "we might use a restoratively-based process but arrive at nonrestorative outcomes" (p. 46). To prevent this from happening, it is therefore vital to first understand the historical origin of restorative justice.

Historical Origin and Definition

The origin of restorative justice traces back to Indigenous wisdom and Judeo-Christian beliefs (Vaandering, 2011). Borrowing from these tribal and religious values, we see an emergence of restorative justice in the 1970s as an alternative approach to the conventional Western legal systems. Its introduction is considered a major development in criminological thinking (Braithwaite, 1999) as it departs from the traditional retributive model of justice.

The retributive-restorative dichotomy has been, and continues to be, heavily debated with little consensus on how to properly address wrongdoing (Armstrong, 2014). The retributive approach views crime as an offense against a nonhuman entity, such as the state; whereas, under the restorative paradigm, crime is seen as a violation against people, with emphasis placed on the victim and the victim's family (Holtham, 2009; Zehr, 1990). The retributive model contends that the offending agent must suffer in proportion to the harm caused; that they should get what they deserve. It sees the *eye for an eye* philosophy as central to determining punishment. The restorative model diverges significantly from this punitive approach. Its focus is on addressing harm and restoring relationships; or in other words, making things right. It sees forgiveness and closure as integral to the restorative process (Wenzel et al., 2008).

In the judicial system, restorative justice manifests itself as peacemaking and sentencing circles, family group conferencing, victim-offender mediation, or reparation boards (Braithwaite, 1999). The primary purpose of each process is to initiate interactive dialogue through a face-to-face encounter between the victim, offender, and the affected community. The intention behind the meeting is to repair relationships, and when possible, prevent a recurrence of the offense. Albeit, the process of restorative justice seems fairly straightforward; its definition is both multilayered and complex (Reimer, 2018).

Critics of restorative justice argue that it lacks conceptual consistency (Vaandering, 2011). At times, its varied definitions has resulted in major confusion and misunderstanding. While there is no universally accepted definition of restorative justice (and will likely never be according to most restorative justice scholars), to reduce linguistic ambiguity, Zehr (1990) in his early writings offers an insightful way of thinking about restorative justice within the context of criminology. He states:

> Crime is a violation of people and relationships. It creates obligations to make things right. Justice involves the victim, the offender and the community in search for solutions which promote repair, reconciliation, and reassurance. (p. 181)

Tony Marshall (1999) goes on further to define what is meant by restorative justice. He offers the following working definition:

> Restorative justice is a problem solving approach to crime ... whereby parties with a stake in a specific offense collectively resolve how to deal with the aftermath of the offense and its implications for the future. (p. 5)

It is Zehr (2015), however, who provides the most commonly accepted and widely cited definition. He contends that restorative justice is:

> An approach to achieving justice that involves, to the extent possible, those who have a stake in a specific offense or harm to collectively identify and address harms, needs, and obligations in order to heal and put things as right as possible. (p. 48)

It is this definition that has traditionally guided restorative practice within the juvenile justice system and schools.

Juvenile Justice Systems and Schools

Restorative justice gained international prominence in the early 1990s during a time of heightened public and political focus on youth justice reform. Particularly, in New Zealand there was public dissatisfaction with the treatment of youth offenders in the criminal justice system (Carruthers, 2012; Van Ness & Strong, 2015). In response, the *Children, Young Persons, and Their Families Act of 1989* was introduced as law. This marked the first major legislative step toward institutionalizing restorative justice (Carruthers, 2012; Maxwell & Morris, 2006). Although the 1989 act does not explicitly mention restorative justice, it integrates many of its core values through the introduction of family group conferencing—a process that allows families and communities to engage in collaborative decision-making and problem solving concerning matters of child protection and youth justice (Levine, 2000).

The New Zealand model gives primacy to family group processes with the intention of redirecting youth away from formal court proceedings.

Van Ness and Strong (2010) contend that "conferencing [takes] the power to decide what should happen [away] from the judge and [places] it in than hands of the conference" (p. 28). In other words, the victim, offender, their families and friends or support group—not the court—come to a consensus about how best to respond to the harm caused by the offense. Overall, family group conferencing has been uniquely successful in diverting New Zealand youth from courts and custody (Maxwell, 2006). For this reason, we have seen an increasing emergence of adaptations of restorative justice in the United States education system.

Schools in the United States have come under intense scrutiny for their zero tolerance approach to school discipline. Zero tolerance policies "punish all offenses severely, no matter how minor" (Skiba & Peterson, 1999, p. 373). While these policies were originally intended to keep schools safe, arguably they caused more harm than good. Zero tolerance policies unfairly label and stigmatize students of color, leading many of them to be excluded and pushed out of school for relatively minor offenses (Skiba & Peterson, 1999). This get-tough approach to school discipline—intentionally or not—has been associated with racial disparities in school suspension (Skiba et al., 2002).

In searching for a viable alternative to zero tolerance policies, some U.S. schools have turned to restorative justice (Schiff, 2018). However, a major criticism is that, when implemented, practice tends to march ahead of theory (Vaandering, 2011). This means that in a haste to use restorative justice, schools sometimes lose sight of the very values that make it most effective. When this happens, the focus shifts way from the original purpose of restorative justice to a schools' desired outcome for its use—with more emphasis placed on decreasing the number of suspensions, rather than on building relationships. In turn, fidelity is compromised and most—if not all—of the benefits and possibilities of restorative justice are lost.

If restorative justice is not implemented as designed, it can perpetuate the very inequities it intended to disrupt. Poor implementation is usually the result of schools adopting restorative justice initiatives without carefully vetting them against its core values. With no regard for the foundational principles of restorative justice, racial disparities are likely to persist—with a disproportionate number of suspensions being meted out to Black students. This overrepresentation creates a vicious cycle of blaming and shaming Black students, even in times when they have done nothing wrong. Because a substantial percentage of suspensions stem from subjectively defined offenses, such as defiance and disrespect, it is not uncommon for Black students' behaviors to be misunderstood or misinterpreted (Monroe, 2006). Thus, forcing a student who is wrongfully accused to apologize for someone else's mistake deviates from the principals of restorative justice. This type of misuse/abuse is not only traumatizing for the student, it is simply just bad practice. Unless schools attend to and prioritize the principles of restorative justice, its viability and relevance as an alternative to overly punitive discipline policies can never be fully realized.

FOUNDATIONAL RESTORATIVE JUSTICE PRINCIPLES: A NOTE OF CAUTION TO SCHOOLS

Scholars have identified a number of foundational philosophies for understanding the nature of restorative justice in educational environments (Amstutz & Mullet, 2005; Evans & Vaandering 2016; Reimer, 2018; Wachtel, 2013; Zehr, 2015). Using this work, a list of the most salient restorative justice principles were identified and compiled and then grouped thematically as follows: (a) *a mindset, not a program*; (b) *a compass, not a map*; (c) *proactive, not (only) reactive*; and (d) *for everyone, not just students*. These principles are presented to differentiate the current application from the intended application of restorative justice in education. This section is written as a note of caution to schools against using restorative justice outside its original purpose.

It's a *Mindset*, NOT a *Program*

Zehr (1990) and Holtham (2009) remind us that restorative justice is a mindset, not a program. It is more than a process, more than a means to an end. Yet, in education, restorative justice continues to be reduced to a set of strategies. Professional development in schools often focus on the facilitation of restorative circles, and not on the restorative justice framework. To compound matters further, training is generally administered online through independent learning or through 1- to 2-day workshops (referred to as a sit-and-get wherein participants passively take in information over a short span of time), neither of which provide opportunities for follow-up and ongoing support. Hundreds of dollars are funneled into packaged programs annually, though few of them produce significant results. Money is wasted and racial disparities in school discipline persists. Because of this, buy-in is low. When a program fails, schools should not abandon restorative justice altogether, but instead, evaluate the program against the core values of the restorative framework to understand why it did not work. Oftentimes as a program, the central principle that makes restorative justice most effective is omitted. That is simply this: restorative justice is a mindset.

Restorative justice works when educational practice is guided by theory. There is no getting around this basic fact. Schools must remain mindful that restorative justice requires a paradigm shift in one's thinking about school discipline. The switch from punitive to restorative discipline policies is not easy, but it is necessary. School discipline under a restorative framework is based upon respect, dignity, and mutual concern (Evans & Vaandering, 2016; Zehr, 2015). It refocuses the disciplinary process from punishment to interconnectedness and empathy. As a note of caution, a restorative justice mindset begins with a new way of thinking about both problems and solutions. Schools start to prioritize relationships over rules, connection over correction, people over policies, asking over telling, and well-being over success when responding to discipline concerns (Amstutz & Mullet, 2005; Evans & Vaandering, 2016). Having this mindset shapes school culture and yields lasting results.

It's a *Compass*, NOT a *Map*

Zehr (2015) and Evans and Vaandering (2016) remind us that restorative justice is a compass, not a map. Much like a needle on a compass points us in the right direction to get to our desired destination; in education, restorative justice—when rooted in principled values—provides guidance for mitigating inequities in school discipline. Holtham (2009) tells us that "restorative justice compliments a school's comprehensive discipline system—it does not replace it" (p.12). It is not a panacea for all disciplinary situations. School suspension may be appropriate and necessary in some cases. The point is that there is no strict blueprint for implementing restorative justice in education—it is not a one-size fits all approach. There is no guarantee that schools will see a decrease in suspension by a certain percentage point if using restorative justice. However, if restorative justice is implemented correctly, schools would naturally rely less on the use of suspensions, thereby reducing the number of students traditionally impacted by exclusionary practices. Even still, what works in one school may not work exactly the same way in another school. For instance, one school might find it beneficial to use restorative justice alongside culturally responsive positive behavioral intervention supports (Bal et al., 2012), whereas another might find that restorative justice is more effective when integrated with culturally responsive classroom management (Weinstein et al., 2004). Because each school's needs are uniquely different how they integrate restorative justice principles to fit their environment will also be varied. To a great extent, restorative justice is context specific. Its success depends largely on how well schools can identify and understand their own problems and then use restorative principles to make things right.

As a note of caution, just as there are different paths to arrive at the same end point when using a compass, so will there be different ways to eliminate racial disparities in school discipline using principles of restorative justice. How far you have to go really depends on where you start. Once you know where you are and where you want to go, the compass—if used appropriately—will guide you to your destination. Some journeys will be longer than others, but with time and patience everyone gets to their final destination if they can simply follow the compass.

It's *Proactive*, NOT (Only) *Reactive*

Thorsborne and Vinegrad (2003), along with Wachtel (2013), remind us that restorative justice is not only reactive, but also proactive (Baily, 2019; Morrison et al., 2005). In education, restorative justice should never be used for the sole purpose of responding to a discipline issue. If students' first and only encounter with restorative justice is the direct result of their involvement in the disciplinary process, something is terribly wrong. Restorative justice is proactive. Its application starts the moment the doors of the school are opened. It begins with a simple hello or good morning. This level of communication, no matter how seemingly insignificant, can either build or destroy relationships; it can develop or divide a community.

Restorative justice in education is the proactive development of what Amstutz and Mullet (2005) refer to as "peaceable schools" (p. 33). Peaceable schools are primarily characterized by an ethos of care, compassion, and nonviolent communication (Rosenberg, 2015). They offer everyone a safe and inclusive environment to learn and work. Cultivating healthy relationships and communities is at the heart of restorative justice principles; without it, equitable discipline is more difficult to achieve. Should conflict arise, both the relationship and community have a far better chance of being restored if it is strengthened beforehand and not after the fact. Relationship building is not just essential for restoration, it is equally vital for prevention.

There is an old adage that says students don't care what you know, until they know that you care. This is certainly true when it comes to school discipline. By following restorative justice principles, schools communicate to students that they matter, that they have worth. As a note of caution, restorative justice in education—in its truest form—strives to make students feel connected and supported at all times, not just in response to disciplinary concerns.

It's for *Everyone*, NOT Just *Students*

Reimer (2018) reminds us that restorative justice is for everyone, not just students. In education, seldom does restorative justice, as it is widely practiced, directly address adult behavior. Students are seen as the ones in need of correction, while teacher behaviors and attitudes often remain unchecked. Reimer (2018) questions whether teachers, and possibly other adults (e.g., principals, counselors, lunch staff, custodians, bus drivers, etc.), are held to the same standards as students. Do they abide by the golden rule, which instructs us to *treat others the way that we want to be treated*, or do they assume a more authoritative stance that says, *my way or the highway*? The latter represents a commonly held belief that children should stay in their place and never talk back to an adult. This type of one-way communication does not align with the principles of restorative justice. Zehr (2015) stressed that restorative justice is an inclusive and collaborative process where everyone's voice is heard and respected equally.

Apart from student-teacher relationships, Reimer (2018) also contends that teacher-teacher relationships are not carefully attended to in many of the current applications of restorative justice in schools. This oversight is one with severe implications for practice. Teacher-teacher conflict exists. No matter how well teachers attempt to mask their emotions, students tend to know when teachers do not get along. If adults cannot model basic restorative principles, how can schools expect students to take restorative justice seriously? The expression *students will do as they see, not as they are told* is not just an old proverb; it is a foundational element of social learning theory (Bandura, 1971). Students model the behavior of the adults around them, this includes their teachers. As a note of caution, restorative justice in education holds everyone accountable. There are no exceptions and no exemptions.

CONCLUSION

Ten years ago, I began studying school discipline. The data led me to many provocative discoveries and conclusions. Yet, I was not completely satisfied. Something was missing—where were the solutions, I asked. This marked a turning point in my research. I began reading the work of Howard Zehr and other restorative justice scholars. I drew connections between restorative justice and school discipline. My hope was restored and my passion was reignited. I started to believe in the transformative power of research once again. No longer do we have to accept racial disparities in school discipline as the norm. There was a solution, and her name is restorative justice.

Restorative justice is not a new idea necessarily. Although its early origins have been traced to long-standing indigenous and spiritual wisdoms; its placement in education is still in its infancy. Schools have embraced restorative justice as a strategy to address discipline concerns. While well-meaning, many have discarded its foundational principles, which has led to poor implementation. The most common mistake that schools have made is limiting restorative justice to circle processes. Restorative justice, when used correctly, is much more than this.

The purpose of this chapter was to take a closer look at the restorative justice framework to differentiate its current application from its intended application to school discipline. To do this, I introduced what I believed to be the most important principles of restorative justice. This was not a comprehensive undertaking, but valuable nonetheless. I argued, here, that if schools were to implement restorative justice—in its truest form— they would recognize that restorative justice is a mindset, not a program; it is a compass, not a map; it is proactive, not (only) reactive; and it is for everyone, not just students.

The understanding of the principles of restorative justice, alone, is insufficient. If schools want to experience the full potential of restorative justice, if they desire to achieve equity in school discipline, then they must take necessary action. By this, I mean, schools have to ensure that they are evaluating their restorative justice initiatives against the basic foundational principles laid out in this chapter and, where appropriate, revise their approach to school discipline with these considerations in mind. Not doing so damages the credibility of restorative justice and weakens perceptions of its effectiveness.

As I see it, restorative justice is the best solution we have, at the moment, to address disproportional trends in school discipline data. This said, we are relying heavily on schools to bridge the gap between theory and practice to correctly apply the principles of restorative justice. I can only hope that the note of caution to schools presented here is taken seriously. The state of school discipline depends on it.

REFERENCES

Amstutz, L. S., & Mullet, J. H. (2005). *The little book of restorative discipline for schools: Teaching responsibility; creating caring climates.* Good Books.

Armstrong, J. (2014). Rethinking the restorative-retributive dichotomy: Is reconciliation possible? *Contemporary Justice Review, 17*(3), 362–374. https://doi.org/ 10.1080/10282580. 2014.944796

Bailey, M. H. A. (2019). Restorative justice: Moving from punitive sanctions to proactive interactions. In F. Villegas & J. Brady (Eds.), *Critical schooling* (pp. 47–74). Palgrave Macmillan.

Bal, A., Thorius, K., & Kozleski, E. (2012). *Culturally responsive positive behavioral support matters*. The Equity Alliance at Arizona State University.

Bandura, A. (1971). *Psychological modeling: Conflicting theories*. Aldine Atherton.

Braithwaite, J. (1999). Restorative justice: Assessing optimistic and pessimistic accounts. *Crime and Justice, 25*, 1–127.

Blake, J., Butler, B. R., Lewis, C., & Darensbourg, A. (2011). Unmasking the inequitable discipline experiences of urban Black girls: Implications for urban educational stakeholders. *The Urban Review, 43*(1), 90–106. https://doi.org/10.1007/s11256-009-0148-8

Blake, J., Butler, B. R., & Smith, D. (2015). Challenging middle class notions of femininity: The cause of Black females' disproportionate suspension rates. In D. Losen (Ed.), *Closing the school discipline gap: Equitable remedies for excessive exclusion* (pp. 75–88). Teachers College Press.

Butler, B. R., Joubert, M. D., & Lewis, C. (2010). Who's really disrupting the classroom: An examination of African American male students and their disciplinary roles. *National Journal of Urban Education and Practice, 3*(1), 1–12.

Butler, B. R., Lewis, C., Moore, J., & Scott, M. (2012). Assessing the odds: Disproportional discipline practices and implications for educational stakeholders. *Journal of Negro Education, 81*(1), 11–24.

Butler, B. R., Robinson, D., & Walton, C. (2014) A perfect storm: How pose, perception and threat converge to perpetuate discriminatory discipline practices. In C. Lewis & J. Moore (Eds.), *African American male students in preK–12 schools: Informing research, policy, and practice* (pp. 151–175). Emerald Group.

Butler, B. R., & Triplett, N. P. (2019). The influence of administrative leadership on racial disparities in school discipline: A closer look at white male principals. In B. J. McMahon & L. R. Merriweather (Eds.), *Convictions of conscience: How voices from the margins inform public actions and educational leadership*. Information Age.

Carruthers, D. (2012). Restorative justice: Lessons from the past, pointers for the future. *Waikato Law Review, 20*, 1–29.

Evans, K., & Vaandering, D. (2016). *The little book of restorative justice in education: Fostering responsibility, healing, and hope in schools*. Good Books.

Farinde-Wu, A., Allen-Handy, A., Butler, B. R., & Lewis, C. (2017). The urban factor: Examining why Black educators teach in urban schools. In A. Farinde-Wu, A. Allen-Handy, & C. Lewis (Eds.), *Black female teachers: Diversifying the United States' teacher workforce* (pp. 73–92). Emerald.

Holtham, J. (2009). *Taking restorative justice to schools: A doorway to discipline*. Homestead Press.

Levine, M. (2000). The family group conference in the New Zealand Children, Young Persons, and Their Families Act of 1989 (CYP&F). *Review and Evaluation. Behavioral Sciences and the Law, 18*, 517–556. https://doi.org/10.1002/1099-0798(2000)18:4<517::AID-BSL402>3.0.CO;2-E

Lewis, C., Butler, B. R., Bonner, F., & Joubert, M. D. (2010). African American male discipline patterns and school district responses resulting impact on academic achievement: Implications for urban educators and policy makers. *Journal of African American Males in Education, 1*(1), 7–25.

Maxwell, G., & Morris, A. (2006). Youth justice in New Zealand: Restorative justice in practice. *Journal of Social Issues*, *62*(2), 239–258. https://doi.org/10.1111/j.1540-4560.2006.00449.x

Marshall, T. (1999). *Restorative justice: An overview*. Home Office, Research Development and Statistics Directorate.

Monroe, C. (2005). Why are "bad boys" always Black? Causes of disproportionality in school discipline and recommendations for change. *The Clearing House*, *79*(1), 45–50.

Monroe, C. (2006). Misbehavior or misinterpretation? Closing the discipline gap through cultural synchronization. *Kappa Delta Pi Record, 42*(4), 161–165. https://doi.org/10.1080/00228958.2006.10518021

Morrison, B., Blood, P., & Thorsborne, M. (2005). Practicing restorative justice in school communities: The challenge of culture change. *Public Organization Review: A Global Journal, 5*, 335–357. https://doi.org/10.1007/s11115-005-5095-6

Pranis, K. (2015). *Little book of circle processes: A new/old approach to peacemaking*. Good Books.

Reimer, K. (2018). The kids do a better job of it than we do: A Canadian case study of teachers addressing the hypocritical application of restorative justice in their school. *The Australian Educational Researcher, 46*, 59–73. https://doi.org/10.1007/s13384-018- 0286-7

Rosenberg, M. (2015). *Nonviolent communication: A language of life*. Puddledancer Press.

Sawin, J., & Zehr, H. (2013). The ideas of engagement and empowerment. In G. Johnstone & D. W. Van Ness (Eds.), *Handbook of restorative justice* (pp. 41–58). Willan.

Schiff, M. (2018). Can restorative justice disrupt the 'school-to-prison pipeline?' *Contemporary Justice Review, 21*(2), 121–139. https://doi.org/10.1080/10282580.2018.1455509

Skiba, R., Michael, R., Nardo, A., & Peterson, R. (2002). The color of discipline: sources of racial and gender disproportionality in school punishment. *The Urban Review, 34*(4), 317–342. https://doi.org/10.1023/A:1021320817372

Skiba, R., & Peterson, R. (1999). The dark side of zero tolerance: Can punishment lead to safe schools? *The Phi Delta Kappan, 80*(5), 372–382.

Thorsborne, M., & Vinegrad, D. (2003). *Restorative practices in schools: Rethinking behavior management*. Routledge.

Vaandering, D. (2011). A faithful compass: Rethinking the term restorative justice to find clarity. *Contemporary Justice Review, 14*(3), 307–328. https://doi.org/10.1080/10282580.2011. 589668

Van Ness, D., & Strong, K. (2015). *Restoring justice: An introduction to restorative justice* (4th ed.). Anderson.

Wachtel, T. (2013). *Defining restorative justice*. International Institute for Restorative Practices.

Weinstein, C. S., Tomlinson-Clarke, S., & Curran, M. (2004). Toward a conception of culturally responsive classroom management. *Journal of Teacher Education, 55*(1), 25–38. https://doi.org/10.1177/0022487103259812

Wenzel, M., Okimoto, T., Feather, N., & Platow, M. (2008). Retributive and restorative justice. *Law and Human Behavior, 32*(5), 375–389. https://doi.org/10.1007/s10979-007-9116-6

Williams, J. W., III, Davis, A., & Butler, B. R. (2020). Reducing discipline disparities by expanding the Black teacher pipeline: A descriptive analysis of the Charlotte-Mecklenburg School District. *The Urban Review.* https://doi.org/10.1007/s11256-020-00558-y

Zehr, H. (1990) *Changing lenses: A new focus for crime and justice.* Herald Press.

Zehr, H. (2015). *The little book of restorative justice: Revised and updated.* Good Books.

ABOUT THE AUTHORS

Amy Allen is a PhD student and elementary social studies methods instructor at the University of Oklahoma in Norman. Throughout her time teaching at the elementary level, Amy focused on engaging young students in complex and thoughtful dialogue and integrating social studies concepts throughout all subject areas. These experiences served as a catalyst for many of her teaching and research interests which broadly include elementary social studies, integration of social studies with other subject areas, and service learning. In writing about elementary school, her research focuses primarily on the ability of young students to participate in classroom discussions. She is also interested in researching various ways teachers integrate children's books about social studies topics into the time and space devoted to language arts, using them as an avenue to enter into discussion and dialogue about issues of diversity, equity, inclusion, and social justice that can be neglected in the elementary classroom.

Kristen D. Beach, PhD, is an associate professor of special education in the department of Special Education and Child Development at UNC Charlotte. Her research centers on the design and evaluation of reading and language interventions for struggling adolescent readers and students with reading disability. Her research also focuses on the prevention of reading difficulties and early identification of children with reading disability. She is currently engaged in multiple research projects in local school districts, including an evaluation of a summer reading clinic for elementary aged struggling readers and a multistate research project aimed at designing and evaluating academic vocabulary instruction for middle school students with reading disability. Dr. Beach teaches preservice and graduate certificate courses in adolescent reading development, diagnostic assessment, and writing development. She provides professional development and consulting services to local school districts on issues related to reading development, curriculum selection and evaluation, assessment, and teacher preparation.

Chara Haessler Bohan is a professor in the Department of Educational Policy Studies in the College of Education & Human Development at Georgia State University. She specializes in educational history, with a focus on curriculum, race, and gender. She has more than 80 publications and authored or coauthored several books, including *Go to the Sources: Lucy Maynard Salmon and the Teaching of History* and *Histories of Social Studies and Race, 1865–2000*. She served as president of the American Association for Teaching and Curriculum in 2014–2015. She is also the current editor of *Curriculum and Teaching Dialogue*. Her most recent research focuses on how Lost Cause mythology was perpetuated in "Mint Julep" history textbooks.

Bettie Ray Butler, PhD, is an associate professor of urban education and the director of the MEd in urban education program at the University of North Carolina, Charlotte. Her specialized research interest is in culturally responsive practices (i.e., instruction, classroom management, leadership, and mentoring). Her scholarly research has appeared in publications including, *Teachers College Press*, *Journal of Negro Education*, *The Urban Review*, and *Multicultural Perspectives* (recipient of the 2019 Emerald Literati Award for Outstanding Paper/Article).

Amanda R. Casto is an instructor of STEM Education and a preservice teacher guide at Southern Oregon University. She is also a recent graduate of the curriculum and instruction PhD program in the Cato College of Education at the University of North Carolina at Charlotte. Before she became a teacher educator, Amanda taught in a variety of K–8 settings, including public, STEM magnet, private, and charter schools. Her research interests include STEM education, multicultural education, teacher preparation and professional development.

James E. Davis is the retired executive director of the Social Science Education Consortium, a position he held from 2000 to 2018. He holds two degrees in economics from Montana State University and a doctorate in social science education from the University of Colorado, Boulder. He has taught economics at Pacific Lutheran University; the University of Colorado, Boulder; and the University of Nevada, Las Vegas. Davis has authored over 50 publications, including textbooks in economics and civics, as well as supplementary textbook materials, teacher resource guides, and has published articles in the field of social studies/social science education. He has directed more than 15 programs funded by the U.S. Department of Education and the National Science Foundation. He has extensive international training experience in Prague, Czech Republic; Kiev, Ukraine; Vilnius, Lithuania; various sites in Armenia, Croatia, and

Kazakhstan; and several American schools in South America. He also served as program evaluator for the United States Institute of Peace, the Colonial Williamsburg Foundation, and Junior Achievement International. Davis has been a member of the SSEC since 1973 and a member of the National Council for the Social Studies since 1968. He is married to Sharryl Holloway Davis and has five grandchildren.

Paul Fitchett, EdD, is an assistant dean of teaching and innovation and professor in the Cato College of Education. He currently oversees revisions and other initiatives across the college's various teacher education programs. His research interests include the intersections of education policy, teacher working conditions, and student learning outcomes with an emphasis on the social studies. Dr. Fitchett's research has been featured in *Theory & Research in Social Education, Educational Policy, Teachers College Record*, and *Teaching and Teacher Education*

Laura K. Handler, PhD, is an adjunct professor and associate member of the graduate faculty at the University of North Carolina at Charlotte. Her teaching and research focus on educational equity and diversity, particularly in relation to immigrant Latinx populations. Laura has authored publications on educational policy pertaining to school choice and integration; curriculum connected to inquiry, service learning, and technology; as well as teacher preparation, professional development, and recruitment. At UNC Charlotte, she instructs students at all levels through social studies, service learning, and TESL methods courses in addition to those focused on urban education and equity. Her work is continually informed by service in and with schools, families, and community partnerships.

Tina L. Heafner, PhD, is a professor in the Department of Middle, Secondary, and K–12 Education at the University of North Carolina at Charlotte. Tina's teaching and research focus on effective practices in social studies education with particular emphasis in online learning, technological integration, and disciplinary literacy. Her research also examines curriculum and policy issues in social studies education. Tina's publications include seven coauthored books and four edited books including titles such as *Beginning Inquiry: Short Texts for Inexperienced Readers in U.S. History, Seeds of Inquiry: Using Short Texts to Enhance Students' Understanding of World History*, and *Exploring the Effectiveness of Online Education in K–12 Environments*. Tina has received four research awards from the American Education Research Association for her contributions to the fields of social studies and online learning, two research awards from the National Council for the Social Studies College and University Faculty Assembly and the Society for Information Technology and Education, and four awards in teaching, research and service at UNC Charlotte.

Yvonna Hines-McCoy is a doctoral student in the Department of Middle, Secondary, and K–12 Education (Urban Education) at the University of North Carolina at Charlotte. She also works as a social studies teacher and instructional coach. Her research interests include addressing issues of equity and achievement in K–12 urban settings. She can be reached via email at yhines@uncc.edu.

Jeanneine Jones, EdD, is an awarded professor of middle grades education at the University of North Carolina at Charlotte. A former eighth-grade social studies and English teacher, she took her 15 years' classroom experience to Charlotte, where she has continuously directed the middle grades education program and embraced multiple leadership opportunities. She has published many articles and book chapters based on her experiences and has frequently shared her knowledge through presentations, professional development, and service to those schools and organizations who value education as much as she, including the Association for Middle Level Education and its North Carolina affiliate, the College Board, the Lilly Endowment, and the North Carolina Department of Public Instruction. Her areas of expertise and special interest include topics such as creating successful middle schools; adolescent development; teacher leadership; and effective classroom curriculum, instruction, and assessment practices.

Wayne Journell is a professor and associate chair of the Teacher Education and Higher Education Department at the University of North Carolina at Greensboro. An award-winning scholar, his research focuses on the teaching of politics and controversial issues in secondary education. He is also the current editor of *Theory & Research in Social Education*, which is the premier research journal in the field of social studies education. His most recent book is an edited volume, *Unpacking Fake News: An Educator's Guide to Navigating the Media with Students*, published in 2019 by Teachers College Press.

Jill Leet-Otley (BA, MEd, PhD) is an assistant professor in the Department of Education at Luther College. She uses critical whiteness studies to explore White preservice teachers' understanding of racism/White supremacy. Her research also focuses on students who are marginalized by structural inequalities, in particular Somali youth and students with dis/abilities.

Wade H. Morris is a dean's fellow at Georgia State University's College of Education and Human Development. Prior to joining Georgia State, he taught high school history and economics for 15 years in Atlanta, Beirut, and Washington, DC. He earned his master's from Georgetown University and his BA from the University of Virginia. His article on the desegregation of Episcopal schools has been published in volume 46 of *American Educational History Journal*. He is currently working on a book about using primary sources to facilitate the teaching of the history of slavery. He is also researching education in wartime Beirut.

Jessica Norwood, PhD, completed her doctorate in the PhD in curriculum and instruction for urban elementary education at the University of North Carolina at Charlotte. Her research interests include elementary social studies pedagogy, the sociology of education, and critical Whiteness studies. A former elementary school teacher, she now works with first-year education students as a graduate assistant in the Prospect for Success program and teaches sociology at a community college. She is currently working on her dissertation, which examines a diversity curriculum in place at an elementary school serving a predominantly White student population. After graduating, she hopes to work in higher education researching social studies pedagogical practices and teaching preservice teachers. Dr. Norwood teaches sociology at Central Piedmont Community College.

Antoinette (Toni) Rochester is a doctoral student in the Department of Middle, Secondary, and K–12 Education (Urban Education) at the University of North Carolina at Charlotte. She is also the Graduate Research Assistant at the University of North Carolina Charlotte. Her interests include addressing issues of equity amongst minority students and the intersection between race, policy, and education. She can be reached via email at aroches1@uncc.edu.

Tracy C. Rock, PhD, is a professor in the Department of Reading and Elementary Education in the Cato College of Education at the University of North Carolina at Charlotte. Her teaching and research interests include inquiry models of teacher professional development, social studies education, and service learning. She teaches courses in the undergraduate, masters, and doctoral level programs in the Cato College of Education. She is a faculty fellow for the Center for Teaching and Learning at UNC Charlotte where she provides professional development workshops, webinars, private consultations, and peer observations for faculty across the campus. Tracy is the recipient of several teaching awards including the Teaching Fellows Teaching Excellence Award in 2007, the

2014 Bank of America Award for Teaching Excellence and the 2015 Board of Governor's Award for Teaching Excellence.

Dean P. Vesperman (BA, MSE, PhD) is an assistant professor of education in the Teacher Education Department at the University of Wisconsin River Falls. His primary focus of research is on using sociocultural and activity theory approaches to examine how pre-service teachers construct knowledge of themselves, their discipline, and democracy.

Greg Wiggan, PhD, is a professor of urban education, adjunct professor of sociology, and affiliate faculty of Africana studies at the University of North Carolina at Charlotte. His research addresses school processes that promote high achievement among urban and minority students. He was recipient of the 2015 Cato College of Education Award for Excellence in Teaching and the college's diversity award. He has authored over 100 publications, inclusive of 28 education books, with notable titles such as *Global Issues in Education*; *Power, Privilege and Education*; and *Teacher Education to Enhance Diversity in STEM* among others.

Daniel Yonto is a lecturer at Georgia Southern University. He is a human geographer interested in social mobility and neighborhood change. He advocates actionable research through analyzing and visualizing open sourced data to improve the quality of life in people he meets.

Portia M. York, PhD, earned a degree in the curriculum and instruction: urban education program at the University of North Carolina at Charlotte. She also holds a bachelor's degree in sociology from Clark University, and a master's degree in management, with a business concentration from Cambridge College. Portia has been in education administration for more than 12 years and has extensive experience in funding and development of youth programs. As a trained fiber artist, Portia also holds a master of advanced crochet stitches and techniques certification from The Crochet Guild of America. She teaches fiber arts incorporating math, science and social justice. Her research addresses issues of equity and achievement among Black students and other underrepresented student populations, particularly around STEAM education and culturally relevant arts education.

CPSIA information can be obtained
at www.ICGtesting.com
Printed in the USA
BVHW041952201220
595723BV00001BA/1

9 781648 023002